NEW FOUNDATIONS OF
COST-BENEFIT ANALYSIS

Matthew D. Adler

Eric A. Posner

New Foundations of Cost-Benefit Analysis

HARVARD UNIVERSITY PRESS

Cambridge, Massachusetts, and London, England   2006

Library of Congress Cataloging-in-Publication Data
Adler, Matthew D.
  New foundations of cost-benefit analysis / Matthew D. Adler, Eric A. Posner.
     p.   cm.
  Includes bibliographical references and index.
  ISBN-13: 978-0-674-02279-9
  ISBN-10: 0-674-02279-3
  1. Cost effectiveness.   2. Decision making.   3.Public administration.   I. Posner, Eric A.
II. Title.

HD47.4.A35 2006
352.24'3—dc22   2006043377

To our families:
Julia, Jonathan, and Spencer
Emlyn, Nathaniel, and Jacob

Contents

Acknowledgments

We thank the many friends and colleagues who helped us develop the ideas that have found their way into this book. Special thanks go to Adrian Vermeule, who read and commented on the entire manuscript. We have also benefited from conversations over the years with Steve Coate, Jason Johnston, Chris Sanchirico, and Cass Sunstein, and from the comments of a pair of anonymous referees. Many people have commented on the articles on which this book is based, but we do not have the space to thank them all here. Additional thanks go to Ross Tucker, Abby Wright, and Iman Lordgooei for research assistance, to Bill Draper for library assistance, and to our deans, Mike Fitts (Penn) and Saul Levmore (Chicago), for research support.

Chapter 2 builds upon our prior scholarship, in particular: Matthew D. Adler and Eric A. Posner, "Rethinking Cost-Benefit Analysis," *Yale Law Journal* 109 (1999): 165, 197–216; Matthew D. Adler, "Risk, Death and Harm: The Normative Foundations of Risk Regulation," *Minnesota Law Review* 87 (2003): 1293, 1303–1310; Matthew D. Adler, "Beyond Efficiency and Procedure: A Welfarist Theory of Regulation," *Florida State University Law Review* 28 (2000): 241, 262–267, 288–313.

Chapter 3 builds on our previous work, in particular Matthew D. Adler and Eric A. Posner, "Rethinking Cost-Benefit Analysis," *Yale Law Journal* 109 (1999): 165, 216–225. Special thanks to Resources for the Future Press for allowing the use of tables from their publication *Economic Analysis: Benefits, Costs, Implications* by Richard D. Mortgenstern and Marc K. Landy.

Chapter 4 is a heavily revised version of Eric A. Posner, "Controlling Agencies with Cost-Benefit Analysis: A Positive Political Theory Perspective," *University of Chicago Law Review* 68 (2001): 1137.

Chapter 5 is a revised version of Matthew Adler and Eric A. Posner, "Implementing Cost-Benefit Analysis When Preferences Are Distorted," *Journal of Legal Studies* 29 (2000): 1105.

Chapter 6 draws on our prior work, in particular Matthew D. Adler and Eric A. Posner, "Rethinking Cost-Benefit Analysis," *Yale Law Journal* 109 (1999): 165; Matthew D. Adler, "Beyond Efficiency and Procedure: A Welfarist Theory of Regulation," *Florida State University Law Review* 28 (2000): 241; and Matthew D. Adler, "Incommensurability and Cost-Benefit Analysis," *University of Pennsylvania Law Review* 146 (1998): 1371.

We would also like to thank the copyright holders for permission to reprint sections of Matthew D. Adler and Eric A. Posner, "Rethinking Cost-Benefit Analysis," 109 *Yale Law Journal* 165 (1999); Adler and Posner, "Implementing Cost-Benefit Analysis When Preferences Are Distorted," 29 *Journal of Legal Studies* 1105 (2000), reprinted in Adler and Posner, eds., *Cost-Benefit Analysis: Legal, Economic, and Philosophical Perspectives* (University of Chicago Press, 2001); and Eric A. Posner, "Controlling Agencies with Cost-Benefit Analysis," 68 *University of Chicago Law Review* 1137 (2001).

NEW FOUNDATIONS OF
COST-BENEFIT ANALYSIS

Introduction

Our lives are governed by regulations issued by administrative agencies of the federal government. The Environmental Protection Agency (EPA) regulates what factories emit into the air, water, and ground. The Food and Drug Administration (FDA) evaluates and approves drugs. The Department of Agriculture (USDA) regulates farms. The Interior Department regulates the uses of public lands. The Federal Trade Commission protects consumers from unsafe products and misleading advertisements, and challenges anticompetitive practices. The Department of Transportation regulates highway safety. The Occupational Safety and Health Administration (OSHA) evaluates risks in the workplace. Every aspect of daily life bears the imprint of a regulatory agency.

It was not always so. In the nineteenth century, most statewide and nationwide regulation was performed by courts—only in cities were there regulatory agencies with significant powers. Courts regulated through tort law, which, generally speaking, made a person who harmed someone else liable for damages only if the harm was produced by negligence. In some areas—the activities of common carriers, dangerous activities, and, later, the production of certain consumer goods—courts would hold people liable despite the absence of fault, so long as it was clear that the activity caused the harm.

Judicial regulation of this kind, which continues today but in an interstitial manner, had three distinctive characteristics. First, the courts did not explicitly adopt an economic standard for regulating behavior. Although it was claimed later by Judge Learned Hand that the negligence standard had an implicit economic logic, the cost-benefit analysis performed by courts was, at best, extremely casual.[1]

Second, the courts had no expertise in any particular activity that a dispute brought to their attention. Judges then, as now, were generalists, and could rely on expert testimony but also had to take it on faith, subject to the constraints created by an adversarial system.

1

Third, the judicial system then, as now, was decentralized. The judge's task is to decide the case before him or her. In doing so, the judge will set a precedent that other courts will usually, but not always, follow. State judges were frequently influenced by out-of-state precedents but had no obligation to follow them; and although federal courts attempted to harmonize state law, this effort was piecemeal, and it was ultimately abandoned.

The technological advances of the late nineteenth century created a nationwide market. State-by-state judicial regulation was seen as unsuited to the new challenges posed by huge corporations that had resources all across the country. Led by members of the Progressive movement, elected officials took the first steps toward a federal regulatory system around the turn of the century. The modern system fell into place during the Great Depression. Roosevelt's regulatory state survived a succession of Republican congresses and presidents, and even prospered. Although the deregulatory movement of the 1970s and 1980s produced significant reform, and even raised hopes in some quarters of a counterrevolution against the New Deal, it is now clear that the deregulatory movement was a reaction to the excesses of the early 1970s, and did not mark a return to the nineteenth century. The federal courts now have a supervisory role: rather than regulating directly through the tort system, they review agency regulations for errors and inconsistencies.

The terrain of academic debate has shifted as well. Twenty years ago, the Left and the Right split over the regulatory state itself. The Left urged expansion; the Right urged deregulation, including the abolition of whole agencies and jurisdictions. The Left prevailed; antiregulation arguments no longer have political salience and have played a minor role in recent academic scholarship. Since around 2000, the debate has become an apparently more technical one about the decision procedures that agencies should use when evaluating regulations, and the relationship between agencies, courts, Congress, and the president.

However, this debate has not been as technical as it might seem to outsiders. The main issue—and the topic of this book—is agencies' use of cost-benefit analysis to evaluate regulations, and cost-benefit analysis has become the symbol around which the forces of Left and Right have regrouped.

To simplify greatly, cost-benefit analysis (CBA) requires the regulatory agency to sum up the costs and benefits of a proposed regulation, and issue the regulation if the benefits exceed the costs. For many readers, this formula will seem obvious; for many others, this formula will seem plainly wrong—

and we will discuss the problems of CBA in subsequent chapters. For now, one needs to understand the historical context in which it emerged. Prior to 1981, agencies did use CBA from time to time, but mainly as a way of rationalizing regulations, not as a justification for resisting calls for regulation, and the analyses were so poorly done that it is hard to believe that they played much of a role in decision-making. All this changed in 1981, when President Reagan issued his Executive Order 12,291, which directed regulatory agencies to perform CBA on all major regulations.

The origin of this executive order has not been fully studied, but it appears that it had two main constituencies. The first constituency consisted of technocrats, who believed that agencies should regulate but that their regulations should be sensible rather than unreasonable. Cost-benefit analysis would be a device for preventing agencies from issuing unreasonable regulations. The second constituency consisted of opponents of regulation; these were the deregulators, who believed that the federal government should stop regulating industry, or at least should regulate significantly less than it did. For them, the main function of CBA would not be to distinguish the good regulations from the bad regulations but to slow down all regulations, which now would have to survive a new round of bureaucratic evaluation. It is not clear whether this constituency was large or powerful, but it played a large role in the imaginations of environmentalists and other proregulatory forces, who feared that Executive Order 12,291 would be the first step in the demolition of everything they had built over the last fifty years.

These fears turned out to be exaggerated, though perhaps only because the critics mobilized proregulatory forces to resist deregulation. Although the Reagan administration completed some of the deregulatory projects begun by the Carter administration, this task was not accomplished through the vehicle of CBA. Prodded by the Office of Management and Budget (OMB), agencies began to perform CBA more routinely than in the past, but these early cost-benefit analyses did not seem to play a decisive role in regulatory decision-making, and indeed, for most regulations, they continued to be thin rationalizations for decisions made on other grounds. If CBA had an effect, it was marginal, and more to the liking of the technocrats than the conservatives.

This might explain why President Clinton did not reverse course but instead continued the policy of requiring agencies to perform CBA. Clinton's executive order also required agencies to consider equity and other factors absent from Reagan's, however; in addition, Clinton's OMB did not appear to put as much pressure on agencies to perform CBA as Reagan's had. These factors might explain why the Republican-dominated Congress after 1994 tried repeatedly to incorporate cost-benefit requirements in statutes, and why President George W. Bush's administration could revoke on cost-benefit grounds regulations proposed, also presumably on cost-benefit grounds proposed by Clinton's agencies. Formal empirical work does not establish that CBA has improved the quality of regulations, but there are also too many confounding variables to have much confidence in these results. Casual empiricism does suggest that even if CBA has not improved regulation, it has improved regulatory reporting: agencies now often conduct relatively professional cost-benefit analyses and publicly report them, even if they do not always obey them.

In academia, the main defenders of CBA are no longer the Reaganauts of the 1980s but relatively moderate and even liberal commentators who seek to improve the quality of government decision-making. The political moderation of this view is symbolized by the collaboration of the American Enterprise Institute and the Brookings Institution in a joint center on regulatory policy.[2] Many of the papers issued by this center criticize or defend the cost-benefit analyses used by agencies to justify various regulations, the implicit assumption being that CBA is the proper decision procedure and that the role of scholars is to criticize poorly executed cost-benefit analyses, not the decision procedure itself.

The Left continues to fear that CBA is a subterfuge for accomplishing deregulation, but its most troubling charge is that CBA is morally indefensible.[3] The moral problem with CBA, according to the critics, is that it discounts important values, such as the value of the environment; rests on narrow assumptions about human welfare; ignores the claims of poor people and future generations; and neglects concerns about rights. However, the critics have failed to advance an alternative regulatory procedure that is plausible.

Today's defenders of CBA acknowledge the force of the critique but believe that they are minor and surmountable: CBA needs to be tweaked, or used with care, but not abandoned.[4] The defenders have not, however, responded persuasively to the foundational issues raised by the Left's moral critique. There has been little serious study of the philosophical basis of CBA.[5]

What explains this lacuna? We think the answer is that CBA emerged from the economics literature, not from the literatures on philosophy or political philosophy. This should be surprising. Cost-benefit analysis is applied moral philosophy. The claim that regulations should be issued if they comply with a CBA is a claim about how the government should act. The paucity of philosophical analysis shows the closeness of the association of CBA and economics.

Economists, however, have thought philosophically about CBA. This might seem a peculiar division of labor, but there have been stranger events in intellectual history. However, the economic method put constraints on the economists that eventually killed the project of defending CBA.

The story is complex, but a few brief comments here will be helpful.[6] Welfare economics, the branch of economics that concerns policy, what the government should do, tried to establish itself on an uncontroversial assumption—just as positive economics, which predicts behavior, tries to. This assumption was called the Pareto principle, after its inventor. The Pareto principle holds that a project (including a regulation) is desirable if it makes at least one person better off while making no one worse off. Although not everyone agrees with the Pareto principle, its critics are few.

It is immediately clear, however, that the Pareto principle is too strong— few, if any, government projects would satisfy it. In an effort to provide a useable principle, economists tried to develop the Pareto principle into what they would call the *potential* Pareto principle, also known as the Kaldor-Hicks principle. The potential Pareto principle holds that a regulation is desirable if those who benefit from it gain enough so that a transfer of resources from winners to losers that compensates the losers and still leaves the winners better off would be possible, assuming the transfer itself is costless. For example, a forestry regulation that satisfies this criterion would produce more benefits to users of the resource—say, hikers—than costs to the users of the product that is restricted: purchasers of wood. This standard is similar to CBA, although CBA requires one more step involving the conversion of gains and losses into money.

But this research project ran into difficulties. The main problem is that the potential Pareto principle is not as uncontroversial as the Pareto principle. A regulation that satisfies the potential Pareto principle harms people, and could harm all kinds of people, including many sympathetic people. And there are additional problems. The effort to mathematically derive CBA from the Pareto principle or the potential Pareto principle revealed paradoxes, intransitivities, and all kinds of irresolvable ambiguities involving the problem of determining valuations in the first place. This research project stalled and appears to have failed.

The failure of the welfare economic defense of CBA, however, does not entail the rejection of this decision procedure. From a philosophical perspective, the economic project was idiosyncratic from the start. Moral philosophers have never believed that the Pareto principle could be the only possible basis for government action. The purpose of this book is to plumb the other resources of moral philosophy and bring them to bear on the debate about CBA.

Our argument is that CBA is best defended as a *welfarist* decision procedure. Cost-benefit analysis is justified as a decision procedure to the extent that it advances overall well-being—that is, the well-being of the public generally, if not necessarily every member of the public—relative to alternative decision procedures, including the null case of doing nothing. Overall well-being is not the same thing as the Kaldor-Hicks criterion. The two notions can conflict—a crucial point that will become clearer as our analysis proceeds. As for the Pareto principle itself: although it is consistent with overall welfare, the latter is a more capacious standard, and permits government regulations that make some people worse off. Thus a welfarist decision procedure is more useful than a decision procedure derived from the Pareto principle.

However, we do not deny that moral considerations other than overall well-being matter, too. Nor do we deny that many complicated second-order issues arise as one converts the notion of overall welfare to a useable decision procedure. The bulk of this book is devoted to exploring these issues. We come down on the side of CBA, and approve the trend in regulatory decision-making; but we also have many criticisms, and our preferred version of CBA is weaker than the version found in economics textbooks.

Chapter 1 discusses the traditional economic case for CBA and shows why it has failed. Chapter 2 provides firmer philosophical foundations for CBA. We examine the nature of well-being, arguing that welfare and preference-satisfaction are not equivalent. Preferences must survive idealization and be self-interested to make a welfare impact. This chapter goes on to defend a position we call "weak welfarism," which argues that interpersonal welfare comparisons are possible and that overall well-being is a fundamental moral criterion but may not be the sole such criterion.

In Chapter 3 we begin our defense of CBA, arguing that, compared with alternative decision procedures, it best advances overall welfare. A project that passes a cost-benefit test does not necessarily improve overall welfare, but it is more likely to improve overall welfare than a project that passes an alternative test. The key to our argument is that cost-benefit analysis enables agencies to take account of most of the welfare effects of regulations without placing an impossible burden on agency decision-makers.

Chapter 4 continues the comparison of CBA and alternative decision procedures, adding a note of realism to the argument by recognizing that administrative agencies may have a multitude of bureaucratic or ideological goals other than the maximization of welfare. The emphasis here is on the political and institutional context for administrative decision procedures. One of the main virtues of CBA is that it enhances the transparency of regulation, so that citizens and elected officials can monitor agencies and discipline those that go awry.

Chapter 5 describes important ways in which textbook CBA, as constructed by economists schooled in the Kaldor-Hicks criterion and in a view that equates welfare with preference-satisfaction, needs to be modified. Some of these modifications already occur in administrative practice. One set of modifications flows from the account of welfare defended in Chapter 2. Agencies should, at least to some extent, "launder" preferences that are poorly informed or otherwise nonideal, and should also ignore "disinterested" preferences that are based on moral views rather than being connected to the individual's well-being. A second set of possible modifications involves correcting CBA to compensate for the declining marginal utility of money. Cost-benefit analysis is an imperfect proxy for overall welfare, and is likeliest to diverge from that underlying criterion where those who benefit from a project are much richer or poorer than those who lose.

Chapter 6 addresses recurrent objections to CBA: that it does not respect moral rights, distributive considerations, or other putative moral criteria that have a nonaggregative structure quite different from overall well-being; that it runs afoul of the "incommensurability" of different goods; that the difference between willingness-to-pay and willingness-to-accept means that CBA may be indeterminate; that it overly discounts future goods; and that the monetary valuation of life is morally reprehensible. We conclude that none of these objections is persuasive.

Although the book endorses CBA, we reiterate that the procedure we advocate is a modification of the textbook version—both in contemplating the "laundering" of preferences and sensitivity to the variable marginal utility of money and in recognizing that CBA tracks only one part of the moral landscape (overall welfare) rather than being a "superprocedure." Further, although we certainly do aspire to provide practical advice to governmental decision-makers (Chapters 3–6 are full of concrete recommendations), our deeper aims are theoretical. Above all, we hope to restructure the debate about CBA—by letting loose problematic intellectual ballast, such as Kaldor-Hicks efficiency, or the equation of welfare and simple preference-satisfaction, or straight utilitarianism, to which CBA has long been tied, and by drawing the crucial distinction between foundational moral criteria and the decision procedures that implement them.

Cost-benefit analysis, itself, is not part of the moral bedrock. Rather, it is a workable proxy for something that is part of the moral bedrock—overall welfare. We will make progress in deciding whether agencies should employ CBA, as opposed to some competitor procedure, only by undertaking both abstract normative argument and hardheaded, empirically informed, institutionally sensitive discussion of the pros and cons of different decisional structures. This should be the template for arguing about cost-benefit analysis, we believe, and it is the template we follow in this book.

CHAPTER 1

The Traditional View

To understand CBA, one needs to understand its theoretical basis. This chapter does three things. It explains how CBA works; it describes the standard theoretical defense of CBA; and it explains why this defense has failed to satisfy theoretical welfare economists even as applied economists and government agencies have forged ahead with CBA of particular projects.

Some History

Economists have long sought to ground policy proposals in a principle of welfare that would be regarded as self-evidently correct. Nineteenth-century economists were, for the most part, utilitarians, who assumed that some version of Benthamism provided the basis for welfare economics: the desirable project maximized the utility of the greatest number. But as the nineteenth century ended and the twentieth century began, this view lost favor. The major problem was that of interpersonal comparability: if an apple were taken from John and given to Mary, how would we determine the effect on aggregate utility? Bentham himself believed that the project would be welfare maximizing if Mary gained more utils than John lost, but how are we supposed to calculate the number of utils?

Vilfredo Pareto, considered one of the founders of modern economics, believed that such interpersonal comparisons were impossible, or at least too impractical to provide a foundation for policy evaluation. One of Pareto's contributions to economics was his reorientation of economics so that henceforth utility would be understood in ordinal rather than cardinal terms. The Benthamite view that people's utils could be counted and summed was rejected, and in its place economists accepted the Paretian argument that utility functions represent a preference ranking or ordering. Thus, we can say that John is better off with the apple than without, or technically that John prefers having the apple to not having the apple, but we cannot associate a particular utility level with having the apple or not having the apple.

This reorientation provided many advantages to the study of economics from a positive perspective, but it does not solve the John/Mary problem. If all we can say is that John is worse off without the apple and Mary is better off with the apple, we cannot say whether aggregate utility has increased—whether the improvement in Mary's well-being, and the decline in John's, is such that "society"—the two of them together—is better off as a result of the transaction.

Pareto would probably have said that this comparison is meaningless; certainly, Lionel Robbins, another important critic of the Benthamite tradition, thought so.[1] In any event, Pareto proposed another approach to project evaluation, an approach that has become associated with his name. According to what economists now call the Pareto criterion, a project is Pareto-superior if it (colloquially) makes at least one person better off without making anyone worse off, or (more technically) it places at least one person on a higher indifference curve while placing no one on a lower indifference curve. As we will discuss later, economists take people's preferences as given, and so the Pareto principle does as well: a Pareto-superior project gives at least one person something he or she actually wants (or money or wealth with which to buy something he or she wants) while taking away nothing from anyone else.

The Pareto principle avoids the problem of interpersonal comparisons of welfare. Consider the transfer of the apple from John to Mary. This project fails the Pareto criterion because it makes one person—John—worse off. By contrast, the type of project that would pass the Pareto criterion would be, say, a pollution law that both eliminated harmful pollutants and fully compensated the owners of factories. The problem with the Pareto principle is that most government projects do not provide for *any* compensation: pollution laws rarely, if ever, provide for compensation of the losers. Yet most people would regard pollution laws that create substantial benefits to nearly everyone, and that impose relatively low costs on factory owners, as desirable projects. The Pareto principle, then, cannot be a realistic basis for project evaluation; it is simply too strong.

These difficulties led to the invention of hypothetical compensation tests by various economists.[2] They tried to relax the rigor of the Pareto test without giving up on ordinal utility functions. The solution was what is now usually called the Kaldor-Hicks principle. A project passes the Kaldor-Hicks test if its beneficiaries gain enough from the project that they could compensate the losers and have something left over for themselves. Actual compensation is not required; if it were, then we would have the Pareto principle. The hypothetical pollution regulation mentioned above would pass the Kaldor-Hicks test, despite the absence of compensation for the losers, as long as the people who breathe cleaner air gain enough that they could more than compensate the people who incur the cost of the regulation—whether consumers or owners of capital.

Compensation tests do not rely on cardinal utilities because they do not depend on the assumption that people's utility can be measured in units. Nor do they assume the feasibility of interpersonal comparisons of utility. They accomplish this trick by measuring the intensity of people's preferences for certain outcomes in terms of forgone goods. Roughly speaking (more details below), we can determine how many of their other goods the breathers would give up in order to obtain cleaner air, and compare this amount with the amount of goods that consumers give up as a result of higher prices. If the first amount exceeds the second amount, the regulation is justified. Modern CBA, we will see, is a further elaboration of this method, one that reduces the amounts obtained or given up to monetary values, which can be more easily measured and aggregated.

But we are getting ahead of our story. The compensation tests of Kaldor, Hicks, and others were received frostily by theoretical welfare economists.[3] The gist of their criticisms was that the compensation tests did not solve the problem of interpersonal comparisons but merely avoided it, in a theoretically unsatisfactory way, which had the unfortunate consequence of generating paradoxes, intransitivities, and other problems. Other approaches also failed. Welfare economists have never warmed up to the compensation tests, or CBA, and indeed welfare economics itself has sputtered out.[4]

Despite the formidable objections to it, CBA obtained a foothold among applied economists and government officials, who believed that, whatever its problems, it was superior to the alternatives. Cost-benefit analysis even survived the hostile climate of the 1970s, when technocratic approaches to regulation were regarded with skepticism, and many of the practical problems with CBA—the problem of valuing environmental goods, for example— were pointed out.[5] In the 1980s, President Reagan's forceful endorsement of CBA ensured its spread through the bureaucracy, and in the 1990s, President Clinton's failure to repudiate CBA (to the surprise of some people) gave the decision procedure a further boost. Today, CBA is more popular than ever. Yet it is a practice that has no theoretical justification. The original objections to CBA have never been rebutted.[6]

What Is Cost-Benefit Analysis?

Basic Assumptions

Welfare economics assumes that individuals have preferences over states of the world, and that an individual's welfare or utility increases when preferences are satisfied. "Preference" refers to how people rank or order states of the world: if a person "prefers" one good to another, the only practical implication is that the person would choose the first good over the second. Preference and choice are thus tightly linked: one would never, absent mistake, prefer X but choose Y. Further, "preference" refers to how people actually rank states of the world, not how they would rank states of the world if they were better informed, more enlightened, or otherwise different from the way they really are. A person who prefers heroin over bread will choose heroin over bread, and his preference ordering tells us nothing about whether he regrets the choice, feels himself compelled to act against his wishes, or would choose otherwise if he had more information.

As noted above, there has long been a controversy in welfare economics about the proper criterion for social choice. But whatever the proper criterion, the assumption that it is good to satisfy actual preferences is generally accepted. Adherents of the Pareto principle, for example, would say that a project that makes one person better off, according to her actual preferences, and no one worse off, is socially desirable. It does not matter if the one person who is made better off is the heroin addict who is given more heroin.

We do not mean to make too much of the heroin example. Most economists are pragmatists, and would probably agree that heroin should be regulated because of its negative social effects, even that the preferences of heroin addicts should not be taken too seriously. We will address all of the philosophical difficulties with the economists' position in Chapter 2. For now, it is sufficient to understand that actual (not ideal or enlightened or informed) preferences are the atoms of welfare economics, as they are for positive economics—that welfare economics assumes that a person is better off when his preferences are respected, and that society is better off when its members are better off.

Measuring Individual Utility Changes

In simple terms, CBA is a device for converting the utility losses and gains from a project or regulation into dollar values, and aggregating. To each person affected by the project (whether for good or ill), one can calculate a "compensating variation," the amount that would make her as well off as she would be in the status quo—based on her actual preferences. If the sum of the compensating variations is positive, the project is approved; otherwise, it is rejected. This is the simple version; now let us provide some more detail.

A project is any government action, including a law or regulation, that causes a change in the status quo. A project could be the construction of a new highway, repair of an old bridge, creation of a national health insurance system, investment in research and development, enactment of a law against age discrimination—any action that changes the productive capacities of an economy or the distribution of resources. To evaluate a project, we compare the future "project state of the world" (P) with the "status quo state of the world" (S). In order to avoid biasing the decision in favor of the status quo, one should imagine that S and P are both "projects" between which the agency must choose, where the first project involves not changing the status quo. Any benefits from maintaining the status quo, such as minimization of uncertainty, should be treated explicitly as benefits that project S enjoys and project P lacks.

Some people think that a CBA of S and P is conceptually straightforward and that the only problem posed by CBA is the practical difficulty of collecting data. Suppose that P is the creation of a new dam. The status quo, S, means not constructing the dam. Clearly, a new dam would create benefits: people would enjoy cheaper electricity than under S. Just as clearly, a new dam would be costly in materials and labor (which could be used for other projects) and in environmental degradation as well. One might believe that if one could accumulate data on these benefits and costs, the CBA itself would be a simple matter of determining whether the benefits exceed the costs. Unfortunately, matters are not so straightforward.

To understand how CBA works, one must rely on a more precise model of the economy. Consider a two-good and two-person economy, with goods E and F, and individuals A and B. P's effect, relative to S, will be to change the amount of E or the amount of F or both. Usually, a project will not increase both E and F but instead will increase the amount of one good while reducing the amount of another. For example, a dam will increase the supply of electricity but reduce the supply of fish. Assuming that P does not substantially change the relative allocations of the goods between A and B, if P increases the amount of E relative to the amount of F, the price of E (in terms of F) will fall.[7] Depending on their preferences for E and F, this change in relative purchasing power will make one party better off and the other worse off, both better off, or both worse off.

In our example of the dam, P represents the construction of the dam, and S represents the decision not to construct the dam. Let E represent electricity and F represent fish. It is useful to choose one good as the numeraire, by which we mean the baseline good that is used to measure the other good. If E is the numeraire, then we talk about measuring fish in terms of electricity. (F could also be the numeraire.) But, more generally, we think of the numeraire as representing all the goods in the economy except the other good under consideration. So if E is the numeraire, then F represents fish, and E represents everything else, which is denominated in dollars. Then we can measure F in terms of dollars. Although one can thus extend the two-good case to the real economy without causing analytic problems, we will stick to the two-good case, despite its lack of realism, because it is simpler.

P can have a variety of influences on A and B. Suppose that in S a person can trade one fish for one unit of electricity, and that in P a person can trade one fish for two units of electricity. If A has a relatively intense preference for electricity, and his share of total endowments does not substantially change, P will make A better off. He can exchange the fish for electricity at a higher rate than under S. If A has a relatively intense preference for fish, and his share of total endowments does not substantially change, P will make A worse off. Whereas under S he can trade one unit of electricity for one fish, under P he must trade two units of electricity in order to obtain one more fish. The same comments apply to B. So P can have four effects on the utility of the two people in the economy: it can make both better off relative to S, both worse off, A better off and B worse off, or B better off and A worse off.

Figure 1.1 illustrates these effects. It shows the effect of the project on a person, say, person B. The y-axis of the graph represents units of electricity and the x-axis represents units of fish. Under S, B's budget line is represented by m_S, which intersects B's highest indifference curve, U_S, at point s^*. A plausible effect of the dam is to make electricity cheaper and fish more expensive, so if P were implemented, B's budget line would shift to, say, m_P. The steeper slope reflects the fact that electricity is cheaper and fish are more expensive. If B does not buy any fish ($F = 0$), then B can buy more electricity under P

than under S (represented by the fact that m_P intersects the y-axis at a higher point than m_S does). If B does not buy any electricity ($E = 0$), then B can buy fewer fish under P than under S. Assuming the indifference curves as drawn, P improves B's utility. The project budget line, m_P, intersects a higher indifference curve, U_P (at point p^*).

This is just a formal way of showing that the decrease in the cost of electricity benefits B more than the increase in the cost of fish. But this is not necessary; it depends on the relationship between B's willingness to trade off fish and electricity and B's total endowments of both. If B's preferences were different, U_P could be to the left of U_S, so that p^* lay behind U_S. For example, suppose that B's preference for fish is strong when she is poor, but declines as her endowments increase. When B is poor, she will exchange a lot of electricity for a few fish; when she becomes wealthier, she will value the two goods more equally. At S, she is relatively wealthy. P increases the cost of fish so much that she will have to exchange a tremendous amount of the (cheap) electricity in order to satisfy her increased desire for fish, so much that she is worse off than she was under S.

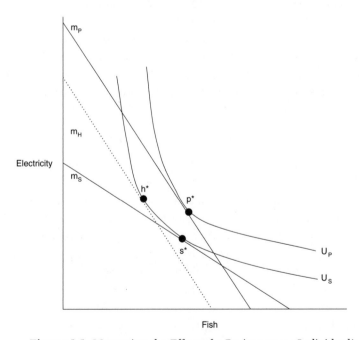

Figure 1.1 Measuring the Effect of a Project on an Individual's Utility

Cost-benefit analysis requires that the project's effect on B's utility be converted into units on a metric that enables comparison of the project's effect on B with its effect on other people. One possible solution to this problem is to determine how much one could take from B in the project state of the world, such that B's utility would be reduced from U_p to U_S. To calculate this amount, one draws a new budget line parallel to m_p and tangent to U_S, which is labeled m_H. The distance between the points where m_p and m_H intersect the y-axis represents the amount of E that one could take from B in the project world in order to reduce her utility to the level in the status quo. In our example, E is electricity, so we have converted a utility change into an equivalent change in the amount of electricity that B would consume. At a higher level of abstraction, E, as the numeraire, represents all goods except F and is measured in dollars. So the distance between the points where m_p and m_H intersect the y-axis is the amount of dollars that would have to be taken from B in the project world in order to reduce her utility to its status quo level. This amount of money is called the compensating variation (CV). Cost-benefit analysis assumes that B's CV is an adequate representation of the difference in B's utility as between the status quo and the project state of the world.[8]

In our example, B is made better off by P. If B were forced to pay her CV to someone else, then B would fall back to indifference curve U_S. However, B would be at a different point on U_S than under S; she would be at point $h*$. B is consuming more electricity and fewer fish than under S, thanks to the change in prices caused by P, but B is no worse off. If P reduced B to a lower indifference curve, then the CV would be negative and would represent the amount of money necessary to raise B's utility to the level that would prevail under S.

Aggregation

The purpose of determining B's CV is to enable a comparison of the effects of P and S on B and A. Recall that in our example, P placed B on a higher indifference curve. Now P might also place A on a higher indifference curve, in which case P is Pareto-superior to S. We will discuss Pareto superiority below. For now it is sufficient to note that Pareto superiority may be a sufficient condition for approving a project, but few, if any, actual projects are Pareto-superior to the status quo, and the reason for using CBA is that the Pareto standard cannot be used to justify the vast majority of government projects. For the purpose of the example, suppose that P injures someone.

Since we assumed earlier that P benefits B, let us assume that it hurts A. Because A, a fisherman, likes fish more than electricity, P's effect of increasing the price of fish in terms of electricity reduces the extent to which A can satisfy his preferences. A's CV is calculated in the same way B's CV is calculated, but this time CV is a negative number. A would have to be given money in the project state of the world in order to make him as well off as he was in the status quo, unlike B, from whom money would have to be taken. Then the project is approved if the sum of A's CV and B's CV exceeds zero; otherwise, the project is rejected.

One should be clear about what is shown by aggregating CVs. One does not show in a straightforward way that B's well-being is enhanced more than A's well-being is reduced. Rather, one shows that B satisfies her preferences to a greater extent under P than under S; that A satisfies his preferences to a smaller extent under P than under S; and that B's improvement is such that B could more than compensate A for his loss. One reason for this result may be that B's preference for the electricity made cheaper by P is more intense than A's preference for the fish made more expensive by P. B prefers electricity much more than fish; A is close to indifference. Thus, if B gave A some extra units of electricity, A would be compensated for his loss of fish and B would still be better off. Holding everything else equal, this difference in intensity of preferences—so long as unrestricted preferences are entitled to respect—may justify a project that makes electricity cheaper and fish more expensive.

But another reason for the result may be that as B accumulates more fish and electricity, her relative preference for electricity increases—her stomach being full of fish, she wants to watch more television—whereas A, at a low endowment, is indifferent between fish and electricity but still eager for both. A needs fish for food and electricity for warmth, and wants them intensely, but also wants them equally, so he is not willing to give up a lot of one good in order to obtain a little of the other. One's CV reflects not just the intensities of one's preferences but also how these preferences change as one's endowments increase. And yet this strikes a false chord. If B has plenty of fish but a modest appetite, she may be willing to trade lots of fish at the margin for a little electricity. So she is willing to pay a lot for P. Meanwhile, A does not have very many fish or much electricity and values fish slightly more than electricity, but still values both a great deal. P makes him worse off because he must reduce his consumption of fish, and the increased warmth does not offset that loss. But he is not willing to pay much (in terms of electricity units) to avoid P, because at his low endowment, electricity matters as much to him as fish do. At a more abstract level, wealthier people have higher CVs for a given welfare impact than poorer people do, because the marginal welfare productivity of dollars diminishes. Millionaires do not reap the same welfare benefit from $100 as poor people do.

Some scholars argue that this bias in favor of wealthy people is a decisive objection to CBA.[9] One response is that if CBA benefits wealthier people more than poor people, but at the same time makes wealthier people better off by more than it makes poor people worse off, the bias can be reversed through redistribution of wealth, in which case enough people will be better off as a result. This response correctly points out that an undesired consequence of CBA can be remedied, but it does not deal with the deeper philosophical difficulty that CBA may not measure anything that we care about.[10] CBA reflects both preference intensity, which we do care about, and wealth, which we do not care about; but can these influences be disentangled?

An Example

Let us sum up with an example. The regulation in question will reduce the amount of lead in gasoline. For refiners to comply with the regulation, they will have to adjust the production process at their refineries. Suppose that the cost of doing so is $100 million. The cost will probably be passed on to consumers in the form of higher prices, but whether it is or is not is immaterial. On the benefit side, suppose that the reduction of the amount of lead in gasoline will have various health benefits: the rate of a cancer will decline, there will be fewer birth defects, and so forth. These benefits must be monetized, and though doing so remains difficult and controversial, methods have been devised. One might, for example, calculate the medical costs attributed to exposure to lead in gasoline, multiply these costs by the probability of having the condition in question, and multiply this product by the number of people exposed. Or one might determine, using questionnaires or market surveys, how much people are willing to pay to avoid having the diseases (or even death) caused by exposure. In either case, the costs occur over time, so they must be discounted to present value. The resulting figure is then compared to the $100 million cost, and the regulation is approved if the figure—the benefit, or avoided cost—is greater than the cost of complying with the regulation.

Numerous objections will occur to the reader. What if people do not understand what it is like to have cancer—can their valuations be trusted? What if wealthy people are willing to pay more to avoid having children with birth defects than poor people are—does it follow that a regulation may be cost-justified if wealthy people are affected but not if poor people are affected? The first question corresponds to the concern about relying on actual preferences; the second question corresponds to the concern about distortions introduced by wealth differentials. But there are other questions as well. Can death be monetized? What about birth defects? Can future costs be discounted? We will address some of these questions elsewhere in this book.

The Conventional Defenses of Cost-Benefit Analysis

Economists have defended CBA in several ways. These defenses have in common an implicit commitment to the view that people's unrestricted preferences should be respected.[11] As discussed in the next chapter, we reject this view. However, because the view is important, and the conventional defenses contain influential ideas, we will spend the remainder of this chapter describing and criticizing them. We classify these defenses as the Pareto defense, the Kaldor-Hicks defense, and the utilitarian defense.

The Pareto Defense

A standard defense of cost-benefit analysis is that it provides a sufficient approximation of Pareto-superior projects. This argument naturally assumes that the Pareto standard is ethically desirable. Let us begin with that claim.

At first glance, the Pareto standard appears normatively attractive. A project that harms no one, and makes at least one person better off, is apparently consistent with a wide variety of moral commitments, including classical liberalism and utilitarianism. It seems to be consistent with commonsense morality.

Standard objections to the Pareto principle include the obvious point that people may make incorrect choices, so their indifference curves will not describe distributions that are systematically related to their actual welfare. A drug addict may reach a higher indifference curve as a result of a project that reduces the price of drugs, but most people would condemn such a project as likely to make the addict worse off. Another objection is that a Pareto-superior allocation may be distributively unjust. A project that generates $1,000 for a rich person and nothing for a poor person aggravates wealth inequality. A third objection is that the Pareto standard assumes a commitment to ethical individualism, with the satisfaction of preferences taking priority over the enhancement of community values. But, it is claimed, ethical individualism does not accord with our moral intuitions. We will ignore these objections for now, and address them in the next chapter.

More significant for our purposes is the problem that the Pareto standard cannot supply a complete ordering of projects. It is likely that the Pareto standard would reject desirable projects that would be approved under an uncontroversial social welfare function. For example, a vaccine that improved the health of millions of people but required a tax of one dollar on someone unaffected (who is not altruistic) would violate the Pareto standard but surely is morally required or at least permissible. Indeed, all utility-enhancing government projects probably violate the Pareto standard. Although one might argue that Pareto superiority could be a sufficient condition for a project, we doubt that this claim is of any practical importance.

This is where CBA comes in. Defenders of CBA argue that it provides a useful approximation of the Pareto standard, while also allowing a more complete ordering. This defense has two versions.

The first argument is that although CBA does not require that losers be compensated, the government can (and should) compensate the losers by taxing the winners after the project is implemented.[12] The problem with this argument is that if the government could and did tax the winners and compensate the losers, the project would be Pareto-superior to the status quo, and CBA would not be necessary. But very few projects are truly Pareto-superior, because the administrative costs of identifying everyone injured by a project and of transferring money to those people from the winners would overwhelm the project's benefits. Practical and institutional reasons also militate against permitting regulatory agencies to compensate people who are injured by regulations.

The second argument is that people will in the aggregate, over time, be benefited by projects as often as they are injured by projects.[13] Suppose we must decide today whether henceforth the government should use CBA. If CBA increases the wealth of everyone in the aggregate, then every person expects ex ante to be better off with CBA than without it. In this ex ante sense, CBA is Pareto-superior to the status quo.

The argument relies on some very strong assumptions about how projects affect people. It might be true that tomorrow's project will benefit people who were injured by yesterday's project, but it might also not be true. A regulation that shuts down an industry may well impose transition costs on workers that they will never recover as a consequence of consumer product regulations and environmental regulations that do benefit them. In addition, CBA has a built-in bias in favor of people who have a low opportunity cost for money. Regulations that benefit these people will enjoy an advantage over regulations that benefit poorer people, thus reducing the chance that all will be made better off as a result of CBA. Thus, the Pareto standard will not be satisfied.[14]

The Kaldor-Hicks Defense

Some scholars defend CBA on the ground that it approximates the Kaldor-Hicks standard.[15] This standard says that a project is desirable if it makes the winners better off by an amount sufficient to overcompensate the losers, if the losers could be compensated through a costless lump-sum transfer. More precisely, state P Kaldor-Hicks dominates state S if it is possible to (costlessly) redistribute goods in state P so as to produce a distribution that is Pareto-superior to the distribution in state S. This defense assumes that the Kaldor-Hicks standard is normatively defensible. The difference between CBA and Kaldor-Hicks is that the former uses money as the numeraire, whereas the latter, a more general criterion, does not.

Cost-benefit analysis is not analytically identical to the Kaldor-Hicks standard. It is more powerful than the Kaldor-Hicks standard because it allows one to use dollars; but it purchases this power by relying on some empirical assumptions about the distribution of preferences in the population. If these assumptions are false, then CBA does not approve the same projects as Kaldor-Hicks does; indeed, relying on CBA may produce certain paradoxes.[16] But our focus here is not the empirical basis of the connection between CBA and Kaldor-Hicks but the normative basis of the Kaldor-Hicks standard itself.

The Kaldor-Hicks standard is vulnerable to well-known objections. Consider a regulation that improves the aesthetic qualities of a shoreline while increasing the cost of launching fishing boats. The result is higher prices for poor consumers who live nearby, but more pleasurable recreation for wealthy vacationers. Because the wealthy vacationers already own many goods, they are willing to give up a lot for the improved aesthetics, but they do not actually give up anything, while the consumers must reduce their consumption of fish. The Kaldor-Hicks test lacks what made the Pareto test attractive: under the Pareto standard, no one is made worse off by a regulation.

In addition to approving regulations that are perverse, the Kaldor-Hicks standard bars regulations that appear sensible. Suppose that the shoreline is already aesthetically satisfying, and the proposed regulation would make it more commercially viable but reduce its aesthetic quality. Such a regulation could benefit the poor consumers a great deal while harming the vacationers very little, and still fail the Kaldor-Hicks standard.

There have been various efforts to avoid these objections. None of them has been successful.

First, the Kaldor-Hicks standard is sometimes defended by reference to the Pareto standard. Indeed, it is often called the "potential Pareto" standard. The argument is that although an individual might lose as a result of one project, he or she is also likely to win as the result of another project, so over time the gains and losses will even out, and everyone (or almost everyone) will be better off if the Kaldor-Hicks standard is used than if some alternative is used. In addition, distributive problems can be solved with the tax and welfare system. But this argument is no different from the claim that CBA approximates the Pareto standard, an argument we rejected in the preceding section. As noted above, the only difference between using CVs and using the Kaldor-Hicks criterion is that the former approach uses money as a numeraire; but this difference does not affect the conclusion that the standards are biased in favor of people who are wealthier. Because Kaldor-Hicks is, taken as a moral principle, unsound, CBA cannot be justified by reference to Kaldor-Hicks. To defend CBA, one must appeal to some other moral principle.[17]

Second, it is sometimes argued that the Kaldor-Hicks standard satisfies the Pareto test in the aggregate or in the long run. This argument is virtually the same as the argument that CBA satisfies the Pareto test in the long run, and as we discussed the latter argument above, there is no reason to discuss the slight variation here.

Third, the Kaldor-Hicks standard is sometimes said to be broadly consistent with utilitarianism or the goal of maximizing overall well-being (however defined). Regulations that pass the Kaldor-Hicks test will maximize utility, and regulations that fail the test will not maximize utility. But there is no point in defending CBA on the basis of Kaldor-Hicks, and Kaldor-Hicks on the basis of overall well-being. One would better disregard Kaldor-Hicks and instead determine whether CBA can be justified directly by its effects on overall well-being. We return to this argument below.

Fourth, some economists argue that the Kaldor-Hicks test is attractive because the government or an agency can compensate the losers. The Kaldor-Hicks-with-compensation approach could then be justified on the basis of the Pareto principle (because losers are compensated) or on the basis of overall welfare. But this argument is based on a confusion. Kaldor-Hicks-with-compensation just is the Pareto test, and thus has the same problems as that test: it is too strong for real-world projects.

In sum, the Kaldor-Hicks test is simply not an attractive normative criterion, and for that reason there is no point in trying to defend cost-benefit analysis on the ground that it implements the Kaldor-Hicks test.

The (Unrestricted) Utilitarian Defense

A final defense of CBA is that it is justified on (unrestricted) utilitarian grounds. We do not know of any sustained defenses of this position, but it seems to be implicit in the work of some authors.[18] We also do not think that this version of utilitarianism is plausible. But assuming it were, how could CBA be defended on the ground of unrestricted utilitarianism?

Welfare economists conceptualize the problem of social choice as one of maximizing a social welfare function. The social welfare function is a function that aggregates the utilities of all individuals. A very simple social welfare function, for example, is the sum of the (cardinal) utilities of all individuals. If marginal utility declines with income, then one can increase this social welfare function by taking a dollar away from a rich person and giving it to a poor person: the latter person's utility will go up by more than the rich person's utility will go down. Similarly, a regulation that feeds more goods or dollars to poor people will increase the social welfare function more than a regulation, otherwise identical, that feeds those goods or dollars to rich people.

Using the idea of the social welfare function, one can make sense of the idea that agencies should use CBA in order to maximize utility. Suppose that every person in society had identical endowments. Then it could plausibly be assumed that each valued an extra dollar by the same amount. People's CVs would reflect their utilities exactly, and a project that passed a CBA would also increase aggregate utility. Now suppose that people's endowments were not identical. In order to aggregate utility, one could not use CVs, because they are distorted by the differences in endowments. A rich person might be willing to pay more for a project than a poor person is, yet it is likely that his or her marginal utility of money is less than the poor person's, so approval of the project would result in a reduction in aggregate utility. However, if one could weight CVs in order to eliminate this distortion, then projects that pass the cost-benefit test would increase overall utility. People's CVs would be multiplied by a factor that reflects their degree of poverty (or discounted by a factor that reflects their degree of wealth).

Welfare economists have not proposed a practical way of determining the appropriate method of weighting. The problem is that there does not seem to be a reliable way of determining people's marginal utility of money. Some have suggested using the marginal utilities implicit in the actual redistributive policies of governments, but redistributive policies do not necessarily reflect well-being; they reflect the distribution of political power. Although most economists continue to support CBA, it is fair to say that most economists also think that the practice does not have a firm theoretical basis: it cannot be derived from a plausible social welfare function.

Cost-benefit analysis cannot be justified with the Pareto principle, and the effort to derive it from the Kaldor-Hicks principle foundered on the Kaldor-Hicks principle's own moral unattractiveness. The attempt to ground CBA in a social welfare function also failed. But if it cannot be justified in these ways, shouldn't it be abandoned? The answer is no; the remainder of this book explains why.

CHAPTER 2

The Moral Foundations of Cost-Benefit Analysis

The previous chapter was critical. We challenged existing defenses of CBA, particularly the traditional view that sees it as implementing the criterion of Kaldor-Hicks efficiency. A substantial critical literature, summarized in the previous chapter, makes clear that Kaldor-Hicks efficiency has zero moral relevance. The fact that the winners from a project could, hypothetically, compensate the losers is—without more—no moral reason whatsoever for government to implement the project. The criterion of Pareto-superiority is, to be sure, morally significant. But Kaldor-Hicks efficiency asks about potential, not actual, Pareto-superiority.

Practitioners of CBA, confronted with criticisms of Kaldor-Hicks efficiency, sometimes respond by offering a pragmatic, negative defense. "What's the alternative to CBA?" they ask. But there are alternatives to CBA—for example, eliminating Pareto-inferior options and then choosing between the remaining options by flipping a coin. If nothing affirmative can be said in favor of CBA, current governmental practices are on shaky ground indeed.

We believe that an affirmative case for CBA can be made. Over the course of the next three chapters, we present that case. We detach CBA from Kaldor-Hicks efficiency, and argue instead that CBA is a *welfarist decision procedure*. Cost-benefit analysis is a rough-and-ready proxy for overall well-being. It is an imperfect but practicable tool by which governmental decision-makers implement the criterion of overall welfare—a criterion that differs from Kaldor-Hicks efficiency in important ways.

Our argument for CBA has two basic parts. This chapter examines moral foundations. We begin by surveying existing views about the nature of well-being, and conclude this discussion by arguing for a *restricted, preference-based account of well-being*. This view—our view—is that well-being involves the satisfaction of preferences that are self-interested and survive idealization.

25

Then, we turn to the problem of interpersonal welfare comparisons and—contrary to traditional economic wisdom—claim that interpersonal comparisons are indeed possible. Finally, we argue for a moral position we term *weak welfarism*. Utilitarianism is the (in)famous position that says that morality reduces to the maximization of overall welfare. Weak welfarism is a less hard-edged view; it says that overall welfare has moral relevance but that other considerations, such as distributive or rights-based considerations, may have moral relevance as well.

In Chapters 3 and 4, we shift our attention from the moral foundations for CBA to the problem of governmental decision procedures. In those chapters, we compare CBA to competitor procedures (for example, a safety-maximization procedure, "feasibility" analysis, cost-effectiveness analysis, or an intuitive rather than monetized balancing of the pros and cons of governmental projects), in light of the moral criterion of overall welfare. We consider the accuracy of these various procedures in tracking overall well-being; their decision costs (both direct costs and delay costs); and the possibility of agency error and opportunism. Our conclusion is that CBA is the welfare-maximizing procedure across a substantial range of governmental choice situations.

The reader might be tempted to skip the current chapter and jump to the more concrete discussion of decision procedures in Chapters 3 and 4. We advise against that. An affirmative case for CBA, we believe, hinges on the nature of well-being and presupposes the possibility of interpersonal welfare comparisons and the moral significance of overall welfare. These are large, somewhat abstract questions, but anyone who wants to think seriously about CBA must engage them. That is what this chapter attempts to do.

A Preliminary Worry: Who Cares about Morality?

Economists and policy analysts might be alarmed by our focus on "morality." We conceptualize overall well-being as a "moral" criterion, and CBA as a "morally" justified decision procedure. But isn't talk of "morality" just empty verbiage? And even if it isn't—even if there are moral truths, in some sense—what is the relevance of morality to *governmental* choice? Aren't governmental officials obliged to follow the law, rather than their own sense of moral duty?

Skepticism about the existence of moral truth and facts was the dominant position in philosophy a half-century ago, during the formative years of modern welfare economics.[1] A tone of moral skepticism thus characterizes much of the foundational scholarship in welfare economics, and remains prevalent in the contemporary literature.[2] By contrast, moral skepticism has become a minority view within contemporary philosophy.[3] And we believe the case for nonskepticism is persuasive.

We will not elaborate that case at any length here. Suffice it to say that ordinary moral discourse is nonskeptical; that moral facts and truths need not be understood as esoteric, supernatural things; and that welfare economists, like the rest of us, have core moral commitments that a thoroughgoing skepticism would force them to abandon. Ordinary discourse condemns certain activities (murdering the innocent, rape, torture) as truly morally wrong, notwithstanding the contrary beliefs of those who engage in the activities or the cultures in which these actors are embedded. Moral truths, plausibly, can be reduced to the judgments or preferences of well-informed observers: nothing supernatural there.[4] And real moral skepticism would preclude welfare economists from asserting *any* moral truths, thus undercutting the bedrock normative tenets of the field.

Consider the proposition that governmental officials "should" choose Pareto-improving projects. If this "should" isn't a moral "should," what is it? Welfare economists who argue for Pareto-optimality or other standard principles of normative social choice theory (nondictatorship, anonymity, etc.) are doing more than articulating their personal tastes for these principles.[5] Rather, these are (implicitly) put forward as true moral principles that genuinely bind social planners.

Economists might have a different worry about our presentation of a "moral" argument for CBA. Morality might be seen as explanatorily inert: even if there are moral truths, in some sense, these truths have no role to play in explaining why governmental or private actors make certain choices. In particular, it might be claimed, sophisticated political science has no need for the notion of "overall well-being." Policy-makers have various sorts of preferences, perhaps including but hardly limited to preferences for "overall well-being," "the public good," or other moral or normative constructs. In general, governmental choices are best explained and predicted by appealing to *whatever* policy-makers prefer, plus their beliefs, and not by one or another moral ideal.

This objection misconstrues our project, which is normative, not predictive/explanatory. Normative analysis articulates norms and principles that some class of actors "ought" to follow. The "ought" here might be a moral "ought," a legal "ought," or perhaps some other kind of "ought." In any event, it is not a precondition for normative advice that the actors addressed will actually follow the advice. They might not. "Ought" implies "can," not "will." To be sure, if governmental actors were universally and relentless amoral, a scholarly work analyzing the moral obligations of governmental actors would be pointless. But the claim that governmental officials are wholly amoral, like the claim that they are wholly altruistic, is much too extreme. There is plenty of evidence that political actors have a range of preferences, including some public-regarding or "moral" preferences.[6] So our project— along with the rest of normative welfare economics—is not pointless.

A final worry is that our normative focus is on morality, not law. Even if we do succeed in showing that overall well-being has moral relevance, and that CBA is the welfare-maximizing choice procedure across a wide range of policy contexts, why do these moral propositions have any normative traction for governmental officials? Aren't these actors tightly constrained by law, as opposed to morality? One answer is that law—even in a modern administrative state—affords decision-makers some leeway. The language of governing statutes and regulation is never wholly determinate. There is always some zone of indeterminacy, larger or smaller, and within this zone officials will be legally free to advance moral goals (such as overall well-being).[7] A different answer is that law may incorporate moral considerations. For example, the Fourteenth Amendment to the Constitution incorporates the moral principle of equality. Analogously, some statutes explicitly require agencies to engage in CBA. Other statutes use language (for example, a mandate to regulate "unreasonable" risks) that points in the direction of overall welfare and CBA, or at least permits agencies to be guided by overall welfare and CBA.[8] And, as already noted, presidential orders (a kind of legal directive) have, since 1981, instructed agencies to follow CBA where statutorily permissible.

In short, there is plenty of legal "space" for CBA, and Congress if persuaded of CBA's moral merits can create yet more "space." Although policy-makers may sometimes be legally precluded from employing CBA, there is no such prohibition as a general matter, and even if there were, it could be repealed. Our moral case for CBA is not mooted by countervailing legal constraints.

What Is Welfare?: Existing Accounts

What is welfare? This is surely a fundamental question for any work in welfare economics: not just our particular account but any scholarship that advances some welfarist construct, such as Pareto-efficiency, Kaldor-Hicks efficiency, overall well-being, or the equal distribution of welfare. These criteria invoke "welfare"; but what does that consist in? More precisely, given a set of possible outcomes (for simplicity, a pair of outcomes O_1 and O_2), under what conditions is some person P better off in O_1 as compared to O_2?

Traditionally, theorists of welfare have answered this kind of question in three different ways, offering *mental-state* accounts of welfare, *objective-good* accounts, or *preference-based* accounts.[9] In this section of the chapter, we criticize mental-state and objective-good accounts. We also criticize the simple preference-based account, which is adopted by many welfare economists. The flaws in the accounts of well-being criticized here lead us to adopt a different view— a restricted preference-based view—which is presented in the next section.

Start with mental-state views of welfare. The generic idea is to identify some attribute of experiences or mental states, such that P is better off in O_1 than O_2 if and only if his experiences in the two outcomes differ with respect to that attribute. This general approach goes back to Jeremy Bentham; was pursued, in a different way, by the great nineteenth-century utilitarians John Stuart Mill and Henry Sidgwick;[10] and has plenty of contemporary defenders. These include modern philosophical hedonists;[11] revisionary economists within the burgeoning subfield of "happiness" studies, who focus on maximizing "happiness" or "subjective well-being" rather than preference-satisfaction;[12] and the prominent psychologist Daniel Kahneman, whose current research agenda is to develop metrics for the quality of experiences.[13]

One kind of mental-state view, pressed by Bentham, focuses on "pains" and "pleasures," understood as positive or negative sensations or feelings.

> There is a core of physical pleasures which are the counterparts in every respect of physical pains: they have a purely organic basis, they are often localized in one part of the body, they can have a quite specific duration, they vary in intensity, and we employ a similar vocabulary for describing the way they feel. The paradigm instances [in the case of pleasures] are the pleasures caused by stimuli such as scratching an itch, being massaged, taking a hot bath, quenching a thirst, using a recreational drug, urinating, defecating, and sexual arousal and orgasm. What these sensations have in common, in virtue of which we distinguish them from physical pain, is just the fact that they feel good.[14]

It is impossible to deny that pain and pleasure sensations do occur, and hard to dispute that they are one component of welfare. If P spends a month in pain and is not a masochist, then, *ceteris paribus*, P is worse off. But it is implausible to think that welfare *reduces* to pleasures and pains: that O_1 is better for P than O_2 if and only if O_1 feels better for P than O_2. James Griffin, a leading philosopher of welfare, offers the following counterexample to hedonism:

Freud, wracked by pain at the end of his life, refused painkillers because they would have impeded his thinking. He preferred the more painful mental state (thinking clearly but suffering great pain) to the more pleasant mental state (thinking fuzzily but suffering no pain) and, intuitively, was better off with the more painful mental state.[15] The Benthamite, hedonic equation of welfare with pleasure and the avoidance of pain is too narrow, not just in its mental-statism but also in ignoring the attributes of mental states that we care about other than how they feel.

A more sophisticated mental-state view, originating with Mill and Sidgwick, focuses on the subject's preference for diverse mental states, and not the pain/pleasure aspect of mental states per se. On this view, P is better off in O_1 than O_2 just in case he prefers his mental states in O_1 to his mental states in O_2. This handles the Freud example: P *might* have a strong desire for pleasure and the avoidance of pain or, like Freud, his "tastes" for experiences might be more complicated.

But the Mill/Sidgwick account of welfare, and mental state accounts generally, remain vulnerable to a powerful objection. All such accounts insist that welfare is solely a function of our mental states. If P's mental states are identical in O_1 and O_2, then, regardless of the other ways in which the two outcomes might differ, P's welfare must be the same in both states. This is implausible. Imagine that P wants to be reputed a great scholar, and has been systematically tricked by his colleagues into thinking that he has that reputation; in fact, they are unimpressed by his scholarship and belittle it behind his back. O_1 is the actual outcome, namely, one in which P incorrectly believes he has a good scholarly reputation; O_2 is a counterfactual outcome, in which P believes he has a good scholarly reputation and really does (his colleagues admire his work). Then P's mental states are identical in O_1 and O_2, but, intuitively, O_2 is better for P's welfare than O_1. No mental-state account of welfare can validate this kind of intuition.

The philosopher Robert Nozick famously exposed the implausibility of the view that welfare reduces to mental states by describing an "experience machine" that, he suggested, subjects would plausibly refuse to enter.

> Suppose there were an experience machine that could give you any experience you desired. Superduper neuropsychologists could stimulate your brain so that you would think and feel you were writing a great novel, or making a friend, or reading an interesting book. All the time you would be floating in a tank, with electrodes attached to your brain. Should you plug

into this machine for life, preprogramming your life's experiences? If you are worried about missing out on desirable experiences, we can suppose that business enterprises have researched thoroughly the lives of many others. You can pick and choose from their large library or smorgasboard of such experiences. . . Would you plug in?[16]

Nozick concluded: "We learn that something matters to us in addition to experience [mental states] by imagining an experience machine and then realizing that we would not use it."[17]

Do these philosophical objections to mental-state views of welfare, exemplified by Nozick's "experience machine," really have relevance for policy choice? We think they do. Ordinary citizens really do have some preferences for things other than their own experiences. An individual may prefer not to be exposed to a toxin. This is not the same as a preference not to perceive a risk from the toxin. Governmental reassurance may change the individual's perceived risk, but will do nothing to reduce her actual exposure. Or an individual might strongly prefer not to become physically disabled, even though she recognizes that those who become physically disabled tend to adapt and return to their predisability level of happiness. More generally, there is considerable research to suggest that an individual's happiness is substantially, if not exclusively, a matter of her basic disposition—that many of the things individuals care about and strive for don't affect mental well-being very much.[18] These preferences, which are reflected in market prices and contingent-valuation surveys, would be discounted by policy analysts implementing a mental-state view of well-being. But they should not be discounted—at least if they are sufficiently well-informed (on which more below).

So much for mental-state views of welfare. Consider, now, the second major family of welfare theories: *objective-good* accounts. This was Aristotle's view. More recently, it has been defended by Martha Nussbaum, John Finnis, and other distinguished thinkers.[19] Objectivists are typically pluralists; they typically offer a list of "values" or "goods" that represent different dimensions of human welfare, different ways a human life can go well or badly. For example, Finnis claims that these goods are: life itself, knowledge, play, aesthetic experience, sociability, practical reasonableness, and religion. Nussbaum's list includes: life, bodily health, bodily integrity, the use of the "senses, imagination, and thought," the emotions, practical reason, affiliation, interaction with other species, play, and control over one's environment. Derek Parfit, describing (without endorsing) objectivism, writes that "[t]he good things might include moral goodness, rational activity, the development of one's abilities, having children and being a good parent, knowledge, and the awareness of true beauty." James Griffin offers: accomplishment, autonomy, understanding, enjoyment, and deep personal relations.[20]

In short, there is disagreement, within the objectivist camp, as to the content of the canonical list of goods or values. There is also disagreement about the basis for that list. Some objectivists argue that human values or goods are grounded in the human essence—in the properties, such as a capacity for rational belief and action, that a being necessarily possesses if she is human.[21] A different proposal is that "what unifies the diverse elements of a good life is their connection(s) to near-universal, near-unavoidable goals."[22] This, in turn, differs from an objectivist view that places more emphasis on culture and language: humans, living together, develop shared understandings of what valuable and worthless lives consist in.[23] Despite these differences, objectivists all concur in the claim that welfare depends upon some set of objective goods or values: objective in that what is truly good or valuable for a given person transcends the subject's own perspective, because it can differ from what she desires, or believes to be good.

Objective-good views of welfare are vulnerable to the following criticism: O_1 cannot be better for P's welfare than O_2, if P does not (at some time) prefer O_1 to O_2. Listening to opera might be, objectively, a better use of someone's time than watching sitcoms, but unless she prefers opera to sitcoms (at least ex post, having been exposed to opera, if not ex ante) the world in which she listens to operas is not better for her than the world in which she watches sitcoms. Similar examples might be constructed for any objective good. An "objective" good (as we use that term) is necessarily some feature of the world that can occur without the subject preferring it. This is true, in particular, of the various "goods" proposed by Finnis, Nussbaum, Griffin, and other acknowledged objectivists. Thus, all these accounts overlook the crucial point that each individual is a (partial) sovereign with respect to his own welfare. Something that P doesn't want for himself, and never comes to want, can't make him better off.[24]

Ronald Dworkin expresses this point eloquently.

> How far and in what way does my having a good life depend on my thinking it good? . . . [To be sure,] a particular life cannot be good for me just because I think it is, and I can make a mistake in thinking a particular life good. But convictions seem to play a more important part in ethics than

that flat statement allows. It seems preposterous that it could be in someone's interests . . . to lead a life he despises and thinks unworthy.[25]

In short, "my life cannot be better for me in virtue of some feature or component I think has no value."[26]

We agree with Dworkin. Welfare is, we think, essentially responsive to
the welfare subject's point of view. That is the nub of the difference between
welfare and value. Some state O_1 involving P can be more valuable than another state O_2—more beautiful, more heroic, more perfectly human—without
being better for P. But to say that O_1 is better, in light of P's welfare, than O_2
is just to say that O_1 is better *for P* than O_2[27]—and that entails, we think, that
P actually rank O_1 over O_2 at some point in time, that he actually prefer O_1
ex ante or ex post. Preference-satisfaction is a necessary if not sufficient condition for a welfare improvement.[28]

This is a fairly weak claim, and in making it we do *not* mean to endorse the
simple preference-based view of welfare commonly held by welfare economists. Our account makes preference-satisfaction one element of welfare; the
simple, economic view makes preference-satisfaction both necessary and
sufficient for welfare. It says that P is better off in O_1 than O_2 *if and only if P*
prefers O_1 to O_2. Welfare-improving states are those, and only those, that the
subject prefers. But this theory of well-being is deeply flawed. While preferences surely have some role to play in the best account of welfare—that was
the nub of our criticism of objectivist views—economists traditionally go
much further and *reduce* welfare to preference-satisfaction. Two important
criticisms—with large implications for policy practice—can be leveled against
this reductive view.[29]

First, it seems quite plausible that people can prefer states that do not improve their welfare because their preferences are evil, ignorant, adaptive, or
otherwise misshapen. Jim prefers torturing his stepson, who (like most
people) strongly prefers not to be tortured. On a simple preference-based
view of welfare, the world in which Jim's stepson is tortured is worse for the
stepson but better for Jim. Reactions to this sort of case do differ, but many
have the intuition—as we do—that the torture world is better for no one,
neither Jim nor the stepson.

Here's another hypothetical case to get the intuitions flowing. Frank has
dedicated his life to leading the Ku Klux Klan and working for the oppression
of blacks. Frank prefers that they be subordinated. The traditional welfare
economist is committed to saying, in this case, that a race-based caste system

might be worse for the oppressed but is better for Frank—better quite apart from any change in Frank's material welfare or any other tangible benefit that racial oppression might produce. A somewhat different example, suggested by Amartya Sen: the housewife who prefers to remain subordinate to her husband because she has been trained, since childhood, that a woman's role is to follow a man's lead.[30]

Let us call the general problem illustrated by these examples the *problem of nonideal preferences:* preferences for states that may well be closely related to the subject's life (in the Ku Klux Klan case, the subject has dedicated his life to racial subordination) but whose occurrence seems nonetheless not to improve the subject's welfare.

The second difficulty with the simple preference-based view of welfare is that people can prefer states that are, intuitively, unrelated to their own lives. Derek Parfit provides an example that is well known in the philosophical literature.

> Suppose that I meet a stranger who has what is believed to be a fatal disease. My sympathy is aroused, and I strongly want this stranger to be cured. We never meet again. Later, unknown to me, this stranger is cured. On the [simple preference-based theory], this event is good for me, and makes my life go better. This is not plausible. We should reject this theory.[31]

Or P might prefer O_1 to O_2 on moral grounds. One outcome involves, say, the continued existence of the Sri Lankan squirrel, an endangered species; the other is the extinction of this species. Sheila has never traveled to Sri Lanka, and never intends to, nor is she an environmentalist who's made species preservation her life's work, but she still (slightly, say) prefers the first outcome because she believes that morality includes environmental values disfavoring the disappearance of species. It seems odd to say that the non-extinction of the squirrel makes Sheila better off.

After all, preferences are simply "proattitudes" that are connected to our choices. P prefers O_1 to O_2 if he's more positively valenced toward O_1 and thus will perform an action that he believes leads to O_1 rather than an action that he believes leads to O_2, all other things equal. More simply: P prefers one state to another if he ranks, and therefore is disposed to choose, the first state over the second.[32] But a very wide range of considerations can motivate someone's ranking of states: moral reasons, detached sympathy, aesthetic reasons, national or ethnic loyalty, legal reasons, and so on. Why insist that the occurrence of one outcome rather than another benefits P as long as P perceives some reason, whatever it might be, for preferring the outcome that occurs?

Note, too, that the states someone prefers might be temporally and spatially disconnected from her. If P prefers O_1 to O_2, then O_1 can occur—thereby satisfying P's preference—without P ever learning of this occurrence. John spends a year in Spain, working to lay the foundations for what he hopes will become a beautiful garden. John returns to the United States and stays there; the seeds he planted indeed flower, so that his preference for a beautiful garden is satisfied, but he never learns of the garden's flowering, and, more generally, it never causally impacts him (in the sense of causing any changes in his mind or body). Does that occurrence benefit John? Maybe not.

In this example, someone's preference has been satisfied by a state that, given its temporal and spatial location, could have a causal impact on his mind or body but, as it happens, does not. An intuitively even stronger case for the welfare-irrelevance of certain kinds of preferences involves states that, given their temporal or spatial location, necessarily do not causally impact the individual who prefers them. Consider preferences regarding posthumous states. Many intuit—and we share the intuition—that the occurrence of states after P's death may harm his survivors, and may constitute harmless wrongs to P, but cannot be welfare-reducing for P.[33] And even if some posthumous states can affect P's welfare, it seems quite untrue that any posthumous state will affect P's welfare just in case P had a preference regarding that state. It should be stressed, here, that preferences regarding posthumous states are perfectly kosher qua preferences: although O_1 and O_2 might differ only in events that occur after P's death, P might well rank O_1 over O_2 and take actions to promote O_1 and thwart O_2.

Stranger-on-the-train, Sri Lankan squirrel, the garden in Spain, and the case of posthumous states illustrate the second general problem with the simple preference-based account of welfare. Call this the problem of *disinterested* preferences: preferences that may well satisfy whatever criteria of idealization we propose (P's sympathy for the stranger's health and the squirrel's existence are in no way distorted, evil, etc.) but concern states that are, intuitively, remote from the subject's own life and therefore do not change the subject's well-being.[34]

Our Proposal: A Restricted, Preference-Based Account of Well-Being

In the previous section we criticized mental-state and objective good accounts of well-being, but also described two problems with the simple preference-based view of well-being: the problem of nonideal preferences and the problem of disinterested preferences. It is *not* true that P is benefited by an outcome if and only if he prefers it, because P's preferences can be poorly informed or otherwise nonideal and, even if ideal, might have nothing to do with his own life.

This analysis leads us to an account of well-being that depends on preferences, but is more nuanced than the simple view. Call our view a *restricted preference-based view* of well-being. This account shall undergird our defense and elaboration of CBA. The account stipulates that an outcome benefits a person if she has an appropriately "restricted" preference for that outcome— a preference that survives idealization and concerns her own interests.

A Restricted, Preference-Based Account of Welfare

Outcome O_1 is better for P's welfare, as compared to outcome O_2, just in case:

(1) P actually prefers O_1 to O_2 (at some time);

(2) P's preference for O_1 over O_2 survives idealization;

(3) the preference is self-interested.

This account, we believe, synthesizes the key insights that emerge from the philosophical and economic literature on well-being. What improves P's welfare is constrained by P's own point of view. P cannot be made better off in the teeth of her actual preferences; objective-good theories of welfare as well as Benthamite hedonism overlook this crucial point. But traditional economists go too far in the other direction, by making preference-satisfaction not only necessary but also sufficient for welfare improvements. Preferences can be nonideal; people can be mistaken about their own welfare. It is this insight that, at bottom, animates the objectivist strain within philosophical writing on welfare. And preferences have too wide a potential scope for it to be the case that preference-satisfaction (even the satisfaction of idealized preferences) is automatically welfare-improving. It is this insight that, at bottom, animates the mentalist strain within philosophical writing on welfare. The distinction between what goes on inside P's head and what occurs outside is an attempt (albeit unsuccessful) to delineate the boundaries of P's own life—to provide a noncircular characterization of just those outcomes that can make a welfare difference for P.

The theoretical work we have done here has direct implications for the actual practice of CBA, as we shall demonstrate at length in Chapter 5. Cost-benefit analysts can and do "launder" preferences that deviate from welfare in the two ways we have described: by failing idealization or by failing the test of self-interest. For example, agencies typically ignore or discount racist or sexist preferences, preferences to use addictive drugs, or preferences to engage in violent or abusive behavior. And, with the exception of environmental law, where disinterested preferences *do* sometimes figure into policy analysis (in the form of so-called existence values for wilderness and endangered species), such preferences are usually ignored by CBA. The simple preference-based view of well-being suggests that CBA analysts should not "launder" preferences; our account says that they should, at least under some conditions.

It should be stressed that our account of well-being is incomplete in a number of ways. These gaps reflect difficult and contested theoretical problems that we will not attempt to resolve. *However* the problems are resolved, our argument for weak welfarism and for CBA as a welfarist decision-procedure holds good (although, to be sure, different answers to the problems will have different implications for how CBA analysts should "launder" preferences— a point we will underscore in Chapter 5).

To begin, we have no easy answer to the thorny problem of conflicting preferences. The conflict can be diachronic: preferences can change over time.[35] Harry is a dedicated climber and prepares intensely for an ascent of Everest, motivated by a preference for mountain climbing over family activities. He succeeds at the climb but soon thereafter comes to regret his recreational choices, wishing that he'd spent time with his family rather than readying himself for Everest. Was Harry benefited by the mountain climbing or not? A conflict between preferences can also occur synchronically: for example, Jane might prefer watching TV to reading but have a second-order preference for reading over TV. Jane wishes she were the kind of person who preferred reading.[36] Is she benefited by watching TV or not?

It might be thought that the idealization "filter" solves the problem of conflicting preferences. If P prefers O_1 to O_2, but later (or at a different level) prefers O_2 to O_1, perhaps only one of these preferences is sufficiently well-informed, authentic, deliberative, and otherwise ideal to constitute a welfare improvement. Even so, a difficulty remains. Imagine that P prefers O_1 to O_2, mistakenly chooses O_2, regrets this choice for the rest of his life, but shortly before death change his preference and now retrospectively endorses O_2. If this retrospective preference survives idealization, has the occurrence of O_2 benefited P? This sort of fact-pattern puts pressure on our claim that an outcome benefits P only if P (at some time) actually prefers the outcome. How long must the actual preference endure for the welfare-improvement to be realized? A moment? A day? A year? A life-stage? A lifetime? A lifetime seems too long, a moment too short, but we have no exact answer for where to draw the line.

A second gap in our account concerns the appropriate idealization of preferences. Consider, as an illustrative case, Sen's example of the housewife who prefers her subordinated status. How to explain why satisfying that preference doesn't benefit the housewife? One general approach to idealization, popular among many philosophers of welfare and some welfare economists, too, is to invoke fully informed preferences.[37] We are attracted to this approach, but the notion of "full information" needs to be fleshed out. Are we imagining that the subject herself is provided with all the information she can handle, up to her cognitive limits? Or that some cognitively unbounded "counterpart" of the subject (whatever exactly that means) is provided a comprehensive stock of information? And is "information" simply propositional information, true facts, or does it also include some nonfactual data (for example, what an experience feels like)? Note also that a "full information" requirement may not achieve the desired result in Sen's housewife case. What if the housewife's preferences are so entrenched by years of subordination that, even with full information, she still prefers the role of underling?

A different sort of idealization "filter" appeals not to full information but to objective goods. Incorporating this sort of filter into our account yields a kind of hybrid theory of welfare: something benefits a person only if he prefers it *and* it is objectively better for him. Yet another way to handle the problem of distorted preferences is to screen out "adaptive" preference, preferences that have resulted from unjust or otherwise unfavorable circumstances. The general idea here is to identify permissible processes of preference-formation and stipulate that only the satisfaction of preferences with the right sort of history is welfare-enhancing.[38]

The objectivist and historical approaches to idealization may handle Sen's case more readily than the full-information approach. Even if the housewife is so thoroughly subordinated that she would prefer subordination with full information, the premise that subordination is objectively worse, or that the crucible of subordination is an ineligible process for preference-formation, may explain why her continued subservience doesn't benefit her. But there are countervailing difficulties with the latter approaches. We will not choose, as a philosophical matter, between full-information, objectivist, and historical specifications of what it means for preferences to "survive idealization." We do believe that "laundering" poorly informed preferences is more feasible for administrative agencies than "laundering" objectively bad or adaptive preferences, and we discuss this point in detail in Chapter 5.

A third and final lacuna in our account concerns the definition of self-interested preferences. This problem has received less scholarly attention than other aspects of the theory of welfare, but is quite significant. The traditional economic view avoids the problem by eliminating the very distinction between self-interested and disinterested preferences—by stipulating that the satisfaction of any sort of preference is a welfare-benefit to the holder—but that strikes us as no solution at all, for reasons already discussed.

The Sidgwick/Mill account of well-being is, in effect, one solution to the problem of defining self-interest: only preferences for mental states are self-interested. But Nozick's experience machine shows the flaws in this solution. A broader definition identifies each person's body *or* mind as the locus of his or her self-interest: *P* is better off just in case a preference (that survives idealization) concerning her physical condition or mental state is satisfied.[39] On reflection, this, too, seems overly restrictive. Consider the example of a scholar's preference for a good reputation among her peers, which certainly seems to be self-interested. The scholar's reputation depends on states external to her mind and body (albeit facts that can potentially impinge on her experience), namely, what others think about her. The philosopher Mark Overvold, in one of the most sustained treatments of the problem of defining self-interest, suggests a yet broader category—subsuming all preferences for states that entail the subject's existence.[40] Matt's preference that Matt have a good reputation is satisfied only if Matt exists; Matt's preference that the stranger on the train survive can be satisfied without Matt existing. The difficulty, here, is that some existence-entailing preferences don't seem to be welfare-enhancing. One example: the remorseful wrongdoer's preference that he be punished.

"Self-interest," like many basic concepts, is difficult to define and has fuzzy applications. But, again like many basic concepts, it also has clear applications. For example, preferences that are morally motivated, and do not concern the subject's mind or body, or entail her existence, are pretty clearly disinterested. The concept, albeit fuzzy to some extent, can still usefully structure agency practice, as we elaborate in Chapter 5.

The Possibility of Interpersonal Welfare Comparisons

We have covered part of the moral landscape on which CBA rests, arguing for a restricted preference-based account of welfare. We now survey the rest of the relevant terrain. We defend *weak welfarism:* overall well-being has moral weight, albeit not conclusive weight. Our defense of weak welfarism, in turn, has two parts. First, in this section, we argue for the possibility of interpersonal welfare comparisons. If interpersonal comparisons are impossible, then the notion of "overall well-being" has no content (more precisely, no content beyond the notion of Pareto-superiority). Then, in the next section, we argue that "overall well-being" is not merely contentful, but has moral weight.

Let us turn, then, to the puzzle of interpersonal welfare comparisons.[41] Consider two outcomes O and O^* that are "Pareto-noncomparable," to use the technical lingo. Neither outcome is Pareto-superior to the other. There is at least one person who is better off in O than in O^*, and at least one person who is better off in O^* than in O.[42] For at least seventy years, going back to Lionel Robbins's famous critique of interpersonal comparisons (1932), the orthodox view in welfare economics has been that overall welfare is a meaningless notion in this sort of case.[43] Pareto-noncomparable outcomes cannot be ranked with respect to overall welfare—or so economists have traditionally believed.[44]

Why this skepticism about "overall welfare"? Some of the skepticism derives from a more general moral skepticism. We have argued that the marriage of general moral skepticism and welfare economics is inherently unstable. Any discipline that hews to some moral truths (for example, the moral truth that social planners should choose Pareto-superior outcomes over Pareto-inferior ones) can't, without contradiction, embrace general moral skepticism.

A more creditable basis for denying the welfare-comparability of Pareto-noncomparable states derives from the preference-based view of welfare. Imagine, for simplicity, that there are two outcomes (O and O^*) and two persons, P_i and P_j. P_i prefers O to O^*. P_j prefers O^* to O. We now posit that overall welfare is greater in one of the outcomes, say O^*. This means that P_i's *loss* in welfare, moving from O to O^*, is less than P_j's *gain* in welfare, moving from O to O^*. In other words, welfare differences or changes are interpersonally comparable. But how *can* welfare differences or changes be interpersonally comparable, if welfare just reduces to preference-satisfaction? Preferences are simply choice-connected rankings. To say that P_i prefers O to O^* is merely to say that he ranks O over O^*, and is thereby disposed to choose O over O^*. Reciprocally, P_j ranks O^* over O and is thereby disposed to choose O^* over O. How can we get from this "thin" information about each individual's personal ranking of outcomes to "thicker" information about a single, interpersonally valid ranking of welfare changes? Note that an individual can rank outcomes without ranking changes between outcomes. And even if each individual does rank changes between outcomes, this merely gives us a multiplicity of such rankings (one for each individual in the population), not a single one.

So there *is* a genuine puzzle about the possibility of interpersonal welfare comparisons and, therewith, the meaningfulness of the notion of "overall welfare." But this is not an insoluble puzzle. Clearly, information about individual preferences over outcomes, *without more*, will not enable interpersonal welfare comparisons. But it is a fallacy to leap from this premise to the conclusion that interpersonal comparisons are impossible. The construct of overall welfare must incorporate, and can incorporate, information beyond individual rankings.

A variety of scholars have advanced diverse suggestions as to what that information might be, and we shall survey this scholarship in the next section. To begin, however, it is vital to see why the puzzle of interpersonal welfare comparisons must be soluble—why there are strong reasons to resist the orthodox economic view that such comparisons are impossible.

First, a little reflection will show that the orthodox view is deeply counterintuitive. In one world, Felix feels fine but thousands die painful, premature deaths; in another world, the deaths and pain are averted but Felix has a headache. In one world, many workers lose their jobs, and suffer depression, family strife, or other ill effects of protracted unemployment; in another world, the unemployment doesn't occur but a small number of top executives can now only afford to buy BMWs rather than Lamborghinis. Although the two worlds in these scenarios are Pareto-noncomparable, the second world in each scenario is (intuitively) much better for overall welfare than the first. Many similar such cases, real or hypothetical, can be delineated. Why care about our intuitive reactions to these cases? As John Rawls argued, moral reasoning is a process of "reflective equilibrium," in which intuitions play an important role.[45] Here, we are using them to adjudicate between moral views providing different answers to the question whether well-being admits of interpersonal comparisons.

Second, "interpersonal comparisons are an ineliminable part of human life."[46] In day-to-day life, we routinely make judgments of overall well-being, comparing losses to some of our friends, colleagues, or family members with gains to others. Similarly, governmental institutions are constantly faced with policy choices that will increase the welfare of some while causing welfare setbacks to others. An environmental regulation will improve air quality but cause reduced production and job losses in affected firms.

A procompetitive intervention will benefit consumers but lower corporate profits. Raising the speed limit harms those who die in resultant accidents, but helps others by lowering their travel times. Although these welfare trade-offs are *sometimes* seen by the government decision-makers and affected citizens as inscrutable or indeterminate, it is surely not the case that they *always* are.

The orthodox economic view that denies the possibility of interpersonal welfare comparisons thus leads to an "error theory" of ordinary practice. It means seeing our pervasive practices, individual and governmental, of weighing the welfare gains to some persons against the welfare losses to others, as mistaken. This fact, like the (related) fact that the orthodox view is counter-intuitive, would seem to count against the view.

Third, a wide range of moral theories require interpersonal welfare comparisons.[47] Utilitarianism does. So does "weak welfarism," the view we are defending here, which sees overall welfare as one of a possible plurality of morally relevant factors. And, crucially, so do some of the leading competitors to utilitarianism and weak welfarism. As we shall see below, one such competitor is "prioritarianism." "Prioritarians" modify the overall-welfare construct by summing a concave function of utilities, rather than simply adding up unweighted utilities. This has the effect of giving greater weight, in the social calculus, to welfare changes experienced by individuals with a lower level of well-being. "Prioritarianism" is even more demanding, in terms of interpersonal comparisons, than utilitarianism or weak welfarism.[48]

At the limit, prioritarianism becomes the so-called leximin view. This view, widely discussed in social choice theory, builds on Rawls's notion of giving absolute priority to those who are worst off. Leximin says this: in comparing O and O^*, compare the welfare level of the individual who is worst off in O with the welfare level of the individual who is worst off in O^*, then (if these levels are the same) the welfare levels of the individuals who are second worst off in each outcome, and so on.[49] A different view, with some current scholarly adherents, is an egalitarian view that makes the equalization of welfare levels—even if that requires Pareto-inferior moves—a moral desideratum.[50] Leximin does not require the interpersonal comparability of welfare changes, and the egalitarianism just described may not either. However, both views *do* require the comparability of welfare levels. We are aware of no plausible proposal for establishing interpersonally comparable welfare levels that does not also underwrite difference comparisons.

A final set of competitors to utilitarianism and weak welfarism—again, to be discussed below—are "resourcist" views. These views deny that the comparison of outcomes depends on the welfare levels that individuals attain in the outcomes, or on the welfare changes that individuals experience as the outcomes change. Rather, resourcists focus on the "resources" or "primary goods" that individuals possess in the different outcomes: things like money, health, and liberty, which are all-purpose means to attain welfare, rather than welfare itself. Although resourcists are not welfarists, they do need to compare bundles of "resources"; and that comparison, in turn, presumably involves some sense, if only a rough one, of the amount of welfare attainable with different bundles.

To sum up: intuition, ordinary practice, and the widespread use of interpersonal comparisons in moral theorizing all undercut the view that these comparisons are impossible. Overall welfare is a meaningful concept. We have very strong reason to think that Pareto-noncomparable states (or at least some of them) can be compared in light of overall welfare.

Interpersonal Comparisons: Some Specific Proposals

But how, exactly, do interpersonal comparisons occur? Our defense of CBA does not demand an answer to this question. There are a range of plausible accounts of interpersonal comparisons, and all are consistent with our general claims that overall welfare has moral weight and that CBA is a welfare-maximizing decision procedure across a substantial number of choice situations.

Still, the reader who remains skeptical about the possibility of interpersonal comparisons might want to examine some specific proposals for making such comparisons. We therefore survey a range of proposals here, concluding that a modification of a construct for interpersonal comparisons advanced by John Harsanyi fits best with our restricted preference-based view of well-being. Other readers may want to skip this section and turn immediately to our defense of weak welfarism, in the next section.

The specific approaches to interpersonal comparisons proposed in the literature correspond to different families of views about well-being: mental-state views, objective-list views, and preferentialist views. Start with mental-state views. Theorists since Bentham have entertained the possibility of interpersonal *hedonic* comparisons—measuring the pain and pleasure states experienced by different persons on an interpersonally valid scale (call this a scale of interpersonal "hedonic utility") and determining the overall pain and pleasure in each outcome by summing hedonic utilities.[51] Intuitively, this or something reasonably close should be possible. Seemingly, we *can* assign numbers to pain and pleasure states that represent not merely the ordering of those states but the differences between them. As the economist Yew-Kwang Ng observes:

> If your preference [over hedonic states] is really purely ordinal, you can only say that you prefer your present situation (A) to that plus an ant bite (B) and also prefer the latter to being bodily thrown into a pool of sulphuric acid (C). You cannot say that your preference of A over B is less than your preference of B over C. Can you really believe that![52]

How, more precisely, should interpersonally valid hedonic utilities be constructed? The trick, here, is to move from (1) an intrapersonal measure of the hedonic quality of a single moment to (2) an intrapersonal measure of the hedonic quality of an overall experiential episode, that is, a series of pain/pleasure experiences concatenated into an experiential history (at the limit a lifetime hedonic trajectory for a given person) to (3) an interpersonally valid measure of the hedonic quality of an overall experiential episode. In recent work, Kahneman and coauthors demonstrate in detail how to move from (1) to (2), and suggest that it should be possible to move from (2) to (3).[53] Roughly, their idea is this. A given individual can order momentary experiences, and these preferences can be represented by ordinal utilities. *If*, further, there is a hedonically neutral level—the boundary between pain and pleasure—and an individual's rankings of temporally extended experiential episodes satisfy certain axioms, *then* cardinal utility numbers can be assigned to momentary experiences.[54] In particular, the total hedonic utility of a temporally extended episode will equal the sum of its component momentary utilities, and the individual's ranking of episodes will track these sums. As Kahneman explains:

> The subject's ratings correctly order [momentary] experiences . . . but the intervals between ratings may be arbitrary: a pain rating of 7 is reliably worse than a rating of 6, but the interval between 7 and 6 need not be psychologically equivalent to the interval between 3 and 2 . . .
>
> Suppose [now] that the [subject] judges that one minute of pain at level 7 is as bad as two minutes of pain at level 6 . . . [T]his judgment implies that the original reports of pain should be rescaled, assigning 7 a value that is twice as high as the value assigned to level 6. If the [subject's] judgments obey the axioms, the theory asserts that a consistent rescaling is possible, yielding a [cardinal] scale for instant utility that is calibrated by its relation to duration.[55]

Kahneman's theory, thus far, yields cardinal and intrapersonally valid utility numbers: numbers that represent a given individual's preferences over her momentary hedonic states, and that can be summed to derive her preferences over hedonic histories. There is still a gap between these numbers and interpersonally valid hedonic utilities. That gap can be surmounted if individuals converge in their preferences over moments of pain/pleasure and over hedonic histories. If so, a single interpersonal number can be assigned to a momentary pain/pleasure experience, and these can be summed to determine a total utility for each temporally extended episode, representing how everyone would rate that episode as compared to alternatives. And Kahneman suggests that there *is* evidence of considerable interpersonal convergence in ranking pains and pleasures. "For example, the relation between a measure of the physical strength of labor contractions during childbirth and self-reports of pain was generally similar for different women." And in a study where an observer rated the pain of patients undergoing a colonoscopy based on their groans and grimaces, "the observer's ratings correlated quite highly . . . with the patient's own . . . evaluations."[56]

Kahneman's approach to interpersonal comparisons focuses on experiences (specifically, pains and pleasures) and is grounded in a mental-state view of well-being. Objective-good theorists take a different tack. Different objective goods are, in effect, different *dimensions* of welfare: different ways a human life can go well or badly. These dimensions subsume not only pains and pleasures but also other sorts of experiences as well as various nonexperiential features of a life-history. And welfare can be compared interpersonally, because once we have a list of objective goods, we can compare how well different life-histories realize them. As James Griffin argues:

[Consider] Mill's interpersonal comparison of Socrates and the Fool. The Fool attaches no value to Socrates' life. Socrates attaches none to the Fool's life. How would each decide how relatively well off they are? . . . What Socrates [or the Fool] needs to make is a judgment of a very different sort from what we ordinarily understand by a personal preference . . . Socrates [or the Fool] should need to know, primarily, what made life valuable. He should have to appeal to his understanding of what humans, or sometimes humans of a certain type, are capable of, and of the various peaks that human life can reach. Then he should have to decide how close he and the Fool came to some peak. What he should not particularly need to consult is the phenomenological "feel" of their experience, nor their personal tastes and attitudes, nor his own preferences about landing in the one sort of life or the other.[57]

Admittedly, Griffin's objectivist account of interpersonal comparisons is nowhere near as formalized as Kahneman's hedonic account. Imagine that the list of objective welfare dimensions is $D_1 \ldots D_n$. Plausibly, if these dimensions support interpersonal comparisons, then (1) the goodness of a life-history with respect to a given dimension D_i can be represented by a cardinal number; (2) the different dimensions can be commensurated with each other, for example by establishing weighting factors for each dimension; (3) an overall score for a given life-history can be determined; and (4) aggregate welfare in an outcome can be determined by adding up the welfare scores of its component life-histories.[58] A full objectivist theory would specify how these dimensional numbers and weighting factors are assigned, and what exactly they represent. But the basic idea that objective goods would have sufficient content to support such numerical assignments, and therewith interpersonal comparisons, is not implausible—or at least no more implausible than objectivism generally.

Consider Griffin's proposed list of goods: accomplishment, autonomy, understanding, enjoyment, and deep personal relations. One might rebel at the putative "objectivity" of these goods. How can one say that a life-history L_1 is better or worse than an alternative life-history L_2 with respect to (say) the value of "deep personal relations"? What if some individuals prefer the friendships and family relationships that occur in L_1, and others the friendships and family relationships that occur in L_2? The objectivist will have to answer that crucial, threshold question in some way. Once she does, the further claim that numbers measuring objective goods can be weighted and summed is not a huge step. The claim that life-histories can be ordered with respect to "deep personal relations" and the claim that differences between lives can be ordered with respect to "deep personal relations" are *both* assertions of some interpersonally valid ordering that exists despite the heterogeneity of individual preferences.

What about welfare scholarship grounded in the preference-based view of well-being? Here, too, substantial work has been done on the problem of interpersonal comparisons.[59] A central idea in this literature has been that information about individual preferences over outcomes can be supplemented with information about what individuals prefer when confronted with risk or uncertainty—information about preferences over *lotteries* of outcomes—

to yield an interpersonal metric. Von Neumann and Morgenstern, in their seminal work on expected utility theory,[60] demonstrated the following: If an individual's preferences over outcomes and lotteries satisfy certain basic rationality conditions, then utility numbers tracking those preferences (call these "von Neumann–Morgenstern" or "VM" utilities) can be attached to outcomes. Von Neumann–Morgenstern utilities have the following properties: (1) The individual prefers one outcome to another if and only if the preferred outcome is assigned a higher VM utility; (2) the VM utility assigned to each lottery is a weighted average of the utilities of its component outcomes, as weighted by their probabilities; (3) the individual prefers one lottery to another if and only if the preferred lottery has a higher VM utility. Von Neumann–Morgenstern utilities over outcomes are informationally richer than standard, ordinal utilities; these numbers represent, not merely how the individual ranks each outcome assuming it occurs for certain, but also how probabilistic packages of outcomes will be ranked. Mathematically, this means that VM utilities are cardinal, not ordinal. If a given array of VM utilities successfully represents an individual's preferences over outcomes and lotteries, then (in general) another array of VM utilities will also do so only if both sets of VM utilities rank *differences* between outcomes the same way.

This is a neat mathematical trick, but can it be used to generate interpersonal welfare comparisons? J. R. Isbell proposes that each individual's VM utilities be normalized on a 0–1 scale, assigning 0 to her least preferred outcome and 1 to her most preferred outcome.[61] Overall welfare is then the sum of these normalized VM utilities. Isbell's approach makes it axiomatic that individuals are equally productive of well-being—a social choice that moves any individual from his worst to his best outcome must have the same overall effect regardless of the individual involved—and that strikes us as counterintuitive. One person might be capable of a wider range of experiences, cognitions, or accomplishments than another.[62] Recognizing this fact is not inconsistent with egalitarianism. Egalitarians can stipulate that individuals have equal claims to welfare, regardless of physical or mental endowment—which is not the same as insisting that individuals are equally efficient at converting resources into welfare, regardless of physical or mental endowment.

A more plausible preferentialist approach to interpersonal comparisons is John Harsanyi's. Harsanyi formalizes the notion of grounding interpersonal comparisons in the reactions of a sympathetic spectator.[63] This notion goes back to Adam Smith and David Hume and, in recent times, has been endorsed in a general way by such notable philosophers and economists as Kenneth

Arrow, Amartya Sen, R. M. Hare, and Donald Davidson.[64] Harsanyi's formalization runs as follows. If there are N individuals in the population, then each outcome O_i is really a package of N person-state pairs or life-histories: $O_{i,1}$ means "being person 1 in outcome O_i," $O_{i,2}$ means "being person 2 in outcome O_i," and so on up to $O_{i,N}$. An individual ("the spectator") has preferences, which Harsanyi calls "extended preferences," with respect to the different possible person-state pairs. The spectator is capable of *sympathy*—of imagining what it would be like to assume the identity of various individuals in various worlds—and her extended preferences emerge after a process of sympathetic identification. If $O_{1,3}$ is higher in the spectator's extended-preference ranking than $O_{4,7}$, that means the spectator would prefer living the life-history that individual 3 has in outcome 1 to living the life-history that individual 7 has in outcome 4.

Interpersonal comparisons emerge, for Harsanyi, by assuming that the spectator has extended preferences over *lotteries* of person-state pairs as well as the person-state pairs themselves. For a given outcome O_i, the spectator "adds together" the component life-histories $\{O_{i,1} \ldots O_{i,N}\}$ by imagining an equiprobability lottery with the life-histories as the prizes: a lottery where the spectator has a $1/N$ chance that he will live the life of individual 1 in outcome O_i, a $1/N$ chance that he will live the life of individual 2 in outcome O_i, and so on. Overall welfare, Harsanyi proposes, should be defined in terms of these equiprobability lotteries. To say that overall welfare is greater in O_i than in O_j means: the spectator would prefer the O_i equiprobability lottery to the O_j equiprobability lottery.[65] She would prefer a lottery where world O_i occurs for certain and she has a $1/N$ chance of assuming the identity of each person in the population in that world, to a lottery where world O_j occurs for certain and she has a $1/N$ chance of assuming the identity of each person in the population in that world.

Finally, Harsanyi assumes that the spectator's extended preferences over person-state pairs and lotteries satisfy the rationality conditions requisite for VM utilities. This gives us a numerical metric for overall welfare. Each individual life-history can be assigned a utility number, representing the spectator's extended preferences, and the sum of utilities in one outcome is greater than the sum of utilities in another if and only if the spectator prefers an equiprobability lottery involving the first outcome to one involving the second—in other words, if and only if overall welfare is greater in the first outcome.

One difficulty for Harsanyi's account, as for preferentialist theorizing about welfare more generally, is the problem of nonideal preferences. What if the spectator is a twisted sadist who prefers outcomes in which pain is deliberately inflicted, on the chance that he'll be the one who gets to inflict the pain? Harsanyi, recognizing this difficulty, stipulates that the spectator's extended preferences must be fully informed. Other approaches to idealization might also be deployed here. The spectator might be required to have non-adaptive preferences or, perhaps, objectively good preferences.

A second difficulty with Harsanyi's model of interpersonal comparisons concerns disinterested preferences—again, a general problem for preferentialist accounts of well-being. Here's a stark but illustrative example. Imagine that the spectator believes that morality requires an equal distribution of wealth. In O, wealth is equally distributed; in O^*, everyone has greater wealth, and it is unequally distributed. Then the spectator might, on moral grounds, prefer the O equiprobability lottery to the O^* equiprobability lottery, even though he would self-interestedly prefer to be any given person in O^* rather than O (since each individual has greater wealth in O^*). The solution, here, is to define overall welfare by focusing on the spectator's self-interested preferences over person-state pairs and lotteries of person-state pairs. "Launder" the spectator's preferences and wash out the disinterested ones; use the remaining rankings, of life-histories and lotteries, to generate interpersonal comparisons. Admittedly, this refinement to the Harsanyi construct is something of a promissory note, since no one has yet fully explained what the difference is between "self-interested" and "disinterested" preferences.

A third difficulty with the Harsanyi construct is the possibility of divergent extended preferences.[66] Harsanyi assumes that every spectator will have the same ranking of person-state pairs and lotteries of person-state pairs. But this is little more plausible than assuming homogeneity in ordinary preferences. Larry likes playing basketball; Lester likes listening to music. If this sort of mundane heterogeneity can occur, then why mightn't it also be the case that Larry extendedly prefers the basketball player's life-history to the musician's, while Lester extendedly prefers the musician's life-history to the basketball player's? Larry would just rather stand in the basketball player's shoes—Lester in the musician's. Idealizing preferences will not solve the problem, at least if full-information (Harsanyi's preferred approach to idealization) is employed. Larry's genes and upbringing are such that he likes basketball and extendedly prefers lives filled with basketball, while Lester's genes and upbringing cause him to extendedly prefer musical lives. Those are just their "preference endowments," and knowing more about the world or the source of the preferences needn't induce them to change their extended preferences.

Where extended preferences diverge, there is no truth of the matter about interpersonal comparisons. If spectator Sam prefers the O equiprobability lottery to the $O*$ equiprobability lottery, and spectator Sally has the opposite preference, then it is hard to see how either $O*$ or O could be better for overall welfare. So the possibility of divergent extended preferences *is* a real threat to the Harsanyi construct—but not, we think, an insoluble one. The solution, here, is to refine the construct by adding a convergence condition.[67] In short:

Harsanyi's Construct for Interpersonal Comparisons, with Refinements
Given two Pareto-noncomparable states, O and $O*$, O is better for overall welfare if and only if idealized spectators would unanimously (or near-unanimously) self-interestedly prefer the O equiprobability lottery to the $O*$ equiprobability lottery.

Further work would need to be done refining the convergence requirement. For example, if "idealized" means that the spectators possess full information, demanding unanimity in extended preferences is probably too demanding, since some dysfunctional preferences can be so entrenched that they persist with full information.

So where are we? On the table are three approaches to interpersonal comparisons, representing the best work in each of the three main schools of thought about the nature of well-being: mental-state, objectivist, and preferentialist. Kahneman offers a mental-state construct; Griffin, an objectivist construct; Harsanyi, a preferentialist construct. Of these three, we find Kahneman's approach substantially less appealing than the other two. It ignores all the nonexperiential components of well-being—indeed, all the non-hedonic components (including facts about our bodies and about the external physical or social world, as well as those features of our experiences that we care about other than their painfulness and pleasantness). Determining the overall welfare in an outcome by adding up "hedonic utilities" is, at best, a fallback strategy for interpersonal comparisons, given that well-being consists in more than pain and pleasure. If, for some reason, the nonhedonic aspects of welfare were inherently unmeasurable, or unsuited for interpersonal comparisons, we might end up using Kahneman's construct to compare Pareto-noncomparable states. But, as shown by the Harsanyi construct, pain and pleasures are *not* the only elements of our lives that can be measured and compared.

This leaves us with Harsanyi and Griffin. Not surprisingly, we prefer the

Harsanyi construct, as amended to require that the spectators be idealized and self-interested and that their extended preferences converge to a large extent. This approach to interpersonal comparisons meshes neatly with our basic account of well-being. To summarize:

The Nature of Welfare and Interpersonal Comparisons
- A restricted preference-based account of welfare: P is better off in O than O^* if P actually and self-interestedly prefers O at some time, and the preference survives idealization
- Overall welfare is greater in O than O^* if:
  (1) O is Pareto-superior to O^* (i.e., at least one person is better off in O, and none are worse off); or if not
  (2) (Harsanyi) Nearly everyone would ideally and self-interestedly prefer the O equiprobability lottery to the O^* equiprobability lottery.

But it should also be stressed that this account may be fairly close to one that incorporates Griffin's construct, which measures overall welfare by balancing objective goods. Consider the following.

An Alternative Schema
- A restricted preference-based account of welfare: P is better off in O than O^* if P actually and self-interestedly prefers O at some time, and the preference survives idealization
- Overall welfare is greater in O than O^* if:
  (1) O is Pareto-superior to O^* (i.e., at least one person is better off in O, and none are worse off); or if not
  (2) (Griffin) The gain in objective welfare goods realized by those who are better off in O than O^* is larger than the loss in objective welfare goods incurred by those who are worse off in O as compared to O^*.

How different these two approaches are will depend on what the list of objective goods is, and how that list is generated. As noted earlier, there is considerable disagreement within the objectivist camp on such matters. Some philosophers would use the notions of convergence and full-information to *define* objective goods. On this view, there is no difference at all between (1) the ranking of life-histories and lotteries over life-histories generated by the convergent extended self-interested preferences of spectators with full information and (2) how the life-histories and lotteries should be ranked in light of the objective goods at stake. Other philosophers appeal to the human essence—specifically, the human capacity for rational thought and action—

in defining objective goods. Here, there presumably is a larger difference between the Griffin construct for interpersonal comparison and a Harsanyi-type construct framed in terms of full information. There are various things about human lives that we care about, and that we would continue to care about with full information, that aren't part of our nature as rational cognizers and actors: for example, pleasure and the avoidance of pain, or social interaction.

It should be emphasized that the Harsanyi construct is *not* meant as a decision procedure for governmental officials. The best decision procedure is CBA, or so we shall argue in subsequent chapters. Rather, the Harsanyi construct is an analytic device, meant to illuminate the notion of overall well-being. Real-world welfarist decision procedures will track overall well-being in a rough-and-ready way. But given deliberation costs and bounded rationality, the optimal welfarist recipe for decision-making will *not* be direct implementation of the Harsanyi construct. Governmental officials should not rank outcomes by attempting to determine the extended preferences of idealized spectators. That is not our proposal.

We have also said that our commitment to the Harsanyi construct is provisional. It is the best developed model of interpersonal comparisons within the preferentialist school, but a better approach (for example, one that does not depend on preferences under risk and uncertainty) may yet emerge. Further, our arguments in the following sections and chapters of this book—about the moral relevance of overall welfare, about CBA as an excellent welfarist decision procedure, and about how CBA should be conducted—do not generally depend on the Harsanyi construct. It *is* crucial for our argument that interpersonal comparisons be possible, and that money be an all-purpose means to welfare (thus CBA, which measures welfare changes by monetizing them). The particular form that interpersonal comparisons take is less crucial. Still, a purely generic defense of the possibility of interpersonal comparisons, one that made no concrete claims about how to make such comparisons, might well have been frustrating to some readers. We have therefore furnished, at least in outline, a solution to the puzzle of what "overall welfare" means in the case of Pareto-noncomparable states.

The Moral Relevance of Overall Welfare

We have argued for the possibility of interpersonal comparisons. Overall welfare is a meaningful concept; but it remains to be shown that overall welfare has moral weight.

Utilitarians argue that overall welfare is morally *decisive*. They claim that private individuals and governmental officials are always required to choose the course of action that maximizes overall welfare. That is not our view, or at least not a view we shall defend here, given the powerful objections that have been raised against utilitarianism. Utilitarians deny the existence of moral rights, and thus would demand the harvesting of one person's organs to prevent the deaths of two or more others who need transplants, or the execution of an innocent to appease a murderous mob. Utilitarians also deny the moral relevance of distributive considerations, and thus would enact a measure that benefits the superrich at the expense of the desperately poor whenever the net benefit is positive. Finally, utilitarians insist that ecosystems, wilderness areas, endangered species, and other features of the environment can never have moral value except as a resource for humans or nonhuman animals sufficiently advanced to be capable of welfare.[68]

Our position is not utilitarianism, but "weak welfarism." "Weak welfarism" claims that overall welfare is *morally relevant*, not that it is morally decisive.[69] Morality may encompass a plurality of moral factors. It certainly includes overall welfare; but it may also include such factors as moral rights, the fair distribution of welfare, and even moral considerations wholly detached from welfare, such as intrinsic environmental values. To put the point formally: the morally required choice for a given actor, public or private, in a given choice situation, depends on the balance of $\{W, F_1, F_2, \ldots, F_m\}$, where W is overall welfare, the F_i are other considerations, and $m \geq = 0$. In this book, we don't take a position as to the content of the F_i. Nor, for that matter, do we insist that some such F_i exist. But neither do we rule them out. "Weak welfarism" includes both utilitarianism as a limiting case and pluralistic moral views that combine overall welfare with other moral concerns such as rights or fair distribution.

The term "welfarism" has a technical meaning in contemporary moral philosophy and normative economics. It refers to a moral theory that depends solely on well-being, and that ignores information about outcomes other than well-being.[70] The theory we are defending here, it should be stressed, is *not* this theory. We call our theory "weak welfarism" to distinguish it from "welfarism" in the technical philosophical sense. Again: by "weak welfarism," we mean a theory with the structure $\{W, F_1, F_2, \ldots, F_m\}$, where W is overall welfare, the F_i are other considerations, and $m \geq = 0$. Crucially, the F_i might be considerations that depend on information other than well-being. For example, they might be moral rights or intrinsic environmental values.

We claim that welfare (through the construct of *W*, overall well-being) is part of the moral fabric of the universe, but we do not insist that this fabric is exclusively welfare-woven.

"Weak welfarism" is a much more catholic position than utilitarianism, but it still needs a defense. Skeptics might deny that overall welfare has any moral weight whatsoever. The overall-welfare skeptic might be a pure egalitarian, who insists that morality is merely a matter of achieving the equal distribution of welfare or welfare-resources; or a pure rights theorist, who insists that morality is just a matter of protecting moral rights to person and property. What is it, exactly, that confers moral significance on the total amount of welfare in the world?

Our answer to this question and defense of weak welfarism appeals, first, to intuitions. Moral views such as pure egalitarianism or a pure rights-based view (to say nothing of radical environmentalism), which fail to include overall welfare or related constructs as morally relevant factors, are deeply counterintuitive. Dennis McKerlie makes this point about pure egalitarianism:

> Even if we do care about equality for its own sake, it cannot be the only thing that we care about. We also want people to be happier or to have larger shares of resources. The principle of equality must be supplemented by another moral principle to express this concern. It must be part of a combined moral view that also includes something like the utilitarian principle.[71]

Unless the egalitarian principle is thus supplemented with the overall-welfare principle or something like it, the moral view may require us to "level down": to advance equality through Pareto-inferior measures that reduce the welfare of those who are better off, thereby bringing everyone's welfare level closer to equality. Shelly Kagan advances a parallel criticism of a pure rights-based view. For example, in rescue cases, even if the endangered person has no moral right to be rescued, and the possible rescuer has no duty to rescue him, performing the rescue and thereby maximizing welfare is surely morally commendable and (at least sometimes) morally required.

> Suppose a building is on fire. Upon entering, I find a child and a bird trapped within. Needing one hand free to clear a path back outside, I can only save one of the two, and I hastily pick up—and escape with—the caged bird.
>
> Clearly I have done something wrong. . . .
>
> [Ordinary morality] believes that there are cases where I am morally required to act so as to promote the good even though there is some cost to

myself which I am not inclined to take on: for example, I am required to throw the drowning child a life preserver, even though my clothes will get soaked, and I risk catching a cold.

If [the believer in ordinary morality] is asked to account for his judgments here, the best explanation seems to involve the quite general thesis that one always has a [moral] reason to promote the good.[72]

The moral importance of overall welfare can be seen, too, by reflecting on the Pareto principle. Among serious scholars of morality, the Pareto principle is far and away the most widely accepted moral axiom. Virtually all welfare economists and many, probably most, moral philosophers endorse it.[73] A choice that benefits someone and harms no one is morally required or at least morally commendable. The Pareto principle shows that well-being exerts a moral tug on us, independent of moral rights, distributive considerations, or other moral factors. Why? The crucial point, here, is that the Pareto principle applies *even where the benefited person(s) are already well off, and have no moral rights against those who can improve their welfare.*

Imagine a case in which Phil finds in his backyard an odd little rock that is of no use to him, or anyone else, except that it can mitigate the mildly uncomfortable symptoms of a very rare dermatologic condition that periodically afflicts Donald. The condition isn't really that serious, and Donald is otherwise doing very well in his life—so well, indeed, that he is now the richest person in the world in welfare terms. The Pareto principle requires Phil to further enrich Donald by giving him the rock—even though it's Phil's rock, not Donald's, and even though Donald, being already the richest, has no distributive claim on Phil or anyone else. Giving Donald the rock is morally commendable because, and only because, welfare has moral weight as such.

Finally, our governmental practices underscore the point that welfare has moral weight quite independent of distributive considerations or moral rights. Consider food and drug regulation. The pure rights-based view would be that government should ban only those food and drug transactions that violate moral rights. But actual proscription is dramatically broader than that. The sale of a dangerous food or an unlicensed and ineffective drug, fully labeled, to a competent adult, violates no one's moral rights. Purely rights-based food and drug regulation would be little more than a law of labeling. The pure egalitarian, by contrast, would orient food and drug law toward the promotion of equality. The sale of dangerous or ineffective products to the poor should be discouraged, but their sale to the rich should be affirmatively encouraged. Such transactions effect a kind of "leveling down," by reducing the resources of the rich and/or their longevity. But actual food and drug regulators would find ludicrous the notion that they should enact Pareto-inferior, proegalitarian measures.

We have used food and drug regulation as a concrete case, but workplace safety regulation, air and water pollution laws, motor vehicle and highway regulation, the antitrust system, the securities laws, and many other examples would equally well illustrate how existing regulatory practices are radically at odds with pure egalitarian or rights-based views.

Objections to Weak Welfarism

One possible objection to our analysis is that the deficiencies in pure egalitarian or rights-based views can be cured without adopting weak welfarism. Weak welfarism includes factor W: overall or aggregate welfare. But why not supplement (or replace) egalitarian or rights-based factors with a different sort of welfarist factor, namely, overall *weighted* welfare? Overall welfare takes the form $\sum_{i=1}^{N} U_i$, where U_i is the interpersonally comparable utility number measuring the welfare of person i and there are N people in the population. If U_i increases by 1 unit, then overall welfare increases by 1 unit regardless of whether person i is rich or poor. Overall *weighted* welfare uses a "prioritarian" maximand, which gives greater weight to the welfare of those who are worse off. It takes the form $\sum_{i=1}^{N} g(U_i)$, where g is an increasing, concave function of utilities—meaning that g increases as U_i increases, but the rate of increase slows. At the limit, the prioritarian principle becomes leximin. Prioritarianism has been much discussed in recent philosophical work, and leximin has been a central focus of the literature on social choice since Rawls.[74] Weak welfarism rejects prioritarianism or leximin; it is committed to overall unweighted welfare, not overall weighted welfare in a moderate (prioritarian) or stark (leximin) form. What would justify that commitment?

Consider, to begin, the leximin rule. This is the most extreme version of giving priority to the worst off. Given two outcomes O and O^*, compare the welfare of the worst-off person in O to that of the worst-off person in O^*; the welfare of the second-worst-off person in O to that of the second-worst-off person in O^*; the welfare of the third-worst-off person in O to that of his counterpart in O^*; and so on. Proceeding in this order, find the first pair where the welfare levels of the two individuals are different; and choose the outcome where that level is higher. As Dennis McKerlie notes:

[Leximin] has two defining features. [First, i]t gives absolute priority to the interests of the very worst-off group. It counts any gain for them (as long as it leaves them in the position of being the worst-off) as more important than any gain for any other group. Secondly [it] is innumerate. The priority is not affected by the number of people in this group compared with the number of people in other social and economic groups. If we think about the priority view in an intuitive way, it is not obvious that it should have these features.[75]

"[A] philanthropist who has a book to give away would do more good in giving it to a literate person than to an illiterate person, even if the literate person is already better off."[76]

Prioritarianism ($\Sigma g(U_i)$) softens the hard edges of leximin. Even if the worst-off person in $O*$ has a lower welfare level than his counterpart in O, the prioritarian rule might still rank $O*$ as better, if a sufficiently large benefit accrues to other individuals in $O*$. How exactly this works will depend on the shape of $g(U_i)$.

Whatever the precise shape of $g(U_i)$, prioritarianism strikes us as a muddled moral view. Welfare exerts a moral tug on us; that is why we morally ought to choose (or at least are to be morally commended for choosing) Pareto-superior courses of actions, even where the benefited individuals have no distributive or rights-based claims on us. The prioritarian rule, $\Sigma g(U_i)$, is (at a superficial level) consistent with the Pareto principle. Since g increases with increasing U_i, Pareto-superior outcomes will always be chosen by the rule. At a deeper level, however, prioritarianism and Paretianism are in tension. Phil has a moral reason to give his rock to Donald, the richest person in the world, if Phil can do so costlessly and no one else has any use for the rock. Donald's welfare, and nothing else, generates this moral reason. Consider now a case in which both Donald and Ronald can use the rock; they're both richer than Phil, and it remains Phil's rock. Phil now faces two competing moral considerations. He has a moral reason, as before, to give Donald the rock, grounded only in Donald's welfare (not moral rights or distributive claims). But now Phil also has a second moral reason, to give Ronald the rock, grounded only in *his* welfare (not moral rights or distributive claims). Shouldn't these competing reasons be balanced by comparing the welfare gain to Ronald of having the rock with the welfare gain to Donald of having the rock—that is, by determining overall welfare? By contrast with the Pareto case, Phil is now pulled in two directions by welfare, not just one—but it is still only *welfare* that is pulling him. Why, then, introduce an extraneous weighting factor $g(U_i)$ rather than simply calculating ΣU_i?

Derek Parfit, one of the earliest defenders of prioritarianism, writes: "[I]f benefits go to people who are better off, these benefits matter less. Just as *resources* have diminishing marginal *utility,* so *utility* has diminishing marginal *moral importance.*"[77] But this misdescribes the Donald case. If the rock will always ease Donald's discomfort by a certain amount, then Phil has the very same welfare-based reason to give it to him, regardless of how rich Donald is. If Parfit is right that "utility has diminishing marginal moral importance," then, at a certain point, as Donald's riches increase, the moral force of his utility gain might fade to zero. Why wouldn't it, on Parfit's view? But it never does—at least if we're Paretians. A different defense of prioritarianism sees the weighted-welfare rule, $\Sigma g(U_i)$, as a hybrid factor that results from merging overall welfare, ΣU_i, with egalitarian considerations. For technical reasons, we are skeptical that this defense succeeds.[78]

Admittedly, our relatively brief analysis here is hardly a decisive refutation of prioritarianism—a view that meshes with intuitions and practice much better than leximin, and that many contemporary philosophers find congenial. And, as an argument in the alternative, we should point out that CBA with distributive weights is plausibly an excellent decision-procedure to implement the prioritarian rule, just as CBA (without distributive weights, or with less substantial weights) is generally the overall-welfare-maximizing procedure. Still, we are not persuaded that prioritarianism improves on weak welfarism, and for the remainder of this book we will assume that unweighted overall welfare ΣU_i, rather than some weighted variant $\Sigma g(U_i)$, has moral relevance for individuals and policymakers.

A second objection to weak welfarism derives from work by Thomas Nagel. Nagel suggests that we have reason, not to promote overall welfare, but rather to maximize the attainment of certain aspects or preconditions of welfare, such as relief from pain.

> If you and a stranger have both been injured, you have one dose of painkiller, and his pain is much more severe than yours, you should give him the painkiller—not for any complicated reasons, but simply because of the relative severity of the two pains, which provides a neutral reason to prefer the relief of the more severe. The same may be said of other basic elements of human good and ill.
>
> But many values are not like this. Though some human interests (and not only pleasure and pain) give rise to impersonal values, I now want to argue

that not all of them do. If I have a bad headache, anyone has a reason to want it to stop. But if I badly want to climb to the top of Mount Kilimanjaro, not everyone has a reason to want me to succeed. I have a reason to try to get the top, and it may be much stronger than my reason for wanting a headache to go away, but other people have very little reason, if any, to care whether I climb the mountain or not.[79]

Nagel, as we read him, is not defending hedonism about well-being. He is not claiming that welfare reduces to pains and pleasures. That is a view we have already considered and rejected. Rather, Nagel is claiming that there are only certain aspects of a person's well-being—paradigmatically, pains and pleasures—that give rise to moral obligations that are binding on other persons. There may well be a wide range of things that I care about, that enhance my welfare, and that I rationally pursue, but only a subset of the components of my welfare have moral significance for others (or for government).

Nagel's view has the implausible implication that we have moral reason to alleviate the pains that rich persons suffer, but not to make them better off. Laura is very rich, much richer than Lee. In one case, Laura suffers a bad headache; in another case, there is something Laura wants very much (and this preference is self-interested and survives idealization). Assume that Lee can act, at a trivial cost to himself, to alleviate Laura's headache or satisfy Laura's preference. Nagel would argue that Lee has a moral reason to alleviate Laura's headache, but not to satisfy Laura's preference. This seems wrong. Note that in *neither* case does Laura have a rights-based claim to Lee's action (he hasn't previously promised her help, etc.) or a distributive claim (she's very rich). Relieving the headache is simply a way to promote human good—welfare—and that reason obtains as much in the second case as in the first.[80]

Our response to Nagel's and similar views should not be taken as an objection to resourcism about distributive justice.[81] Rawls, an early "resourcist," proposes two principles of justice. Crucially, these principles involve the distribution of "primary goods": rights and liberties, opportunities and powers, income and wealth, and a sense of one's worth. The primary goods are all-purpose means to welfare—in other words, resources—rather than welfare itself. "With more of these goods men can generally be assured of greater success in carrying out their intentions and advancing their ends, whatever these ends may be."[82] Ronald Dworkin, building on Rawls, argues that equality demands equality of resources, not equality of welfare;[83] and broadly similar claims have been made by Amartya Sen, G. A. Cohen, and various other theorists of distributive justice.[84] A central concern, in this literature, is that distributive principles formulated in terms of welfare itself require the channeling of resources to individuals with expensive preferences, and fail to distinguish between individuals who have ended up at a given welfare level but have different degrees of responsibility for that result. Other justice theorists, such as Richard Arneson, have argued that welfare rather than resources is the appropriate "currency" for distributive justice, and that the resourcists' worries can be accommodated by tinkering with this currency rather than abandoning it.[85]

We take no position in the debate between Rawls and other resourcists and Arneson. Weak welfarism might include an egalitarian factor using resources as its "currency," or an egalitarian factor using welfare as its currency, or no egalitarian factor at all. The moral relevance of overall welfare is separate from considerations of equal or fair distribution. Weak welfarism has the structure $\{W, F_1 \ldots F_m\}$. In disputing Nagel, we claim only that the "W" factor requires the maximization of welfare itself, rather than certain aspects or preconditions of welfare; we take no position about the structure of the other possible factors $F_1 \ldots F_m$.

A third objection to weak welfarism runs as follows. "Although it is supererogatory, that is, morally praiseworthy, to promote overall welfare, agents are not morally required to do so. Welfare, per se, is too weak a moral consideration to generate moral requirements and prohibitions." We disagree. Overall welfare is a full-fledged moral factor, one that *will* generate moral requirements if not outweighed by other factors.

The standard rationale for making a moral consideration such as overall welfare merely supererogatory is that a moral requirement to advance that consideration would disrupt the agent's own life. Agents need "breathing room" to pursue their own concerns; morality cannot be too "demanding" of agents; the correct moral view will be one that accords agents a wide range of morally permissible choices in typical choice situations, for after all we cannot expect agents always to ignore their own interests for the sake of morality.[86] Whatever the force of this criticism, with respect to private actors, it has no relevance for *governmental officials* acting in their official capacity. As Robert Goodin notes: "Complete neutrality [as between the agent's interests and those of others] is an ideal which people in their public capacities should strive to realize as best they are able." Although "[t]here is no obvious place within utilitarian theories for people's idiosyncratic perspectives, histories, attachments, loyalties or personal commitments," and "[t]hat rings untrue to certain essential qualities of personal life," it is "the essence of public service . . . that public servants should serve the public at large."[87] Governmental officials, at least, are *morally required* to promote overall well-being, absent conflicting moral considerations. For them (and it is, of course, official action that is our concern in this book), overall welfare and the use of welfare-justified decision-procedures are more than supererogatory.

A final objection is that weak welfarism is just too weak to support CBA. Again, weak welfarism says that morality has the structure $\{W, F_1, F_2, \ldots, F_m\}$, where W is overall welfare, the F_i are other considerations, and $m \geq = 0$. Utilitarianism says that morality has the structure $\{W\}$. If CBA is the welfare-maximizing decision procedure, then utilitarianism requires CBA. But— even if CBA is the welfare-maximizing decision procedure—why would weak welfarism require agency use of CBA? After all, there may be other moral criteria in the picture $\{F_1 \ldots F_m\}$, for example, moral rights or distributive criteria.

Our answer, to be fleshed out in Chapter 6, is that CBA is not a superprocedure for agency choice. It is meant to implement overall welfare, not the totality of moral considerations. Cost-benefit analysis is merely one part of a larger, morally well-designed set of governmental procedures and institutions.

But we are jumping the gun. In the next two chapters, we shift our attention from the basic moral landscape to concrete decision procedures, comparing CBA and competitors in light of overall welfare. We then discuss how to refine CBA's performance as a welfarist tool, given the existence of distorted preferences. Having done that, we can address the question of governmental implementation of rights, distributive considerations, and other moral considerations additional to overall welfare.

CHAPTER 3

Cost-Benefit Analysis as a
Decision Procedure

The previous chapter focused on the moral backdrop for CBA. We presented a "restricted preference-based" account of human welfare, arguing that well-being consists in the satisfaction of preferences that survive idealization and are self-interested. We then defended a moral view we termed "weak welfarism." Overall welfare is a coherent notion, and is one of a possible plurality of moral factors.

In this chapter we shift focus from moral foundations to governmental practices. We first draw a distinction between *moral criteria* and morally justified *decision procedures*. A moral criterion identifies the features of outcomes that make them morally better or worse than alternatives. A decision procedure is a technique for making choices, and the morally justified decision procedure is that procedure the employment of which leads to the best outcomes.

Cost-benefit analysis is not a moral criterion. The fact that the sum-of-CVs is greater in outcome O than in O^* does not mean that O is *in any way* morally better or more attractive than O^*.

Rather, CBA is the welfare-maximizing decision procedure.[1] Or at least it is quite plausible to think that CBA, suitably modified to function as a practicable decision-making tool, is welfare maximizing, as compared to currently available competitor procedures (such as safety maximization, "feasibility" analysis, cost-effectiveness analysis, or an intuitive rather than monetized balancing of costs and benefits), across a wide range of governmental choice situations. Crucially, the status of overall welfare as a bedrock moral criterion does *not* entail that a naïve decision procedure that tells governmental officials to "maximize overall welfare" is the optimal one. Conversely, even though the sum-of-CVs test lacks bedrock moral status, instructing officials to follow CBA could still be welfare maximizing.

Whether a governmental decision procedure is welfare maximizing, as compared to alternative procedures, chiefly depends on (1) its decision costs, both the direct information-gathering and processing costs of carrying out the procedure and the delay costs; (2) its accuracy in tracking overall welfare; and (3) the degree to which the political and institutional context in which the procedure is embedded prevents opportunism or mistakes by the decision-makers who are supposed to be implementing it.

These three desiderata will structure our assessment of CBA as a decision procedure. After clarifying the distinction between decision procedures and moral criteria, we describe a variety of possible modifications to the traditional sum-of-CVs test, many of which are routinely used in current CBA practice, that serve or could serve to optimize the functioning of CBA as a decision procedure—by reducing decision costs, increasing accuracy, or dampening opportunism and mistakes. We then review the chief competing procedures that agencies employ or might employ in lieu of CBA, and begin the task of determining which decision procedure is optimal. We train our attention, in this chapter, on the issues of decision-cost and accuracy. The topic of decision-maker mistakes and opportunism is the subject of the next chapter. The thorny problem of structuring administrative procedures and institutions to maximize welfare, given that administrative officials, as well as the political principals who oversee them, may well have goals other than welfare-maximization, is sufficiently complicated to merit a separate chapter.

Decision Procedures and Moral Criteria

A moral criterion specifies the attributes of actions and outcomes that make them right or wrong, better or worse. Different moral theories offer different lists, longer or shorter, of moral criteria.[2] For example, utilitarianism identifies overall welfare as the sole moral criterion. Pure egalitarianism identifies the equalization of welfare levels as the sole moral criterion. Weak welfarism, our preferred theory, identifies overall welfare as a genuine moral criterion or factor, and leaves open the possibility that there are additional such criteria. According to weak welfarism, outcome O is genuinely morally better than outcome O^*, *ceteris paribus*, if aggregate welfare is greater in outcome O.

Cost-benefit analysis is *not* a moral criterion. To begin, CBA and overall welfare are not equivalent. In other words, it is possible that (1) overall welfare is greater in O^* than in O, but (2) the sum-of-CVs is greater in O than in O^*. The proposition that both CBA and its close cousin, Kaldor-Hicks efficiency, can diverge from overall welfare was defended in Chapter 1, and will not be belabored here. Fundamentally, that divergence occurs because dollars can have variable marginal utility. The contribution that an incremental dollar makes to overall welfare can vary, depending on the characteristics of the person to whose resources that dollar is added (for example, his existing wealth). This point is intuitively obvious. Further, it should be noted that neither our preferred account of interpersonal comparisons—the modified Harsanyi account—nor other plausible accounts would ensure that dollars have a constant marginal utility. And scholars, both philosophers and economists, who accept the possibility of interpersonal welfare comparisons universally accept that dollars need not have a constant marginal impact on overall welfare.[3]

Conceivably, morality could have the structure $\{W,$ sum-of-CVs, $F_1, \ldots, F_m\}$. In other words, overall well-being and CBA might enter morality as separate, bedrock, moral criteria. But that seems wrong. The sum-of-CVs test has moral weight, if any, in virtue of its connection to welfare. Since that connection is a contingent one, the sum-of-CVs test lacks bedrock moral status. The fact that the sum-of-CVs is greater in outcome O than in O^* does not mean that O is a morally better outcome than O^*, even *ceteris paribus*. A project that passes a CBA test, relative to the status quo, is not—without more— better than the status quo *at all*. The choice between a project with net money benefits and a status quo with net money costs may, in principle, be entirely a matter of moral indifference.

This conclusion might dishearten, even shock, the proponents and practitioners of CBA. It is crucial, however, to distinguish between *moral criteria* and morally justified *decision procedures*.[4] A decision procedure is a technique for making choices. Decision procedures are ubiquitous. They are used by private individuals and by governmental officials. They may be adopted on a one-off basis, to resolve particular choices. Or a decision procedure may be general, in the sense that it is adopted for application to a whole set of choice situations.

Our interest, in this book, concerns the general decision procedures for administrative choice that are put in place by statutes or presidential orders, or by agencies themselves in the form of regulations or other legal norms guiding agency staff. The crucial point to see—no less crucial for being pretty obvious, once stated—is this: Given some moral criterion C, the optimal legal directive in light of C need not be "Follow a procedure of maximizing C." It might be optimal, instead, to enact a legal directive that instructs agencies to "Follow procedure D," even though D and C are different, and even though D itself is not a moral criterion.

The distinction we are drawing here, between moral criteria and morally justified decision procedures, will be obvious for those readers familiar with the legal scholarship on "rules" versus "standards."[5] Imagine a legislator with some goal, for instance highway safety, she is trying to maximize. The basic observation of the rules-versus-standards literature is that directly enacting the legislative goal into law may not actually maximize the accomplishment of the goal. The legislator has the option of enacting a provision in the traffic code that says: "Motorists must drive safely." Another option is a provision that states: "Motorists must not drive faster than fifty-five miles per hour." The first provision is a "standard"; it simply replicates the underlying legislative goal. The second provision is a "rule." It deviates, in some instances, from the underlying legislative goal, but is easier to apply.

If motorists, police officers, and traffic court judges were perfectly accurate in sorting between safe and unsafe driving behavior, then the first provision would better accomplish the safety goal. But humans are fallible: for example, police officers applying the first provision might fail to catch some instances of unsafe driving, and reciprocally might pull over some drivers who are actually driving safely. The first provision, which directly enacts the underlying goal, might *in its actual application* be overinclusive and underinclusive relative to that goal, just like the second provision. Indeed, the first provision, in its actual application, might be more overinclusive and/or underinclusive than the second provision. It might produce more "false positives" (genuinely safe behavior that is sanctioned) and/or more "false negatives" (genuinely unsafe behavior that is not sanctioned). After all, it is much easier for fallible humans (with radar detectors and speedometers) to determine rate of speed in miles per hour than to judge safety. So the safety-maximizing choice for the legislator could well be to enact the second provision, the "rule," rather than the first provision, the "standard."[6]

This example, and much of the scholarship on "rules" versus "standards," focuses on the legal regulation of private behavior. Our focus, by contrast, is public law: the legal regulation of choices by administrative officials. Still, the basic insight carries over. An agency overseer aiming at some goal (for our purposes, the criterion of overall welfare) has the option of instructing the agency to directly implement the goal, but may actually do better, in terms of the goal, by instructing the agency to use a different procedure.

This distinction between moral criteria and morally optimal decision procedures has two reciprocal implications for weak welfarism. First, although overall welfare *is* a moral criterion, a legal provision instructing agencies to "choose between policies by identifying the policy that maximizes overall welfare" need not itself be the welfare-maximizing provision, and almost surely is not. Second, and reciprocally, although CBA is not a moral criterion, a legal rule instructing agencies to "choose between policies by following CBA" could still be the welfare-maximizing provision.

Let us start with the first observation. We are imagining a decision procedure—

call it the "direct implementation" of overall welfare—that is structured as follows. The agency decision-maker is instructed to follow these steps in selecting a policy: (1) Identify every possible policy option $\{A_1 \ldots A_n\}$, up to the limits of his cognitive ability; (2) for each policy option A_i, identify every outcome $\{O_{i,1}, \ldots, O_{i,M}\}$ that might result from A_i, up to the limits of his cognitive ability; (3) for each $(A_i, O_{i,j})$ pair, gather all information relevant to refining a probability assessment that A_i would result in $O_{i,j}$; (4) for each $O_{i,j}$, gather all information relevant to refining his evaluation of the level of aggregate welfare realized in $O_{i,j}$; (5) use that information to assign a utility number to $O_{i,j}$; (6) for each A_i, determine expected utility; (7) choose the A_i that maximizes expected utility.

Clearly, a legal provision instructing administrative officials to follow these steps—to "directly implement" overall welfare—is not itself welfare maximizing. To begin, the "direct implementation" procedure would have massive decision costs, both direct costs (in employee wages and other direct expenses) and delay costs. Information gathering is expensive. The "direct implementation" procedure tells agencies to collect all information relevant to determining the probability of the different possible outcomes of policy choices and to determining the level of overall welfare in each outcome. The policy-analytic literature on the "value of information" recognizes that information is not free.[7] The expected benefit of acquiring an incremental unit of information may be less than the expected cost. But no such "value of information" safety valve is built into the direct implementation procedure.

The fact that administrative officials are boundedly rational is a further reason that the "direct implementation" procedure would have massive decision costs. Bounded rationality should be distinguished from the lack of information.[8] Omniscient officials have complete information. Boundlessly rational, nonomniscient officials have incomplete information but can process information, perform mathematical operations, and perform other mental tasks at zero cost and infinite speed. Boundedly rational officials face computational limits, and mental tasks are both costly and time-consuming for them. Classical economic theory assumes actors who are nonomniscient but boundlessly rational. Real humans, of course, are boundedly rational.

Some of the steps of the "direct implementation" procedure involve exhaustively *characterizing* possible choices and outcomes. The official is told to enumerate all possible policy alternatives and, then, all possible outcomes of each alternative. If officials conformed to the idealized model of classical economic theory, then these characterization steps—unlike the information-gathering components of direct implementation—would have zero decision costs (direct costs and delay costs). But given bounded rationality, the costs of exhaustive characterization, in computer time, employee wages, and so forth, can be expected to be huge. Note the symmetry with information gathering. Just as the "direct implementation" procedure does not incorporate a "value of information" safety valve that would halt incremental information collection where net expected benefits become negative, so it doesn't instruct decision-makers to make only cost-justified efforts in adding further options to the set of policy choices and further detail to the consequences of those options.

So much for decision costs. The "direct implementation" procedure is also poorly designed to check decision-maker error or opportunism. Well-motivated officials would make errors in following the procedure—once more, a consequence of bounded rationality. For example, direct implementation asks the officials to ascribe probabilities to a huge number of massively described outcomes, conditional on each possible policy choice. And it asks them to determine the level of overall welfare in all of these outcomes. Specifically, if the modified Harsanyi construct for interpersonal comparisons is employed, it asks the decision-maker to determine or at least estimate the way idealized and self-interested spectators, conceiving each outcome as an equiprobability lottery, would rank them. It is an understatement to say that these are not clear or straightforward tasks, and that real-world decision makers—even those who sincerely cared about overall welfare rather than more parochial goals—would accomplish them far from perfectly.

Note, too, that Congress, the president, other oversight bodies, and citizens would find it difficult to monitor official compliance with the direct-implementation procedure. Thus the rule would effectively, if not formally, grant wide discretion to implementing officials. Badly motivated officials would use this discretion to advance their own interests. A clearer decisional rule, one that would be less costly to apply, easier to apply (thus fewer mistakes by well-motivated agents), and easier to monitor (thus fewer cases in which badly motivated agents depart from the rule and advance their own interests), would promote overall welfare much better than direct implementation, even taking into account the inherent inaccuracy in any clearer rule.

The reader might object that our argument attacks a straw man. "No one would think to tell officials to engage in direct implementation of overall welfare, as you have defined it." But direct implementation is not a randomly constructed procedure. It takes the underlying moral criterion (overall welfare) and, in line with classical economical theory, adapts it for nonomniscient decision-makers—those who don't know for certain which outcome would result from a given choice—using the apparatus of expected utility theory.[9] The direct-implementation procedure *would* be welfare maximizing *if* these officials, albeit nonomniscient, were boundlessly rational, could gather available information costlessly, and could be trusted to aim at overall welfare rather than other goals. But these further conditions are clearly not satisfied, and so a legal directive instructing agencies to employ a direct-implementation procedure is not itself welfare maximizing. That is why no sensible person would ever propose such a directive.

We noted earlier that the disjunction between moral criteria and morally justified decision procedures had two, reciprocal implications for welfarism and CBA: first, that "maximize overall welfare" need not be a morally justified decision procedure, even though overall welfare is a moral criterion; and second, that "use CBA" could be a morally justified decision procedure even though CBA is not a moral criterion. Over the last several pages, we have pursued the first point. "Direct implementation" is no longer on the table as a plausible welfarist procedure. In the remainder of the chapter, and the next, we will pursue the second. How should CBA's sum-of-CVs test be restructured to function as a feasible decision-making tool? What are the current competitors to CBA? And which, of all these procedures, is the welfare-maximizing one? To these questions we now turn.

Cost-Benefit Analysis as a Decision Procedure

CBA is traditionally defined as the sum of CVs. This test, unaltered, is not a feasible decision procedure, let alone a welfare-maximizing one. The informational, cognitive, and motivational limits of real-world decisionmakers not only undercut "direct implementation" as a welfarist procedure but also force modifications in CBA itself. For example, a governmental official will not know for sure, even after expending maximal information-gathering effort, what the actual outcome of a policy choice will be, and thus, presumably, cannot know for sure what any individual's CV for that outcome is.

This section describes a variety of modifications to the sum-of-CVs test—many employed in actual governmental practice—that reduce the decision costs associated with CBA, increase its accuracy in tracking welfare, or increase its transparency to overseers and thereby reduce agency error or opportunism. These modifications make CBA a feasible tool for real humans and, moreover, a plausible candidate to be the welfare-maximizing procedure as against currently available alternative procedures.

One modification is to limit the range of policy options considered by the decision-making official.[10] Consider governmental regulation, the heartland of CBA. At any given moment, there are a multitude (indeed, an infinity) of possible regulations that an agency might enact, differing in their subject matter, their addressees, their language, and so on. Boundlessly rational regulators might employ CBA to value all of these choices (as against the status quo choice of inaction). Actual regulators do nothing like that; it is not unusual for the regulatory impact documents that agencies send to the OMB to evaluate just one policy option.[11] The OMB's current guidance urges agencies to consider a plurality of regulatory approaches, but recognizes that it will be optimal to limit the number of alternatives evaluated using CBA (given the incremental decision and delay costs in evaluating an additional option, and the incremental loss in the transparency of the agency's analysis to overseers and interested parties).

> Once you have determined that Federal regulatory action is appropriate, you will need to consider alternative regulatory approaches. Ordinarily, you will be able to eliminate some alternatives through a preliminary analysis, leaving a manageable number of alternatives to be evaluated according to [formal CBA]. The number and choice of alternatives selected for detailed analysis is a matter of judgment. There must be some balance between thoroughness and the practical limits on your analytical capacity. With this qualification in mind, you should nevertheless explore modifications of some or all of a regulation's attributes or provisions to identify appropriate alternatives.[12]

A second set of modifications to the traditional sum-of-CVs test responds to the inevitable problem of uncertainty about the outcomes of governmental choice. Note that this problem would arise even if governmental officials were boundlessly rational but nonomniscient, and a fortiori arises for boundedly rational choosers. An omniscient official confronting policy choices $\{A_1 \ldots A_n\}$ sees each choice A_i as leading for sure to one outcome O_j. An uncertain official confronting the same array of choices sees each choice as leading to a lottery over outcomes. The measure for quantifying the impact of this choice on a given individual must be sensitive to the probabilistic character of the choice, at least if that measure is to be useful to the deciding official. One standard technique is to redefine each individual's CV for a given policy choice ("project") as her "option price": the amount of money, added to or subtracted from each of the possible outcomes in the project lottery, that makes her indifferent between that lottery and the status quo lottery. Another standard proposal is to redefine the CV as the "expected surplus." Here, the idea is to determine the individual's compensating variation for each possible project outcome, then to discount each such value by the probability of the outcome and aggregate the discounted values. The "option price" and "expected surplus" quantities can differ if individuals are not risk-neutral.[13]

A third set of modifications concerns uncertainty about individual valuations. This problem arises, once more, even if officials are boundlessly rational but nonomniscient, and a fortiori given the human reality of both bounded rationality and incomplete information. Further, the problem arises—it should be noted—even if the standard economic view of well-being is adopted and welfare is equated with the satisfaction of nonidealized, unrestricted preferences. The official is choosing between the status quo and some project; each is seen as a lottery over outcomes, and the official is attempting to determine the CV of a given individual P for the project (defined as P's option price, as her expected surplus, or in some other way). Preferences are not directly observable. They are rankings of possible outcomes and lotteries. To determine P's CV for the project lottery means determining the amount or amounts of money sufficient—given P's preferences—to make her indifferent between the status quo and variations on the project outcomes in which the sum is added to or subtracted from her holdings. Nothing in P's behavior directly reveals that CV number.

A large literature in applied welfare economics engages the problem of estimating CVs, given the unobservability of preferences. One set of techniques attempts to infer preferences from market prices and other (nonlinguistic) behavioral evidence.[14] Another set of techniques attempts, in effect, to infer preferences from linguistic behavior.[15] The latter techniques (so-called contingent valuation or stated preference techniques) involve surveys where respondents are asked about their willingness to pay or accept for goods and bads. There is a heated scholarly debate about the merits of the two techniques.[16] This debate raises complicated econometric issues that we will not attempt to engage in this book. The basic point to see is that CBA, as a decision procedure, must include practicable methods for estimating individual valuations, responsive to the fact that these valuations are unobservable and therefore uncertain. The debate about revealed preference versus contingent valuation/stated preference is a debate about what the optimal estimation methods are.

A fourth set of modifications to the sum-of-CVs test responds to the numerosity and complexity of the possible outcomes of each governmental choice. A nonomniscient but boundlessly rational official would see each policy choice as a lottery across "possible worlds."[17] Each possible world is a completely specified possible history of the universe. Imagining a single possible world, let alone the uncountable infinity of possible worlds that might result from a given choice, is infeasible for computationally limited humans. So the possible "outcomes" that real CBA analysts consider are not outcomes in the strict philosophical sense, namely, complete possible worlds. They are much, much lumpier than that. In effect, these CBA "outcomes" are large groups of possible worlds. Within-group welfare differences are (implicitly) seen as too trivial, or too difficult to estimate, and are ignored by the CBA analyst; between-group differences are highlighted.

Here's an illustrative example. An environmental agency is considering issuing a regulation that lowers the permissible amount of some air pollutant emitted by firms in some industrial category. As costs of this regulation, the agency may well consider its effect on consumer, factor-supplier, worker, and shareholder surplus mediated through a shift upward in the industry's supply curve. As benefits of the regulation, the agency may well consider its effect in reducing mortality. There will be uncertainty about the exact movement in the supply curve, and the exact number of deaths avoided. Focusing on the benefit side, one possible outcome is that reducing the emissions avoids one premature death. Another possible outcome is that it avoids two. Another is that it avoids three. The agency will use risk assessment to estimate a mean number of deaths avoided or (if it's a little more sophisticated) to derive a probability distribution across the number of deaths avoided. That mean, or probability distribution, will then be integrated with the "value of statistical life" number (for example, $5 million), to determine a monetary benefit from the regulation.[18] Clearly, each "outcome" here $(1, 2, \ldots, n$ fewer deaths than baseline) is not a maximally specified possible world. Clearly, too, there can be welfare differences within a single "outcome" that the analysis will overlook. Certain members of the population might be aware of, and anxious about, the pollutant. So the "outcome" in which n deaths are avoided by the regulation will have distinct suboutcomes in which anxiety is reduced by distinct amounts. It will also have distinct suboutcomes that differ in completely welfare-irrelevant ways: say, the number of individuals with green eyes. But given decision costs and transparency, it will surely be optimal for CBA to clump together possible worlds in defining outcomes so as to ignore welfare-irrelevant differences between possible worlds (the number of people with green eyes) and, perhaps, to ignore some welfare-relevant differences too (the level of anxiety).[19]

A fifth and related set of modifications to CBA responds to the numerosity of individuals and the heterogeneity of their preferences. Different members of the population will have different CVs for a given good, as a result of differences in inborn tastes, upbringing, education, social and professional status, wealth, and so on. Even if the problem of identifying a particular individual's CV, given the unobservability of her preferences, is placed to one side, the fact remains that there are hundreds of millions of U.S. citizens. Thus calculating the sum-of-CVs for a given outcome or lottery by determining the individual CV of each member of the U.S. population and aggregating would be quite expensive. Cost-benefit analysis in practice uses different and much cheaper approaches. The cheapest is to assume homogeneity in preferences; for example, agencies typically now use a single "value of statistical life," even though actual CVs to avoid a risk of death are heterogeneous, varying with respect to wealth, age, race, gender, and a host of other individual characteristics.[20] A different approach is to estimate the variation in preferences and CVs as a function of a tractable number of individual characteristics.[21] Yet another approach, in the case of a marketed good, is to use observed price-output combinations to estimate demand curves for the good and therewith the sum of CVs for a change that affects the market. Heterogeneity in preferences for a good will be reflected in the slope of its demand curve.

A different group of possible modifications to CBA derive from the restricted preference-based view of welfare we argued for in Chapter 2. An outcome (or lottery) benefits P, as compared to an alternative, if and only if P actually prefers the outcome (or lottery) *and* this preference is self-interested and survives idealization. Assume that this restricted preference-based view of well-being is correct, and that constructs for interpersonal comparison reflect that (as, for example, a modified Harsanyi construct would). As traditionally defined, CVs focus solely on actual preferences and incorporate neither an idealization filter nor a self-interest filter. So the standard sum-of-CVs test will deviate from overall welfare. "Laundering" CVs to eliminate the effect of nonideal preferences and/or disinterested preferences could increase the accuracy of CBA in tracking overall welfare. For example, P's traditional CV for the preservation of an endangered species might be positive, but his "laundered" CV could be zero (if his preference for preservation is purely disinterested). Similarly, P's traditional CV for using a mind-altering drug might be positive, but his "laundered" CV could be zero or negative (if P with full information, or under other idealizing conditions, would not prefer to use the drug). As we shall see in Chapter 5, agencies in practice *do* "launder" preferences in calculating CVs, at least in some contexts.

Finally, CBA could be modified to counteract the variable marginal utility of money, by adjusting CVs using "distributive weights." Wealthy individuals would have low CV weights; poorer individuals would have high CV weights. Here, too, as in the notion of "laundering" CVs to eliminate welfare-irrelevant preferences, the idea is to reduce the disparity between CBA and overall welfare.

To sum up: CBA, to function as a decision procedure, clearly needs to be refined to limit the number of policy options evaluated, to reflect decision-maker uncertainty about the outcomes of those options and about individual valuations, to limit the number and complexity of the possible outcomes evaluated, and to limit the heterogeneity of individual valuations. In addition, CBA might be refined to "launder" CVs and to incorporate distributive weights. Exactly what the modifications to CBA should be is a large and difficult question—one that is partly engaged in Chapter 5, where we discuss the possibility of "laundering" CVs and using distributive weights, but can hardly be resolved in this book. The crucial points, here, are that CBA should be conceptualized as a decision procedure, not a moral criterion; and that it will be a welfare-maximizing procedure only if the traditional sum-of-CVs test is modified in a host of ways.

In comparing CBA to alternative decision procedures with respect to overall welfare, we will assume that the traditional test has been modified, if not optimally, then at least in substantial, welfare-improving ways. Our basic question is whether CBA *in some form* is a better decision procedure than alternatives; and to answer that question, we should focus on CBA as structured to reduce decision costs, increase accuracy, and increase transparency.

Cost-Benefit Analysis and Its Competitors

What are the competitors to CBA? Start with current administrative practice. CBA is a procedure that measures the impact of agency choice on a plurality of aspects of human welfare using a money scale. Frequently, however, agencies compare the welfare "costs" and "benefits" of their choices in a more qualitative way. Policy effects will be described, and indeed might be quantified on various scales (for example, numbers of deaths, acres of ecosystem destroyed, jobs lost or gained), but no monetary scale for commensurating all these impacts will be deployed. Instead, the trade-off will be done more intuitively.[22]

Sometimes, statutes preclude agencies from using either CBA or the more intuitive balancing just described. Much of environmental, health, and safety regulation is like this.[23] An agency might be told to maximize safety rather than to balance safety against compliance costs and other costs. For example, the FDA is instructed to license only food additives that are "safe."[24] Section 109 of the Clean Air Act, governing pervasive air pollutants such as sulfur dioxide, particulate matter, and ozone, instructs the EPA to set standards that "are requisite to protect the public health" and "allow[] an adequate margin of safety."[25] A different sort of departure from CBA, quite standard in social regulation, occurs when an agency focuses on "feasible" technology.[26] The Clean Water Act, for example, requires certain emissions from point sources to be controlled up to the point that is achievable "through application of the best available demonstrated control technology."[27] Sometimes the "feasibility" idea and the "safety" idea are combined. The provision of the Occupational Safety and Health Act governing toxic workplace chemicals directs OSHA to issue standards that "most adequately assure[], to the extent feasible, . . . no employee will suffer material impairment of health or functional capability."[28]

How are we to categorize these procedures and other techniques actually employed by agencies, as well as possible techniques not currently in use? Our interest here is in identifying the decision procedure that maximizes welfare. The following categorization suggests itself. We might distinguish between *welfare-focused procedures,* that direct the agency to maximize one or more aspects of well-being; and *non-welfare-focused procedures,* that direct the agency to use some other test for evaluating policies. Within the group of welfare-focused procedures, we might further place procedures on a spectrum from *narrow* to *wide.* A narrow procedure will direct the agency to maximize one aspect of welfare, ignoring the others; a wider procedure will direct the agency to consider the impact of its choices on all, or at least many dimensions of welfare, without giving priority to any one.

In thinking about the "dimensions" of welfare, Martha Nussbaum's list of objective welfare goods is useful.[29] This is the most inclusive list proposed within the objective-good school of well-being. Furthermore, unlike lists that are generated by focusing on the human "essence" or other such notions, Nussbaum's list is plausibly close to what people with full information would prefer. So an objectivist construct for interpersonal comparisons that integrates the goods on this list is probably not too distant from the modified Harsanyi construct we prefer.

Nussbaum's List

Life	Practical reason
Bodily health	Affiliation

Bodily integrity	Other species
Senses, imagination, and thought	Play
Emotions	Control over the environment

A wide, welfare-focused procedure will instruct the agency to consider all or most of these dimensions. A narrow, welfare-focused procedure will instruct the agency to consider only a few. A non-welfare-focused procedure will take a different form entirely. This categorization scheme is pragmatic and provisional, meant only to facilitate a comparative welfarist analysis of decision procedures; a different scheme might also do so, but we think this one works pretty well.

A decision procedure that instructs agencies to require reductions in some pollutant or some other hazard up to the point that is "feasible," defined in terms of currently existing technology, or in terms of current practices (for example, the level of the pollutant emitted by the cleanest firms, or the median firm, or the top quartile of firms), is an excellent example of a non-welfare-focused procedure. The feasibility standard tells the agency to evaluate competing regulatory options, not by asking which one maximizes safety, and not by considering the compliance costs of those options, but rather by seeking the lowest risk level that is technologically achievable or actually achieved by a sufficient number of actors. "Feasibility" requirements are widespread in environmental law.[30] Another non-welfare-focused procedure that arises frequently in legal contexts is the procedure of looking to social norms. The "reasonableness" standard of tort law is sometimes understood by scholars as a test that looks to customary behavior, rather than an efficiency or welfare-maximization test as per Learned Hand, and appears to be often thus construed by juries.[31]

Decision procedures that focus on technological feasibility, actual firm practices, or customary practices are important examples of non-welfare-focused procedures, but hardly exhaust the category. The category is really a residual one. *Any* procedure that ranks policies in terms of some characteristic other than their impact on (one or more of the) dimensions of welfare falls in this residual category.

Consider, next, the category of "narrow" welfare-focused procedures. Procedures toward the "narrow" end of the spectrum require the agency to focus on a small number of dimensions of well-being, and to ignore all others. "Safety"-focused procedures are a standard example. Actually, there are a variety of different forms that safety-focused procedures take in regulatory practice. The agency might try to *regulate a particular hazard so that it is "safe"* (so that it imposes a zero or de minimis risk of death on those exposed to the hazard). Alternatively, the agency might try to *minimize the total number of premature deaths,* taking into consideration both the deaths that result from the targeted hazard and from efforts to mitigate it. This is, in effect, what the procedure known as "risk-risk" analysis does. Or it might try to *maximize longevity,* taking into account not just the number of premature deaths but also the number of life-years lost. Or it might try to *maximize life-years adjusted for health quality.* The quality adjusted life-year (QALY) scale, a popular metric in public health research, is a practicable way to measure health-adjusted longevity. There are important differences between these approaches, but for our purposes they share a crucial similarity: all train the agency's attention on Nussbaum's "life" dimension (or in the case of QALY adjustments, the "life" and "bodily health" dimensions), to the exclusion of others.[32]

Safety-focused procedures are a familiar example of narrow welfare-focused procedures, but in principle, any dimension of welfare could be assigned to an agency as its sole maximand. For example, an agency might be told to maximize friendship (a subdimension of Nussbaum's affiliation value). This is, of course, fanciful. Less fanciful are statutes that focus on education, or environmental quality, or species preservation, or the arts, or protecting individuals from discrimination, or religious freedom.[33] The "malum in se" offenses of the traditional criminal law also put in place a kind of narrow welfare-focused procedure. This corpus of law is mainly concerned with threats to particular aspects of well-being, namely life, bodily integrity, and property, rather than to well-being generally.

The "precautionary principle" endorsed by many environmentalists and often employed (or at least avowed) by governments abroad is an interesting example of a narrow welfare-focused procedure. One standard articulation of the principle is this: "When an activity raises threats of harm to human health or the environment, precautionary measures should be taken even if some cause and effect relationships are not fully established scientifically."[34] What exactly this means is unclear. Is it simply a strong statement of the priority of health and environmental values over other considerations, namely, that regulators should regulate potentially dangerous or dirty activities, seeking to maximize expected health and environmental preservation, even if it is uncertain that the activities are dangerous or dirty? Or is the principle, instead, a statement that *new* technologies are presumptively more hazardous and environmentally threatening than old ones? Whatever its precise meaning, the precautionary principle is a welfare-focused procedure that seems wider than death minimization, or even QALY maximization (since it focuses on both environmental values and health) but is still quite restrictive in ignoring everything except safety and the environment.

"Happiness" metrics should also be mentioned here. "Happiness" research is a rapidly growing field within welfare economics.[35] This research uses surveys to quantify "happiness" or "subjective life satisfaction" of different individuals. Much of this work has focused on the determinants of happiness and on intercountry comparisons: for example, by comparing average numerical happiness indices for third world and first world countries and explaining the difference with reference to factors such as gross national product, employment, political freedom, inflation, and so on. But it has also been suggested that happiness indices could be used for policy analysis.

> The use of measures of happiness allows for a new way of evaluating the *effects of government expenditure* . . . The problem has been approached scientifically by using cost-benefit analysis. The benefits are the recipients' marginal willingness to pay, which is best measured by a contingent valuation analysis . . . This method is best suited to relatively small and isolated public projects, but it breaks down when it comes to more extensive expenditure policies. Simulations using microeconomic happiness functions with a large number of determinants may be better able to evaluate the widespread effects of such policies.[36]

"Happiness" is a kind of pleasant *experience*. So a "happiness" maximization procedure for policy choice would be an exemplary narrow welfare-focused procedure. As we argued at length above, pleasure and the avoidance of pain are simply one aspect of well-being, not the totality. This is reflected in Nussbaum's list, which classifies pleasure/pain as a subdimension of "senses, imagination and thought."[37]

"Narrow" procedures can reach outcomes that are at variance with overall welfare, as we shall elaborate below. For example, a safety-maximization statute could require firms to incur huge compliance costs for the sake of small risk reductions. One solution to this problem is to adopt a wide welfare focused procedure, such as CBA. A different solution, often employed in regulatory practice, is to combine a narrow welfare-focused procedure with a *cutoff*. For example, an agency might be told to maximize safety, up to the point of "feasibility" defined in terms of current best practices. (This takes off the table the option of increasing safety further by requiring novel and expensive technology.) Or to maximize "safety" up to the point of technological feasibility. (This takes off the table the option of increasing safety further by shutting down production entirely.) Combining a narrow welfare-focused procedure with a cutoff is a kind of hybrid procedure. The cut-off can be defined in nonwelfarist terms (feasibility, social norms) or in welfarist terms, for example, requiring safety maximization except where the costs of increasing safety are massive.

Note that this last example differs from CBA in that the agency is *not* told to balance safety and other welfare dimensions, as per their actual welfare weight. Rather, nonsafety dimensions have zero weight until the costs along these dimensions become sufficiently large. This is generally the structure of "cost-effectiveness analysis," which we therefore classify as a hybrid procedure.[38] In cost-effectiveness analysis, the agency has some cost budget, which is defined exogenously. The agency is then told to maximize some goal (safety, or something else) up to the point of exhausting the budget.

Let us turn, finally, to wide welfare-focused procedures. Cost-benefit analysis is one example of a wide welfare-focused procedure now employed by governmental bodies. In principle, CVs are sensitive to *all* the dimensions of welfare. This is certainly true if CVs are laundered. And even if they are not—even if they are determined in a more traditional way by looking to willingness-to-pay-or-accept in terms of actual preferences—there should be at least a probabilistic connection between genuine welfare changes and changes in CVs. It is also true that CBA analysts, in practice, ignore welfare dimensions where CVs are just too hard to estimate given current techniques—for example, fear or friendship. Still, a substantially larger set of welfare effects is currently reflected in CBA than in safety-maximization or cognate procedures, and yet more will be reflected in the future as estimation techniques improve.

Other than CBA, the only sort of wide welfare-focused procedure now used by governmental bodies is the intuitive balancing we described earlier. Open-ended statutes instructing agencies to adopt "reasonable" regulatory measures,[39] or otherwise licensing or requiring them to take account of a plurality of values, are sometimes implemented not through monetized CBA but rather through an intuitive balancing of different welfare dimensions.[40] Cass Sunstein, now a proponent of CBA, was once an advocate of intuitive balancing. In a 1995 article coauthored with Richard Pildes, he crisply describes and endorses this procedure.

> We do not do well if we see such diverse goods as greater employment, protection of endangered species, lower prices, distributional effects, and cleaner air along a single [cost-benefit] metric, one that erases the qualitative dif-

ferences among these goods. At least in principle, it would be better to have a disaggregated system for assessing the qualitatively different effects of regulatory impositions. . . .

Through regulatory-impact analyses, people should be allowed to see the diverse effects of regulation for themselves, and to make judgments based on an understanding of the qualitative differences. If all of the relevant goods are aligned along a single metric, they become less visible, or perhaps invisible.[41]

At this juncture, a terminological clarification may be helpful. We use the term "cost-benefit analysis" as applied economists and policy analysts typically do, to mean a *monetizing* procedure: one that reduces all effects included in the analysis to a dollar amount, and then aggregates. Sometimes, however, "cost-benefit analysis" is used more generically, to include *any* wide or multidimensional procedure, not just a monetizing one. "Cost benefit analysis," in this sense, includes both monetized CBA and intuitive balancing as specific instances. Whatever the semantics, the point to see is that the monetized, sum-of-CVs test—what we mean by "CBA"—and intuitive balancing are distinct procedures.

A variant on intuitive balancing, suggested in the philosophical literature, is to use explicit quantitative trade-off rates between the dimensions. James Griffin proposes as much, as does Thomas Scanlon. To quote Griffin:

> [G]overnments—just as you and I in our interpersonal comparisons—would use, for the most part, the list of [welfare] values, supplemented by their necessary conditions. So we should need to know not each person's individual desires with the intensities peculiar to his nature, but what is in general desirable in life. And we should need to know what the unavoidable means to those ends are: usually, the healthier, wealthier, freer, and more knowledgeable we are, the better we can realize our life plans . . .
>
> In simple cases, a legislator can just take an increase of something on the list of [welfare] values and unavoidable means as an increase in general well-being . . . In more complex cases, a legislator has to decide between promoting one item on the list at the cost of another, for which purpose he will need a schedule of the trade-offs that virtually all of us are willing to make.[42]

The procedure Griffin describes here is distinct from CBA, as we shall elaborate below, not merely because money doesn't function as the metric for welfare, but also because the procedure provides for a single set of global trade-off rates between the various welfare dimensions rather than rates that can be different for different persons.

To summarize: as shown in Table 3.1, governmental decision procedures can be categorized as non-welfare-focused, hybrid, or welfare-focused and, within the latter category, as narrow or wide. There are real-world examples within each category. We now begin the task of considering which procedure is welfare maximizing.

Decision Costs

The decision costs of CBA include both direct costs (wages for agency staff involved in the preparation or review of analyses, the cost of information or computational resources used in analyses, overhead costs, fees for analyses prepared by independent contractors) and costs in the delayed undertaking of beneficial policies. One standard complaint voiced by critics of CBA is that its decision costs are too high.[43] Is this complaint on target?

Richard Morgenstern and Marc Landy have collected estimates of the direct costs of preparing cost-benefit documents for OMB review (presented in Tables 3.2 and 3.3 on p. 82).[44] These data suggest that CBA has substantial direct costs, in the vicinity of $1 million–$2 million on average. More precisely, CBA's direct costs, as compared to a decision procedure with zero direct costs—one that involves no information gathering, computation, or analytic effort by the agency—seem to be $1 million–$2 million on average.

It is possible to have an administrative decision procedure with zero direct costs. Imagine a statute that instructs an agency to issue particular rules, with the subject matter and even language of the rules prespecified by the statute. In this case, direct administrative costs are zero, but that is only because the statute leaves the agency no discretion; and although the agency itself incurs no direct costs, the process of information gathering and analysis is simply shifted from administrative officials to legislative staff.

In any event, CBA and the competitor procedures described in the previous section are meant as general devices to structure agency choice in cases where agencies retain statutory discretion—cases where statutes do not specify exactly what regulations agencies should issue or what other sorts of legal steps they should take. All such procedures will involve nontrivial information gathering, computation, and analytic effort by agencies. This is certainly true of welfare-focused procedures, "narrow" or "wide." For example, safety-maximization procedures—the paradigm of "narrow" welfare-focused procedures—require agencies to undertake risk assessments, so as to determine the risks, deaths, or losses of longevity or health-adjusted longevity

Table 3.1. Categorizing Decision Procedures

Non-Welfare-Focused	Welfare-Focused: Narrow	Welfare-Focused: Wide	Hybrid
"Feasibility" —Technological feasibility —Current practices	Safety-focused —Eliminate risk of particular kind —Eliminate risk of particular kind above de minimis threshold —Minimize premature deaths —Maximize longevity —Maximize QALYs (health-adjusted longevity)	CBA	Cost-effectiveness analysis (Maximize some aspect of well-being within cost budget)
Social norms	Maximize environmental quality; education; species preservation; arts; antidiscrimination; or religious freedom	Intuitive balancing	Maximize some aspect of well-being, with "feasibility" cutoff
	Precautionary principle	Balancing with explicit trade-off rates	Any other combination of narrow procedure with cutoff
Any other procedure defined without reference to one or more aspects of well-being	Happiness-focused procedures	"Direct implementation" of overall well-being (not a realistic possibility)	
	Any other procedure focused on one or a few aspects of well-being		

Table 3.2. Estimated Costs of a Regulatory Impact Analysis

Source	Extramural Costs	Intramural Costs	Total Costs
Portney (1984)	$585,000	$164,000	$ 731,000
EPA (1987)	$662,000	$325,000	$ 987,000
EPA (1995)	$875,000	$160,000	$1,035,000

Note: Costs are in 1995 dollars. Intramural costs include employee salary and benefits plus overhead, and are estimated at $100,000 per full-time employee. Extramural costs are fees paid to contractors.

Sources: Richard D. Morgenstern and Marc K. Landy, "Economic Analysis: Benefits, Costs, Implications," in Richard D. Morgenstern, ed., *Economic Analysis at EPA: Assessing Regulatory Impact* (Washington, D.C.: Resources for the Future Press, 1997), 455, 461–462. Paul Portney, "Will E.O. 12291 Improve Environmental Policy Making?" in V. Kerry Smith, ed., *The Benefits and Costs of Regulatory Analysis in Environmental Policy Under Reagan's Executive Order* (Chapel Hill: Universty of North Carolina Press, 1984), 228–33. EPA, *EPA's Use of Benefit-Cost Analysis, 1981-1986* (Washington, D.C.: 1987) 6–5. Letter from EPA Assistant Administrator David Gardiner to Representative Cardiss Collins, May 17, 1995

Table 3.3. Costs of a Regulatory Impact Analysis: Selected Cases

Rule	Extramural Costs	Intramural Costs	Total Costs
Asbestos	$4,000,000	$4,000,000	$8,000,000
Farmworkers	$ 79,000	$100,000	$ 179,000
Lead in gasoline	$715,000	$800,000	$1,515,000
Municipal landfill	$2,300,000	$1,000,000	$3,300,000
Navajo generating station	$575,000	$200,000	$ 775,000
Reformulated gasoline	$1,250,000	$850,000	$2,100,000
Sludge	$1,250,000	$600,000	$1,850,000

Source: Richard D. Morgenstern and Marc K. Landy, "Economic Analysis: Benefits, Costs, Implications," in Richard D. Morgenstern, ed., *Economic Analysis at EPA: Assessing Regulatory Impact* (Washington, D.C.: Resources for the Future Press, 1997), 455, 461–462.

associated with different hazards and regulatory responses. Similarly, non-welfare-focused procedures meant to structure agency choice across a range of choice situations will have nontrivial direct costs. As mentioned, the paradigm of this sort of procedure is one that tells regulators to require all technologically "feasible" steps to mitigate some health or environmental threat. Ascertaining current technology, and determining whether some regulatory requirement (for example, some amount of emissions reduction) is achievable given that technology, is not an effortless matter.[45]

In short, Morgenstern and Landy's $1 million–$2 million is an upper bound on the incremental direct costs of CBA, as compared to the various competitors described in the previous section. This is a powerful result. $1 million–$2 million is hardly a de minimis sum, but it is swamped by the impact of large rules. As Morgenstern and Landy put it:

> The relatively small direct cost [of CBA] . . . means that it would not take too much in the way of increased benefits or decreased costs of a rule to enable economic analyses to pay for themselves [assuming delay costs aren't large]. Given the modest one time costs of these analyses compared to the annual costs of the rules—over $100 million—a reduction in costs or an increase in benefits in the final rule of well under one percent—probably closer to one-tenth of one percent—could easily justify the cost of an economic analysis.[46]

In other words, the direct-cost objection to CBA can be resolved by limiting it to large projects: those that satisfy some threshold test of size, such that the expected (positive) welfare difference between CBA and the next best procedure justifies an analytical and information-gathering expenditure on the order of $1 million–$2 million. This is indeed what the presidential cost-benefit orders since 1981 have done. The orders have *not* required agencies to engage in a full-blown CBA for all decisions or even all regulations. Rather, only "major" rules (roughly, those with annual effects likely to exceed $100 million) are covered.[47] Whether this $100 million cutoff is optimal is another question; our only point here is that a "refined" CBA, limited to sufficiently large projects, should be welfare maximizing relative to other procedures *if* it is welfare maximizing given all considerations other than direct costs. Above the threshold, expected direct costs should be too small to tip the balance against CBA.

A final point about direct costs: The $1 million–$2 million upper bound likely substantially overstates the true incremental direct costs of CBA relative to the other "wide" procedure on the table, namely intuitive balancing. Cost-benefit analysis means both quantifying and monetizing the impacts of policies on a multiplicity of welfare dimensions; intuitive balancing means quantifying, without monetizing, policy impacts along a multiplicity of welfare dimensions. Where agencies employ standard values to monetize welfare effects—as, for example, in valuing lifesaving—the incremental direct costs of CBA relative to intuitive balancing are miniscule. Even where standard values are not employed, the expense of monetization may be spread over a number of decision contexts—for example, where numbers from a single contingent valuation study conducted to value a particular type of benefit are used in multiple rulemakings.[48] And, in any event, the point remains that direct costs for information gathering and analytic effort, short of monetization, are incurred both by CBA and by wide balancing.

What about delay costs? Thomas McGarity, a leading opponent of CBA, argues that it means "paralysis by analysis."

> Most regulatory reformers prescribe an exceedingly ambitious cost-benefit analysis that would inevitably drain scarce agency analytical resources and slow down the rulemaking process. In the past, some cost-benefit analyses for major rules . . . have consumed years of precious agency time. Regulatory paralysis may have been the ulterior goal of some of the regulatory reformers, who were not so concerned with achieving efficient regulation as with throwing sand into the regulatory gears.[49]

This concern about CBA's delay costs is a common theme in the critical literature.[50] It is linked to a more general worry about the structure of administrative rulemaking. The general worry is that the various procedural and analytical elements of rulemaking—not just CBA but the "notice and comment" process that demands detailed agency responses to public comments about rules, intensive judicial scrutiny to determine whether rules are "arbitrary or capricious," legislative review of rules under the Congressional Review Act, and so on—have led to "ossification" of the rulemaking process. This "ossification" claim is now pretty standard in administrative law scholarship.[51] Here, too, McGarity has been a major voice.[52] As he explains:

> By the end of the 1980s, it was becoming increasingly clear that the informal rulemaking model was not faring very well. Its great virtue had been the efficiency with which federal agencies could implement regulatory policy . . . Throughout the late 1970s and early 1980s, however, the executive branch and, to a more limited extent, Congress added analytical requirements and review procedures, often at the behest of the regulated industries. These initiatives and the continuing scrutiny of reviewing courts under the hard look doctrine caused the rulemaking process to "ossify" to a disturbing degree. By the mid-1990s, it has become so difficult to promulgate major rules that some regulatory programs have ground to a halt and others have succeeded only because agencies have resorted to alternative policymaking vehicles.[53]

The "ossification" critique has, as yet, no rigorous basis. There is very little empirical scholarship that actually attempts to test whether CBA, or other elements of the rulemaking process, do in fact tend to substantially delay or block agency rulemaking.[54] One important exception is a study by William Jordan, who focused not on CBA but on D.C. Circuit remands under the arbitrary or capricious standard, finding that in 80 percent of the cases examined the agency was able to reinstate the original rule or at least to substantially achieve the goals of the original rulemaking—and to do so with a median delay of one year.[55] Another is Cornelius Kerwin and Scott Furlong's statistical study of the determinants of the elapsed time in EPA rulemakings. They include OMB review time as an independent variable, and find that its effect on total time is statistically insignificant.[56] Stuart Shapiro has used variation in *state* rulemaking procedures to study the determinants of administrative ossification, in the area of child-care regulation. He examines four kinds of requirements: legislative or executive review of agency rules; a requirement that the agency perform CBA or a similar analysis, such as fiscal impact analysis; public participation; or mandatory, periodic agency review of existing rules. Shapiro finds that these requirements "appeared to have had little effect on the pace of regulatory change . . . [T]hey are less important than the political coalitions in power and the interest groups [affected by child-care regulation]."[57]

More empirical research on the factors that retard agency decision-making is clearly needed. Absent such research, our views about the delay costs of CBA can only be tentative. But the following propositions seem plausible. As with direct costs, we are interested in the incremental delay costs of CBA relative to the various competitors described in the previous section. Presumably agency implementation of specific statutory mandates can typically occur fairly rapidly, even taking into consideration the notice-and-comment process and judicial review, and bracketing agency opportunism; but the issue here is whether CBA is unduly slow as compared to other generic decisional devices designed to guide *discretionary* agency choice, in the absence of specific statutory guidance.

Consider, first, the incremental delay costs of CBA relative to non-welfare-focused procedures, narrow welfare-focused procedures, and hybrids. Cost-benefit analysis might (1) delay internal agency deliberations; (2) produce incremental delay through special review procedures unique to CBA, for example, OMB review; and/or (3) delay the ordinary external steps that occur in all rulemakings, most importantly the notice-and-comment process and judicial review if the parties seek it. As for (1), CBA clearly involves incremental information-gathering and analysis relative to narrow procedures (because they focus on one welfare dimension, while CBA focuses on multiple dimensions) and may involve incremental effort relative to non-welfare-focused procedures and hybrids, too, depending on how they are defined. But it would seem that CBA can be structured so that this incremental effort doesn't result in much internal agency delay, by undertaking the different components of CBA in parallel. For example, a safety maxi-mization analysis of a policy for mitigating some hazard involves a risk as-sessment, while CBA requires both a risk assessment and a cost assessment. But there is no reason that the agency must wait to conduct the cost assess-ment until after the risk assessment is done.

As for (2), external review procedures unique to CBA—such as the pro-cess of OMB review that now occurs, or the process of peer review that some have proposed[58]—can produce some delay. One option is to omit these procedures entirely. That is not an option we support; OMB review is crucial in reducing agency shirking and mistakes in performing CBA, and peer review of agency CBA should be given serious consideration as well.[59] Another option is to streamline the special review process, for example, by setting tight deadlines, or by conducting different external review steps si-multaneously rather than consecutively. The Kerwin and Furlong study, which found no significant effect of OMB review time on total rulemaking time, examined rules dating from the late 1980s, when the presidential CBA order in place had no deadlines for OMB review. The current CBA order does set deadlines, and this suggests that the delaying effect on agency decision-making of OMB review should be even less pronounced now.[60]

As for (3), it is possible that CBA, as compared to safety maximization, "feasibility" analysis, cost-effectiveness analysis, and other non-welfare-focused, "narrow," or hybrid competitors, increases the time spent on the notice-and-comment process and judicial review. But it is difficult for us to see why it would. Given open-ended statutory language, an interest group opposed to some agency rule may well have an incentive to seek judicial review—since, with open-ended language, the probability of success in court is nontrivial—and may also have an incentive to pepper the agency with criticisms during the notice-and-comment round, thereby increasing the chances of a judicial vacatur for agency arbitrariness or for nonresponsiveness to comments. But it is hard to see how these incentives change as the agency decision proce-dure shifts from some non-CBA procedure to CBA. For example, firms who oppose pollution controls may well challenge the agency's risk assessment numbers, whether those are then incorporated into a safety-maximization analysis, a hybrid analysis (safety up to the point of feasibility), or CBA.[61]

Parenthetically, it is unclear whether judicial review and the notice-and-comment process really do delay and "ossify" rulemakings. The Jordan study calls that into question, as does the general observation that putative "ossify-ing" factors do not appear to have slowed the overall pace of rulemaking. As Cary Coglianese notes, both the volume of rulemaking (as measured, for example by the number of pages in the Code of Federal Regulations) and the costs of rulemaking in constant dollars have grown substantially since the 1970s, despite the advent of "hard look" judicial review during that decade.[62]

In any event, the issue for analysis here is whether agency CBA conjoined with the current rulemaking structure, designed to facilitate public participation and to provide a judicial check, ends up being more time-consuming than a narrow, hybrid, or non-welfare-focused agency decision procedure conjoined with that same structure. Although empirical work needs to be done on the issue, we see no theoretical reason in the political economy of the rulemaking process to think that the answer is affirmative.

We have been considering the incremental delay costs of CBA relative to non-welfare-focused, narrow, or hybrid competitor procedures. Consider, now, the incremental delay costs of CBA relative to "wide," intuitive balancing. Assuming that an agency follows the steps of internal deliberation, OMB review, notice-and-comment rulemaking, and judicial review in both cases (as currently occurs), why should the intuitive process be expected to be substantially quicker on average?[63] Intuitive balancing involves all the steps of CBA, save monetization; this presumably means nearly as much internal time, and plenty of grist for critical comments during the notice-and-comment process and for judicial challenges.

To sum up our analysis of CBA's decision costs: The incremental direct costs of an average CBA, as compared to non-welfare-focused, narrow welfare-focused, or hybrid procedures, appear to be no more than several million dollars. Assuming CBA is more accurate in practice than competitors (taking into consideration not just intrinsic accuracy but also agency mistakes and opportunism), this direct cost will be swamped by the expected benefits of CBA as rules becomes sufficiently large. More research needs to be done to determine the sources of delay costs. However, existing evidence and the political economy of rulemaking call into question the claim that CBA produces substantial incremental delay, as compared to non-welfare-focused, narrow welfare-focused, or hybrid procedures. Finally, CBA can be expected to have small incremental decision costs—both direct and delay costs—as compared to its "wide" competitor, namely, intuitive balancing.

A different thought, which might occur to some readers, is that decision costs could be endogenized. Agencies could be instructed to perform a more or less detailed CBA, depending on expected direct and delay costs. Formally, CBA under the presidential cost-benefit orders has not worked like this. As mentioned, agencies under the orders have been required to perform a full-blown CBA for major rules (roughly, those with annual effects likely to exceed $100 million), and have been allowed to perform a much more abbreviated CBA for other rules. The current executive order does incorporate an exception for delay costs, but only for "emergency situations" or where a statutory or court-imposed deadline requires quick action. This means that agencies must perform a full-blown CBA for all major rules, even in cases where expected decision costs are sufficiently high enough to warrant a more truncated analysis, and are allowed to undertake a more abbreviated analysis for other rules, even where expected decision costs might justify a fuller analysis. One reason for not endogenizing decision costs is transparency—although it is an open and, ultimately, empirical question whether CBA with decision costs endogenized would increase or decrease overall welfare relative to the current structure.

In any event, our comparative analysis of CBA and other decision procedures focuses on a CBA directive whereby agencies are told what a full CBA would consist in, and are directed to perform that analysis, for every decision above some size threshold, *without* considering direct and delay costs except in extreme cases. CBA in this sense is being compared to intuitive balancing, narrow welfare-focused procedures, non-welfare-focused procedures, and hybrids. The possibility of a CBA with decision costs endogenized is one we note, but will not pursue.

Accuracy

Whether a legal directive requiring agencies to perform CBA is welfare maximizing, as opposed to alternative directives, depends in large part on the comparative accuracy of CBA and competitor procedures in tracking overall well-being. In this section, we focus on their intrinsic accuracy. The implementing agency is assumed to apply the procedures correctly. To be sure, "shirking" administrators motivated by considerations other than the public good, or well-motivated but fallible administrators, would not always apply the procedures correctly. But for now, we place the problems of agency shirking and mistakes to one side, to be discussed in Chapter 4.

In other words, the analysis here focuses on a subset of the total "error costs" associated with CBA and competitor procedures. A statute, regulation, executive order, or some other legal provision instructs agency officials to employ some procedure D in resolving certain choices that the officials will confront. D will have two sorts of error costs relative to a perfect decision-making device that always makes the welfare-maximizing choice. First, the officials might perfectly conform to D, but D itself might deviate to some extent from overall welfare. Second, the officials might fail to conform to D, because of motivational or epistemic failures. It is the first sort of error cost, which we refer to as "intrinsic inaccuracy" and which we discuss in this section.

Assume a set of agency choice situations: situations in which agency choice will be guided by one or another decision procedure. For simplicity, we will assume that in each choice situation the agency chooses between the status quo of inaction and a single project; that the true overall welfare costs and benefits of the projects are measurable on a utility scale; that the probability distribution of net welfare effects measured on the utility scale is symmetrical, with mean zero; and that this distribution is the same for each choice situation in the set.[64] These assumptions are not crucial to our overall conclusions, but they simplify and clarify the presentation. We will refer to project effects measured on the overall welfare scale as "utility" benefits or costs, and to project effects measured by CBA as "dollar" benefits or costs.

Figure 3.1 graphs the probability distribution (for each choice situation in the set) of different possible net project utility effects.

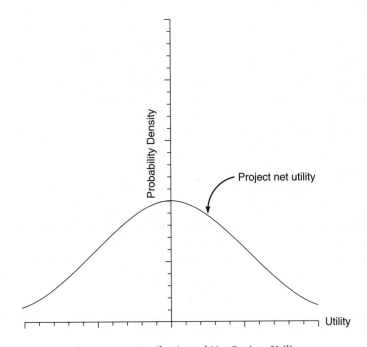

Figure 3.1 Distribution of Net Project Utility

A random procedure (say, flipping a coin and picking the project if the coin comes up heads) would have zero expected utility.[65] A perfectly accurate procedure would always choose projects with net utility benefits, and never choose projects with net utility costs. It would always pick projects to the right of the y-axis in Figure 3.1, and never pick projects to the left. Another way to think about this is in terms of "conditional" distributions: the distribution of project net utility conditional on the project being chosen by the procedure, and the distribution of project net utility conditional on the project not being chosen by the procedure. If the procedure is perfectly accurate, then the first conditional distribution is located wholly to the right of the y-axis, and the second conditional distribution wholly to the left.

Where do actual agency decision procedures—non-welfare-focused, narrow, hybrid, and wide—lie on the spectrum of accuracy, from random to perfect?

Consider, first, non-welfare-focused procedures. Legislators who were cognitively unbounded and cared about overall welfare might (perhaps) perform a welfare analysis for every possible agency choice situation, specifying for each such situation whether the agency should implement the project or not. This represents a kind of non-welfare-focused procedure: the agency in each situation simply follows the legislative directive, rather than itself determining project impacts along one or a plurality of welfare dimensions. And the procedure could be perfectly accurate; it would be if the legislature itself was.

But in practice, of course, given cognitive and communicative limits, legislators do not exhaustively specify. As already stressed, the question here is what generic decisional tools agencies should employ, given the reality that agencies have discretion under their governing statutes. In other words, we are interested in non-welfare-focused procedures that are meant to structure agency choice *in lieu of* welfarist analysis by the legislature, rather than merely implementing the legislature's welfarist analysis.

Designing non-welfare-focused procedures of this sort poses a difficult accuracy problem. The designer must identify some mechanism for sorting between projects with net utility benefits and net utility costs, other than welfare analysis—by the legislature, the agency, or anyone else. It is tempting to say that the problem is just insoluble: non-welfare-focused procedures will end up being no better than the random procedure with zero expected utility. But that conclusion is probably too dogmatic. More plausibly, we suggest, the accuracy problem for this class of procedures is at best partly soluble. Non-welfare-focused procedures will end up having substantial expected utility losses, relative to perfect procedures.

One general mechanism that one might hope could substitute for welfarist analysis is the *market*. But it is well recognized that markets can fail to maximize welfare, for example because of externalities. Indeed, market failure is a standard justification for the very existence of regulatory authority.[66] Legislators (if they care about welfare) will authorize agencies to regulate activities that tend to be characterized by market failures. Remanding the agencies to a market test, rather than welfarist analysis, to decide how to regulate these activities can hardly be expected to be highly accurate. Another general mechanism is *social norms*. Some argue that social norms tend to maximize the welfare of group members.[67] But, as one of us has argued, this claim is suspect;[68] and in any event, no one thinks that social norms are generally sensitive to effects on nonmembers.

The "feasibility" procedure is illustrative. "Feasibility" might be a market test. Regulators might be directed to require pollution reductions up to the point that is achievable, given technology currently existing in the market. But this test is clearly suboptimal with respect to welfare. First, even if cutting-edge technology is optimal for some firms, it will not be optimal for all, given the heterogeneity of the welfare effects of firms' activities and the costs of employing the technology. Second, there is no reason to expect the process of technological development to generate a cutting-edge technology that is optimal on average. On the one hand, researchers motivated by prospects other than market demand, such as fame, may invent expensive technologies that firms or other actors (even if they did internalize all external effects and had good information) wouldn't buy. On the other hand, given external effects or poor information, technologies that result from market demand may fall below the welfare-maximizing level; a "technology forcing" policy might be better.

"Feasibility" might instead be a kind of "norms" test, looking to customary or actual pollution control practices rather than current technology. But because pollution is an externality, there is absolutely no reason to expect customary or actual practices to be optimal.

Our analysis of non-welfare-focused procedures has been complicated—not surprisingly, given the diversity of such procedures. It suggests that even the best such procedures will have substantial utility losses. The analysis of narrow welfare-focused procedures is more straightforward. First, these procedures can be expected to be better than random. Because they track one dimension of welfare, projects that are chosen by narrow procedures are more likely to have net utility benefits and less likely to have net utility costs than randomly selected projects. Projects that are rejected by narrow procedures are more likely to have net utility costs and less likely to have net utility benefits than randomly selected projects. Second, narrow welfare-focused procedures will be worse than perfect procedures, since welfare effects along all but the targeted dimension (safety, education, happiness, antidiscrimination, and so on), etc. are ignored. The size of the loss will depend on the relative magnitude, in utility terms, of project impacts along the targeted dimension versus the remaining welfare dimensions, across the range of agency choice situations where the narrow procedure is to operate.

To see this a bit more formally, imagine that Figure 3.2 represents the probability distribution of project net utility along dimensions other than the targeted dimension. Call this the "background curve." For projects with a given level $S*$ of positive utility along the targeted dimension, the distribution of total utility costs and benefits is the background curve shifted $S*$ units to the right along the x-axis. The expected utility loss, for these projects, corresponds to the area to the left of the y-axis under this shifted background curve. This area represents projects that ideally shouldn't be chosen (because they have net utility costs) but would be chosen by the narrow procedure

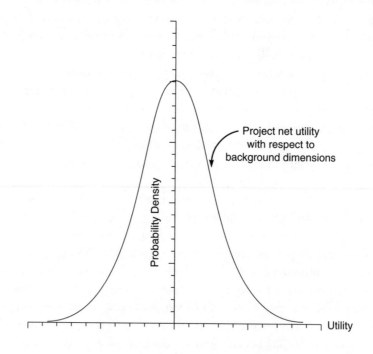

Figure 3.2 Distribution of Net Project Utility
with respect to background dimensions.

(because S^* is positive). Similarly, where projects have a given level S^{**} of negative utility along the targeted dimension, the probability distribution of total utility costs and benefits is the background curve shifted S^{**} units to the left along the x-axis; and the expected utility loss, for these projects, corresponds to the area to the right of the y-axis under this shifted curve.[69] This area represents projects that ideally should be chosen (because they have net utility benefits) but would not be chosen by the narrow procedure (because S^{**} is negative). These effects are shown in Figures 3.3 and 3.4.

If the S^* and S^{**} values encountered by regulators tend to be large, relative to the spread of the background distribution, they will typically shift the "background curve" mostly to the right or left of the y-axis, and the narrow procedure will be quite accurate. If the S^* and S^{**} values tend to be small, relative to the spread of the background distribution, the narrow procedure will be quite inaccurate. Since welfare has a relatively large number of dimensions, and "narrow" procedures focus on only one or a few, the latter scenario seems more plausible than the former. A concrete example: The development of social regulation showed that safety-maximizing statutes would produce

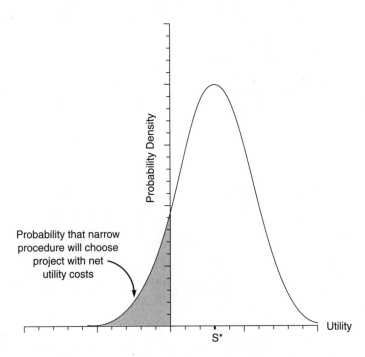

Figure 3.3 Distribution of Net Project Utility for projects with utility S^* along the targeted dimension

some efficient policies but would also regularly induce agencies to choose policies with large costs and small safety benefits.[70] For this reason, a different approach is now used (explicitly or in practice) under many health and safety statutes.[71] Similarly, the absolutism of the Endangered Species Act, which on the face of it "commands that species be protected 'whatever the cost' and 'admits of no exception,'"[72] has in practice been qualified.[73]

It should be noted that the most problematic and controversial examples of safety-maximizing statutes—such as the Delaney Clause, which flatly bars carcinogenic food additives—have been especially narrow in their focus. These provisions have instructed decision-makers to eliminate certain types of fatality risk, without reference to considerations of cost or feasibility *and* without setting forth a de minimis threshold or limiting regulation in cases where elimination of the targeted risk might itself cause some deaths.[74] As explained earlier in the chapter, we have defined "safety maximization" to include a variety of decision procedures focused on life and bodily health.

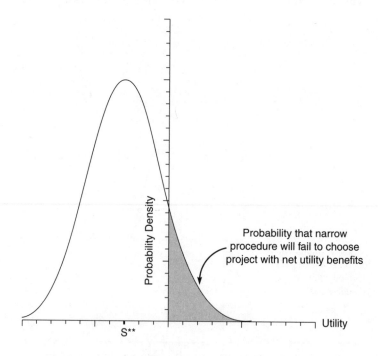

Figure 3.4 Distribution of Net Project Utility for projects with utility S^{**} along the targeted dimension

These include the elimination of all non–de minimis risks of a particular kind, the minimization of premature deaths ("risk-risk analysis"), the maximization of longevity, or the maximization of health-adjusted longevity, as well as the yet narrower sort of procedure exemplified by the Delaney Clause. Our analysis suggests that all of these procedures will be substantially inaccurate, although some certainly do avoid the worst excesses of a Delaney-like concern with specific hazards. Even the most expansive of these procedures—maximizing health-adjusted longevity, using QALYs or some other metric of health—ignores everything that matters to welfare except health and longevity. Consumption, happiness, recreation, art, education, family relationships, productive employment, and the many other things to which people may care to devote their lives are just ignored by QALY maximization, let alone a procedure that focuses only on death rather than death plus health.[75]

Hybrid procedures represent an attempt to reduce the losses associated with narrow procedures. The cutoff might be defined in terms of background dimensions (maximize the targeted dimension, unless the effect on the background dimensions grossly outweighs the target effect). Here, too, there will be some losses (namely, those cases in which the background dimensions outweigh the target dimension but not dramatically so). Alternatively, the cutoff might be defined in terms of some non-welfare-focused criterion (for example, feasibility). Since non-welfare-focused norms won't perfectly track the cases in which the background dimensions outweigh the targeted dimension, hybrid procedures with this sort of cutoff can also be expected to produce losses.

Let us now turn to CBA. A critical point here is that CBA, like the other procedures just considered, *can* be expected to produce some welfare losses. This point is largely obscured by the existing literature on CBA, which tends to see it as a mirror of Kaldor-Hicks efficiency rather than a rough-and-ready tool to implement overall welfare. Since incremental dollars have a variable impact on overall welfare, CBA doesn't perfectly track overall welfare—*even CBA as implemented by a well-motivated, error-free administrator.* Cost-benefit analysis is, to some extent, intrinsically inaccurate in relation to overall welfare.

Consider the probability distribution of net project utility, conditional on the project having net money benefits. This "conditional" distribution will have some area to the left of the y-axis. Projects in this region have net negative utility, but the marginal utility of money for project winners is, on average, less than that of project losers—sufficiently so to skew CBA in the direction of the project. Cost-benefit analysis will select these projects, while a perfect procedure would not. Similarly, consider the distribution of net project util-ity, conditional on the project not having net money benefits (that is, condi-tional on it having either net money costs or being assigned a net money value of zero). This "conditional" distribution will have some area to the right of the y-axis, representing projects that have net utility benefits but where the marginal utility of money for project winners sufficiently exceeds that of project losers so that the project has a zero or negative net money value. Cost-balance analysis will fail to select these projects, while a perfect procedure would. The loss of CBA, relative to a perfect procedure, is a weighted sum of the areas under these two regions.[76]

A bit more formally, let us imagine that W for a given project is the aggre-gate of project winners' CVs divided by their total utility benefit, and that L is the aggregate of project losers' CVs divided by their total utility loss. Then there is a probability distribution of W/L ratios; for simplicity, let us imagine that this distribution is independent of the total utility benefit (B) and cost (C) of a project. Consider a given project, with a given utility benefit to the winners B^* and utility cost to the losers C^*. If B^* is less than C^*, the proba-bility that CBA will produce an inaccurate result in this case—choosing the project when the status quo is better—equals the area under the ratio distri-bution curve (W/L) to the right of the point C^*/B^*. The expected utility loss in this case (relative to the perfect procedure) will be that probability times $(C^* - B^*)$. Similarly, if B^* is greater than C^*, the probability that CBA will pro-duce an inaccurate result—choosing the status quo when the project is better—equals the area under the ratio distribution curve to the left of the point C^*/B^*. The expected utility loss will be that probability times $(B^* - C^*)$.[77]

Note that, if dollars had constant marginal utility, the W/L curve would have all of its mass at 1, and there would be no chance of CBA reaching an inaccurate result. Where the W/L curve doesn't have this shape, the overall expected loss of using CBA will depend on the distribution of project bene-fits and costs (B^* and C^*), plus the shape of the ratio distribution curve. The "tighter" that curve, the smaller the expected loss of CBA.

This analysis shows that CBA, even if perfectly implemented, can be ex-pected to have some utility losses relative to the perfect procedure. This is a vi-tal point, given the Kaldor-Hicks tradition and the uncritical acceptance of CBA by many applied economists and policy analysts. Further, the analysis shows that, in principle, CBA could have greater utility losses than non-welfare-focused procedures, narrow welfare-focused procedures, and hybrids. For example, narrow welfare-focused procedures may accurately track effects along one dimension, but will ignore effects along all others; CBA tracks effects along all dimensions, but measures all somewhat inaccurately, given wealth effects. Concretely, imagine a project that cures a wealthy population with 1,000 individuals of a disease and that results in some incremental consumption, but (somehow) causes a poorer population of 1,100 individuals to suffer the same disease. The disease has the same utility impact on every affected person. Safety maximization will accurately reflect that the project has net safety costs, but it overlooks the consumption benefit; CBA incorporates the consumption benefit, but may misestimate the safety effect, since the wealthier individuals may be willing to pay more not to have the disease than the poor individuals.

Still, the point that CBA *might* have larger expected utility losses than narrow, hybrid, or non-welfare-focused procedures strikes us as a theoretical point. To begin, money is what Rawls calls a "primary good" and Dworkin calls a "resource."[78] Money is an all-purpose means to welfare; it can be used to purchase or facilitate a large variety of welfare improvements. Money's status as a "primary good" derives from its function as the general medium of market exchange. This means that the marginal utility of money, for a given individual in a given scenario, is the marginal utility of whichever marketed good or service (or combination thereof) has the maximum marginal utility at that point. Thus variability in the marginal utility of money can be expected to be less than that of particular goods and services, even important ones. For example, the initial units of food an individual purchases are vitally important; otherwise she starves. But at some point, once the individual is sufficiently fed, consumption of $1 more in food would bring less utility than the expenditure of the $1 on something else. Up to that point, the marginal utility of $1 equals the marginal utility of $1 in food; after that point, the marginal utility of food drops (assuming the food is consumed rather than sold by the individual for cash), and the marginal utility of money exceeds it.

Second, CBA—given its high direct costs—should be limited to large projects, those from which many will gain and many will lose. Therefore, W and L are averages, across large populations, of the CV/utility ratios for particular individuals—the project's effect on the particular individual in money terms, versus its effect on her in utility terms. Because these populations are large, substantial skewing away from unity in the W/L ratio is unlikely. Finally, CBA can, if necessary, be refined to correct the variable marginal utility of money—either by using distributive weights, or by departing from CBA and using some other procedure where the distribution of wealth among project winners (and therewith the distribution of marginal money utilities) is substantially different from the distribution of wealth among project losers.

We have been considering the intrinsic accuracy of CBA as compared to that of competitor procedures in the narrow, hybrid, and non-welfare-focused categories. What about other wide, welfare-focused procedures? As noted earlier, the only such procedure currently in use in governmental practice is an intuitive balancing of welfare impacts. Intuitive balancing, to be practicable, must (like CBA and all the other procedures considered in this section) place some limits on information gathering and analytic effort (for example, the characterization of possible outcomes) by agency officials. That was one upshot of our analysis of "direct implementation" earlier in the chapter. Absent such limits, intuitive balancing would have huge decision costs—but, if correctly implemented by a well-motivated administrator not prone to mistakes, would be perfectly accurate in tracking welfare. Unlike narrow procedures, intuitive balancing captures all welfare dimensions; unlike CBA, valuation of different impacts is not potentially skewed by wealth.

Intuitive balancing, with limits on information gathering and analytic effort, will not be perfectly accurate in tracking overall welfare. It could still be more accurate than CBA. We see nothing to rule that out. The main difficulty with this procedure is not its accuracy in principle but its accuracy in practice—how badly motivated administrators, or well-motivated but fallible ones, will choose among projects without the discipline and transparency of a central, commensurating, money scale. We will consider these points in the next chapter.

The opacity of intuitive balancing might be reduced by the use of quantitative trade-off rates among different welfare dimensions. As noted earlier, various philosophers of welfare have endorsed this sort of procedure; its practicability remains uncertain, since such a procedure would either need trade-off rates among the subdimensions of welfare, as well as the main dimensions, or it would leave lots of intuitive judgments to agencies. Consider again Nussbaum's main dimensions:

Life	Practical reason
Bodily health	Affiliation
Bodily integrity	Other species
Senses, imagination, and thought	Play
Emotions	Control over the environment

A publicly funded park and a publicly funded stadium for spectator sports both underwrite forms of "play." Imagine that building either will lead to some injuries. Even if the legislature or an oversight body such as OMB has announced an overall trade-off rate between the "play" dimension and the "bodily health" dimension, the problem remains of scaling the park and stadium benefits on the "play" dimension. Simply calculating the total number of hours that individuals will spend recreating in the park or watching matches in the stadium assumes that the welfare benefits of the two activities are identical per unit time. Alternatively, the procedure might (1) allow agencies to make intuitive judgments about the relative value of spectator-play and park-play with respect to the "play" aspect of welfare, weighting the time accordingly, or (2) require the legislature or the oversight body to announce trade-off rates among the subdimensions of the main welfare dimensions, such as spectator-play and park-play. The first solution leaves much discretion to agencies; the procedure may end up little more transparent than the intuitive balancing that agencies now engage in. The second solution requires the legislature or oversight body to specify a large number of subdimensions and trade-off rates.

However, these are points about decision costs and transparency/opportunism, not about intrinsic accuracy. It might be thought that a multidimensional procedure with specified trade-off rates, like intuitive balancing, is intrinsically quite accurate. That is incorrect. The inaccuracy arises because the trade-offs are made *globally*, rather than within individual persons. Assume welfare dimensions $D_1 \ldots D_n$. Quantitative multidimensional balancing specifies some social choice function $F(D_1 \ldots D_n)$, where each D_i represents the aggregate level attained by society on some welfare dimension—in other words, the sum of individual levels on that dimension. The most tractable kind of multidimensional function will be a linear function, but the problem we are pointing to arises with nonlinear functions too. Consider a given change ΔD^*, along a given dimension D^*. In one case, that change affects person P_i, who is located at a particular set of levels on the various dimensions $(D_{1i}, D_{2i} \ldots D_{ni})$. In another case, that change affects P_j, who is located at a different set of levels $(D_{1j}, D_{2j} \ldots D_{nj})$. The effect on overall welfare might be different in the two cases. The utility of an outcome for a person depends on where *she* stands with respect to the various sources of welfare, and overall welfare in turn is a sum of individual utilities. U for person $k = U(D_{1k}, D_{2k} \ldots D_{nk})$. Willingness-to-pay values are sensitive to this effect, but quantitative multidimensional balancing is not: the two cases just mentioned are treated identically by that procedure.

To sum up: This section has analyzed the "intrinsic" accuracy of different administrative decision procedures, placing to one side administrative error and opportunism in the implementation of the procedures. How often will these procedures, if correctly applied, select policies that actually reduce overall welfare, and fail to select policies that increase it? In other words, how large is their expected welfare loss relative to a perfect procedure? Our analysis suggests that non-welfare-focused procedures may be no better than random, and at best will have substantial losses. "Narrow" welfare-focused procedures and hybrid procedures will be better than random, but will have substantial losses. Turning to "wide" procedures, CBA will not be perfectly accurate, but losses are kept in check by money's status as a "primary good"—an all-purpose means to welfare—and can be further controlled by limiting CBA to choice situations where the distribution of wealth among project winners does not differ too dramatically from the distribution among project losers, or perhaps by using distributive weights. Intuitive balancing will also not be perfectly accurate (given limits on information gathering and analysis necessary to make the procedure practicable and hold down decision costs) but may perhaps be more accurate than CBA. Its main problem is its lack of transparency, not intrinsic inaccuracy.

These conclusions are theory driven. It would be nice to confirm them empirically, but we have not been able to do that. Although there is a literature on the costs and benefits of various regulatory programs and structures, to be briefly discussed in the following chapter, this literature employs CBA as the metric and focuses on dollar costs and benefits. Our effort, here, has been to evaluate different procedures, including CBA itself, using overall welfare ("utility") costs and benefits as the metric. Further, the observed costs and benefits of a given regulatory procedure are affected by slippage in its implementation, and do not directly reveal its intrinsic accuracy. Still, we think there is substantial theoretical reason to believe that CBA—at least if restructured or limited in application to cope with the possibility of large differences in money utility as between project winners and losers—should be a better proxy for overall welfare than its non-welfare-focused, narrow welfare-focused, and hybrid competitors.

CHAPTER 4

Political Oversight

In previous chapters, we evaluated CBA from a resolutely apolitical perspective. We assumed that an agency is well motivated, in the sense that the agency—that is, the officials and bureaucrats who run the agency—seek to maximize overall welfare. The only problem was that of giving them an instrument or decision procedure for undertaking this task. We also assumed that the agency correctly applied whatever decision procedure it was instructed to use. The choice between CBA and other decision procedures turned on a comparison of the accuracy and decision costs associated with the decision procedure. We assumed away the possibility that an agency might seek to act opportunistically—to achieve ideological goals shared by agency personnel but not by the public or elected officials, to pay off interest groups that offer agency officials jobs when they retire from the agency, and so forth—as well as the possibility that agencies might incorrectly (but in good faith) apply the decision procedures.

In this chapter, we bring back those possibilities. The bulk of the chapter addresses the question: What if agency officials and personnel—what we will sometimes generically refer to as the "agent"—are not well motivated? How might strategic agents affect the case for cost-benefit analysis? At the end, we also briefly consider the possibility that different procedures might be harder or easier for agencies to use. We will argue that both considerations improve the case for CBA. One overlooked virtue of CBA is that it, more than other decision procedures, increases the transparency of agency decisions, thus facilitating oversight by elected officials and the public—for the purpose of correcting errors and deterring opportunism.

Why Agencies Might Be Ill Motivated

Agencies are staffed by human beings, and human beings are not always motivated by a desire to enhance the public's welfare, and even when they are, they do not always agree about what sort of actions enhance the public's welfare and what sort of actions do not.

A typical American regulatory agency has two types of personnel. First, political appointees occupy the top positions. The head of the agency is a political appointee, and most of the heads of the units of the agency are political appointees, as are their assistants. For example, the Department of Justice's head—the attorney general—is a political appointee; so are his immediate assistants, and the heads of the various units—the assistant attorneys general for the Civil Division, the Criminal Division, and so forth. The president chooses the people who occupy these positions, subject to the approval of the Senate; however, some lower level positions may not require Senate approval. The Senate is typically, but not always, deferential; deference is lower for the top positions.

Second, civil servants occupy the lower positions. These are the people who do most of the day-to-day work. Civil servants in the Justice Department try the cases, for example. Civil servants also often occupy relatively high managerial positions. Although civil servants are subject to the supervision of the political appointees, they have a great deal of influence over how the agency operates. Political appointees come and go, serving terms of a few years, usually, while civil servants may remain at an agency for decades or their entire careers. Thus, the culture of the agency reflects the views, ideas, and feelings of the civil servants, who may also have allies in Congress, the media, and elsewhere; and so political appointees may find that they have relatively little influence over an agency, or over some aspect of the agency's practice. Effective political appointees may focus on specific projects, while allowing the agency otherwise to proceed as always; or they might seek to stimulate the agency to action, or act as a drag. But their overall influence may well be marginal.

If overall welfare is the baseline goal of agencies, one needs to ask why the people who operate agencies may pursue goals unrelated to overall welfare.

Part of the answer is simply politics. Political appointees may seek to serve their party loyally, so that they will be rewarded later on; to serve the president loyally, for the same reason; to reward some interest group or constituency to which they owe their position; to obtain visibility with a segment of the public; to satisfy an ideological conviction; or in other ways to advance their political position. It is not hard to see that these motivations are in tension with that of enhancing public welfare. The motivations do not *always* conflict with public welfare: it may be the case, for example, that the president seeks to maximize public welfare—either because that is what he thinks is the right thing to do, or that is what is most likely to win him reelection—and so the loyal officeholders will also seek to maximize public welfare. But theory, evidence, and common experience tell us that political appointees will be influenced by narrower political considerations. Industry and environmental organizations may support environmental regulations that are not good for the public; farmers influence the Department of Agriculture; and logging companies influence the Department of the Interior.

Civil servants are protected from these political influences, but they are not necessarily well motivated either. Scholars have long observed that senior civil servants can expect lucrative jobs in regulated industries when they retire from the government, and these scholars worry that in anticipation of such jobs, civil servants will underregulate while still in office. There is also a crosscutting concern, namely, that civil servants are ideologically committed to the mission of their agency, but in a way that does not reflect the trade-offs that are necessary for maximizing overall welfare. If those who work for the EPA care more about the environment than the public does, they may support regulations that burden the public more than the public would be willing to tolerate. Finally, there are other possible problems: that civil servants just do not work hard enough because they have job security; or that they care more about protecting their turf than regulating; or that they care more about the size of their budget than about regulating.

We should emphasize that scholars disagree about the influence of political forces on agencies. Steve Croley, for example, argues that the evidence for such political influence is limited.[1] It is possible that agencies are able to shrug off lobbyists, that personnel are able to ignore or overcome their own ideological biases or postretirement payoffs, and that political appointees either have little influence over the agency or generally act in a public-regarding way. It is also possible that the influence of lobbyists and interest groups is offsetting. Although we will assume otherwise for the purpose of this chapter, we note here that even in such a world, a requirement that agencies perform CBA would not be otiose. As we noted above, CBA minimizes decision and error costs even when agencies are well motivated.

A Simple Model

The best developed work on the relationship between agencies, the president, Congress, and the courts can be found in the literature on positive political theory.[2] The literature treats this relationship as a principal-agent problem, in which the "principal"—usually Congress, a congressional committee, a legislative coalition, or the president—delegates authority to the "agent," that is, the regulatory agency. Delegation is attractive because the agency can develop expertise and use this expertise to implement projects that best satisfy the principal's goals. But delegation has this attractive character only to the extent that the agency is loyal to the principal. The problem with delegation is that the agency may use its power to pursue its own goals—that is, the goals of the agency's chief or personnel—rather than the goals of the principal. To minimize these "agency costs," the principal sets up laws and institutions designed to monitor the agency and then sanction the agency when it acts improperly. Well-studied examples include the congressional committee system and notice and comment rulemaking under the Administrative Procedure Act.[3]

A simple way of understanding how CBA changes the relationship between principals and agencies is to imagine that it converts a relationship of asymmetric information to one of full information. Without CBA, the principals are not at a complete loss, because they can infer that certain projects benefit or harm them; but they will refuse to consent to other projects that may or may not make them worse off. With CBA, the principals now can accept or reject the project on the basis of direct observation of its consistency with their interests. Understanding CBA, then, involves comparing a model in which principals have complete information about the agency's activities and a model in which they have incomplete information. In both models the agency can take advantage of its expertise and position to propose new projects, and the principals can punish an agency that proposes projects that the principals do not like. All that varies between the two models is how much information the principals have about the agency's actions.

We use a model developed by David Epstein and Sharyn O'Halloran to examine the role of interest groups in congressional oversight of agencies.[4] The model, as reinterpreted for current purposes, involves two characters: President and Agency. Later we will assign the role of principal to Congress and sometimes to general "government principals," that is, either President or Congress. There are three events: (1) Agency, but not President, observes the status quo; (2) Agency proposes a project; and (3) President approves or rejects the project.[5] The relevant variables are depicted in Figure 4.1.

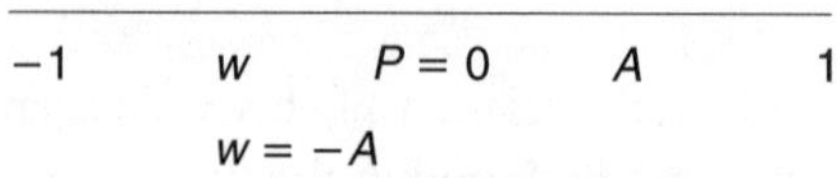

$$-1 \qquad w \qquad P = 0 \qquad A \qquad 1$$
$$w = -A$$

Figure 4.1 Preferences and Outcomes

The line extending from -1 to 1 represents the degree to which there is under- or over-regulation along a particular policy dimension, with w representing the status quo at time 1.[6] When $w = 0$, the welfare-maximizing level of regulation exists. When $w > 0$, too much regulation exists. For example, environmental regulations prevent the production of goods whose value exceeds the cost of pollution. When $w < 0$, too little regulation exists. For example, industry pollution causes significant harm to health and the environment when pollution control devices could be installed at low cost. Note that too much regulation ($w > 0$) is assumed to be as bad as too little regulation ($w < 0$): 0.1 is as bad as -0.1; 0.2 is worse than both, as is -0.2. In Figure 4.1 the status quo is one of underregulation.

The letters P and A represent the "ideal points" of President and Agency. When $P = 0$, as depicted, President seeks welfare-maximizing outcomes. But President may seek outcomes that are not welfare-maximizing. $P < 0$ when President values environmental goods less than the average person does; $P > 0$ when President values these goods more. For the time being, assume that $P = 0$. As for Agency, assume that $A > P$, on the assumption that agencies are generally more interventionist than presidents are.

The players want to minimize the distance between the policy outcome and their ideal point; they do not care whether the outcome exceeds or falls short. For example, a president with an ideal point of 0 is indifferent between policy outcomes 0.5 and -0.5, and prefers 0.4 (or -0.4) to either.

At time 1, Agency but not President observes the value of w. Agency's informational advantage is due to its institutional expertise. At time 2, Agency proposes a regulation or project. This agenda-setting power is due to Agency's special legal authority to issue regulations. The regulation is represented by a number r. If $r > 0$, then the project increases the amount of regulation. An example is the requirement that scrubbers be used in smokestacks. If $r < 0$, then the project reduces the amount of regulation—for example, eliminating the rule that scrubbers must be used. If $r = 0$, the status quo does not change. The outcome of the regulation is simply $w + r$.[7]

At time 3, President approves or rejects the project. Rejection means that the status quo prevails (w). Acceptance means that the regulation is implemented $(w + r)$. Because President does not directly observe w, the decision to accept or reject must be based on inferences from the values of r and A, which President does observe. It should be mentioned that some controversy exists over whether presidents have the power to reverse a project—and it may depend on the legal and institutional setting—but it is clear that the president may fire the agency head if the agency is not an independent agency; and even if he doesn't go that far, he is likely to have some influence over the agency head's political future. Armed with these various sanctions, President can credibly threaten agency heads who approve regulations that deviate too far from President's ideal point.

Because $A \neq P$, Agency and President do not have the same goals, but neither are their interests completely conflicting. Consider the location of w in figure 4.1. Both President and Agency prefer a regulation, $r > 0$, because both seek a more regulated environment. President's ideal regulation is $r = -w$, for such a regulation would bring the status quo to 0, President's ideal point. Agency's ideal regulation is $r = -w + A$, because this higher value regulation would bring the status quo to A, Agency's ideal point. Observe that President would be willing to accept a regulation up to $r = 2w$. The reason is that $+w$ is no worse for President than $-w$; each outcome is the same distance from 0. And a similar point can be made about Agency. Each player is willing to accept a range of outcomes superior to the status quo, but its ideal outcome is just one point within that range.

Finally, it should be observed that the degree to which Agency's and President's goals converge or diverge depends on the location of the status quo. We have already seen a case in which their goals partially converge: when $w = -A$. Their goals diverge when w is, say, $A/2$. When $w = A/2$, Agency benefits only when $r > 0$, while President benefits only when $r < 0$. For example, President believes that pollution controls are too strict, and Agency believes that they are too lax. In the earlier case, President and Agency believe that pollution controls are too lax, but Agency wants to strengthen them more than President does.

We will not go into the details of the equilibrium analysis.[8] It is sufficient here to point out a few general characteristics of the equilibrium.

First, when the status quo is one of extreme underregulation (lots of pollution), Agency will choose too much regulation, in fact, the amount of regulation that results in Agency's ideal point (A). President approves the regulation because he prefers a little too much regulation to extreme underregulation; anticipating this, Agency chooses an amount of regulation that results in its ideal point rather than President's. President can infer the degree of overregulation but cannot do anything about it, because disapproval would result in lack of regulation that would make President worse off.

Second, when the status quo is one of moderate underregulation, Agency will also overregulate, indeed, may even regulate to an extent greater than Agency's ideal point. The reason is that Agency must struggle against President's concern that the status quo is close to President's ideal point; overregulation relative to Agency's ideal point can show that in fact the status quo was far from President's ideal point. This kind of costly signaling is a familiar problem in models of asymmetric information.

Third, when the status quo is one of minimal under- or overregulation, Agency will not regulate at all. Here, President does not know whether the status quo is better or worse than his ideal point; he can only expect Agency to overregulate compared to his ideal; therefore, he won't approve any project. For this reason, Agency does not bother to propose a regulation.

Fourth, when the status quo is one of extreme overregulation, the agency may deregulate, but insufficiently (instead resulting in Agency's ideal point). President knows that Agency will deregulate only if the status quo is one of extreme overregulation; he also knows that Agency will deregulate insufficiently; but he prefers insufficient deregulation to none at all.

From President's perspective, three things are preventing Agency from making optimal choices. First, the divergence between Agency's interests and President's interests causes Agency to prefer different projects. Second, Agency's agenda-setting power—which results from its ability to move first and make a take-it-or-leave-it offer—enables it to choose nonideal projects for President even when President can infer the status quo. Third, incomplete information prevents some mutually beneficial projects from being proposed, and causes Agency to distort other beneficial projects in the direction of greater than necessary regulation.

Cost-Benefit Analysis

Now let us introduce CBA, which is initially conceived to be costless and perfectly accurate. Agency can, without expending any resources, produce a cost-benefit analysis, which will be understood as a statement about the value of w (the loction of the status quo). If $r = -w$, the project passes; otherwise the project fails.[9] This follows from our assumption that the welfare-maximizing outcome is 0 on the policy line. For now, assume that Agency is obligated to produce the cost-benefit analysis, perhaps on the theory that if it does not, it will be punished by President.

These assumptions transform the incomplete information game described above into a full information game. For many values of w, the equilibrium project with CBA is the same as the equilibrium project with incomplete information. But for a range of values, the equilibria diverge.[10]

First, when the status quo is one of extreme underregulation, Agency still overregulates, resulting in Agency's ideal point. The reason is that Agency can continue to take advantage of its agenda-setting power.

Second, when the status quo is one of moderate underregulation, Agency overregulates less than when information was incomplete; it still overregulates somewhat, however. The reason is that although Agency can still take advantage of its agenda-setting power, it can no longer take advantage of the information asymmetry.

Third, when the status quo is one of minimal underregulation, Agency can now regulate optimally. Agency cannot regulate to its ideal point because President prefers the status quo to Agency's ideal point, and would block excessive regulation. Anticipating such interference, Agency engages in moderate rather than excessive regulation.

Fourth, when the status quo is one of minimal overregulation, Agency can no longer regulate. The President observes the status quo, and will not approve any further regulation.

Fifth, when the status quo is one of extreme overregulation, Agency will deregulate, but not enough, as before. Here, Agency can continue to take advantage of its agenda-setting power.

The comparison of the two equilibria yields a number of insights. As one would expect, introduction of cost-benefit analysis results in better projects from the perspective of President and of social welfare. However, even with full information, Agency can exploit its agenda-setting power—that is, its power to propose a project, which President can only accept or reject—and it will do so by biasing most projects in favor of greater regulation. In other words, introduction of CBA will not prevent all forms of overregulation.

Another insight is that the introduction of CBA will result in more regulation but less extreme regulation. The reason is that without CBA, President cannot trust Agency much. A president who does not trust an agency will reject low-value projects, and thus the agency has no incentive to propose them in the first place. In a moderate range, Agency will propose more aggressive projects than even it wants, as a way to signal to President that the status quo is bad. Introducing CBA enables President to trust Agency more, so more regulation will occur. But because signaling is no longer necessary, the regulation will exhibit less variance.

Costly Cost-Benefit Analysis

So far we have assumed that CBA is costless, but it is not. A cost-benefit analysis takes time and costs money. An improperly performed cost-benefit analysis can result in further delay; the OMB may reject the regulation, or a court may reverse it. How do these factors influence our analysis?

There are two variables of interest: the accuracy of a cost-benefit analysis and the cost of performing a cost-benefit analysis. Of course, these variables are related: a more accurate cost-benefit analysis will be more expensive than a less accurate cost-benefit analysis. At some point, there is a point of diminishing returns.

One possibility is that cost-benefit analyses are cheap and accurate. They are cheap relative to the amounts at stake. They are accurate in the sense that they correctly capture the welfare effects of a proposed regulation. If this is the case, then the analysis so far continues to hold. If agencies are required to perform CBA, then there will be more regulations, and the regulations will be better from a welfarist perspective, but there will still be suboptimal regulations because of agencies' agenda-setting power.

Suppose, instead, that CBA is expensive and accurate. If this is the case, then agencies ought to perform it only when the stakes are high enough. Whether agencies should be free to regulate when stakes are low depends on how close their ideal points are to overall welfare.

Suppose, finally, that CBA is expensive and (often) inaccurate. If this is the case, then it may not be desirable for agencies to engage in it. But it also may not be desirable for agencies to regulate at all. If agencies' goals are far enough from overall welfare, then agencies should be forbidden to regulate— this was the extreme view taken by deregulation proponents in the 1970s. If agencies' goals are not too far from overall welfare, and CBA is excessively crude, then agencies should be allowed to regulate without conducting cost-benefit analyses. There is also the possibility that other instruments may be appropriate substitutes, the subject of the next section.

Cost-Benefit Analysis versus Other Decision Procedures

In Chapter 3 we discussed various alternatives to CBA, classified as (1) non-welfare-focused, (2) narrow welfare-focused, (3) wide welfare-focused—the latter category being further divided between quantitative (CBA) and qualitative (intuitive balancing)—and (4) hybrids. In that chapter, we criticized the alternative decision procedures for failing to accurately capture the welfare costs of regulations. Here, we evaluate these alternative approaches according to the degree to which they help elected officials such as the president constrain strategic behavior by agencies.

Non-welfare-focused standards are notoriously vague. An agency that is required to ensure that its regulations are "fair" or respect people's rights is given very little guidance. To comply with non-welfare-focused standards, the agency would, in principle, need to engage in a philosophical analysis. One could imagine how this would work. Suppose an agency must determine rules for the distribution of donated organs; conceivably, it could make arguments based on desert ("People who have accomplished great things should go first in line"), fairness ("People who have been waiting the longest time should go first"), or rights ("people with disabilities should not be discriminated against"). An ill-motivated agency could no doubt come up with a plausible-sounding rationale for a wide range of distributive schemes. The president might as well consult his own conscience, or those of his advisors. The agency's procedures do not enhance transparency.

Another example of a non-welfare-focused standard is the feasibility rule. To show that a regulation is feasible, an agency need show only that the industry will not be bankrupted or perhaps that available technological fixes would satisfy the regulation. But a sufficiently harmful industry should be bankrupted; and a regulation that does not bankrupt an industry may nonetheless lower overall welfare. The president learns little or nothing of relevance from a report that declares a regulation feasible.

Narrow focused welfarist procedures, by contrast, do enhance transparency. Agencies that are, for example, required to report the effect of their regulations on quality-adjusted life years are forced to divulge information that is useful for hierarchical superiors. The information can be verified; the calculations can be checked; and uniform valuations can be determined in advance, further constraining the agencies' ability to rationalize preferred outcomes. The problem is that because narrowly focused procedures exclude welfare-relevant information, the president does not learn from the agency's report whether the regulation actually enhances welfare or not. Agencies are constrained, so strategic behavior is limited; but outcomes may nonetheless be bad.

Wide focused welfarist procedures other than CBA go to the opposite extreme. When agencies are directed by statute to issue regulations that serve the "public interest," they typically issue statements that provide a general, often vague, description of the regulation's effects, along with a conclusory assertion that the regulation meets the statutory criterion. Because this is no agreement about what the "public interest" is, agencies take the easy road and declare regulations in the public interest without divulging the relevant information needed to determine their welfare effects.[11]

One of the great virtues of CBA is that it enhances transparency without forcing agencies to depart too much from the goal of maximizing overall welfare. The cost-benefit analyses issued by agencies are informative, and it is relatively easy to see whether they are well or poorly done. Armed with this information, the well-disposed president can scold, threaten, or punish agencies that do not produce welfare-maximizing regulations.

The Role of Courts

An issue that is neglected in the literature on CBA is whether this instrument is enforced by *political sanctions* or by *legal sanctions*. To understand this distinction, consider the different approaches of two bills proposed in the Senate, one in 1995 and the other in 1999. The 1995 Senate bill states:

(A) No final rule . . . shall be promulgated unless the agency finds that—
   (1) the potential benefits to society from the rule outweigh the potential costs of the rule to society . . .
(B) The requirements of this section shall supplement the decisional criteria for rulemaking otherwise applicable under the statute granting the rulemaking authority, except when such statute contains explicit textual language prohibiting the consideration of the criteria set forth in this section.[12]

In addition, the bill provides that courts "shall set aside agency action that fails to satisfy the decisional criteria of [the section excerpted above]."[13]

The 1999 Senate bill states:

If the agency head determines that the rule is not likely to provide benefits that justify the costs of the rule or is not likely to substantially achieve the rule making objective in a more cost-effective manner, or with greater net benefits, than the other reasonable alternatives considered by the agency, the agency head shall—
(A) explain the reasons for selecting the rule notwithstanding such deter-

mination, including identifying any statutory provision that required the agency to select such rule;

(B) describe any reasonable alternative considered by the agency that would be likely to provide benefits that justify the costs of the rule and be likely to substantially achieve the rule making objective in a more cost-effective manner, or with greater net benefits, than the alternative selected by the agency; and

(C) describe any flexible regulatory option considered by the agency and explain why that option was not adopted by the agency if the option was not adopted.[14]

In addition, the 1999 bill provides that courts shall not review the regulations solely on the basis of the regulations' satisfaction of the CBA, but may treat the latter as relevant for overall review of the rule.[15]

The bills differ along two dimensions. The 1995 bill requires the agency to comply with CBA and backs up this requirement with judicial review. The 1999 bill requires the agency only to report the results of the CBA—not comply with them—and softens judicial review. But what is important for our purposes are the different provisions for judicial review. The bills and the statute show that Congress can either rely on courts to compel CBA, or it can choose not to and instead allow the political branches to punish agencies that fail to use CBA.

The Reagan and Clinton executive orders provide yet another variation. They order agencies to engage in CBA, report the results, and, where statutorily permissible, comply with the results; but the orders leave sanctions to the executive branch to impose on noncomplying agencies if it wishes.

It is thus clear that elected officials understood that CBA can be enforced in two different ways: by political sanctions and by legal sanctions. What is the difference between these two approaches?

Political sanctions enable Congress and the president to retain control over the agency's incentives. In the model above, President's political sanction is to reverse Agency's project. This means that a president who does not care about welfare maximization will approve a regulation that is suboptimal but beneficial to President. When CBA is enforced by political sanctions, it does not cause agencies to act optimally; it causes them to issue regulations closer to President's ideal point, whatever it is, than the regulations the agencies would issue under incomplete information.

Judicial sanctions, which transfer control of the agency's incentives from the political branches to the judicial branch, introduce new issues. Courts have their own ideal points, and these are not necessarily the same as welfare maximization.[16] But even if courts are willing to overturn regulations that violate CBA, they are hampered in two ways. Just like the president, courts have less information than agencies have. And just like the president, courts lack agenda-setting power. So agencies remain able to exploit these advantages in order to produce regulations that are suboptimal.[17]

Still, judicial enforcement of CBA may well be desirable. At a minimum, courts can check for inconsistent assumptions, gaps, and misinterpretations of the evidence. Judicial enforcement also overcomes the danger that agencies and the president will renegotiate after an agency proposes a regulation that fails a CBA at a time that is politically sensitive for the president, or indeed that a president who doesn't care about overall welfare, or who has been successfully lobbied by interest groups, will direct or encourage agencies to issue regulations that violate cost-benefit tests.

If courts are equipped to review CBA, several implications follow. First, it is not as important for courts to insist that agencies use the "right" valuations for any given regulation as that they use consistent valuations across regulations. For example, an agency should not be permitted to value a statistical life at $7 million in one regulation and then $4 million in another, even though both valuations are within the range of plausible valuation. The reason courts should not determine their own valuations is that they are insufficiently specialized. They should, nonetheless, demand consistency on the part of agencies, because the ability to change valuations opportunistically lowers the cost of issuing a plausible CBA of regulations that are not welfare maximizing. Courts should demand consistency within agencies for all kinds of valuations, including items like discount rates. To the extent consistent with statutory frameworks, courts should also demand consistency across agencies.

Second, when costs and benefits are not monetizable, courts should not necessarily demand that agencies monetize them. The problem is that a monetized valuation may be arbitrary.[18] But courts can nevertheless improve the quality of regulation by demanding quantification if possible (for example, the use of life-years), and a reasoned, nonboilerplate discussion of why the valuation cannot be quantified if quantification is not possible.

Third, courts arguably should take account of the ideal point of the agency. The less the agency cares about welfare maximization, the stricter the demands the court should make on the agency. It should be more willing to vacate a regulation issued by an extreme agency than a regulation issued by a moderate agency.[19]

Fourth, courts should take account of the ability of the political branches to sanction the agency. As the ideal points of the political branches converge, and as they become more distant from that of the agency, the court should be more willing to approve a regulation, even one in which the cost-benefit analysis is of low quality. The reason is that the political branches, which have better information than the court about their own ideal points, are in a better position to discipline the agency.[20]

The possible role of courts is illustrated by the famous case of *Corrosion Proof Fittings* v *EPA*,[21] which vacated a regulation of asbestos products.[22] The court criticized the EPA's cost-benefit analysis for:

1. Discounting only the costs of the regulation and not the benefits
2. Discounting from the time of exposure rather than from the time of injury
3. Calculating costs and benefits over a short period (thirteen years) rather than the life of the regulation
4. Treating lives saved beyond the thirteen-year period as "unquantified benefits" that outweigh the expected costs of the regulation
5. Using an unreasonably high valuation for life ($43 to $76 million per life saved) compared to the valuations used in other regulations
6. Double-counting factors by including them in the cost-benefit analysis and using them as a separate reason for regulation
7. Failing to take account of the risks of technologies to which industry would substitute as a result of the regulation
8. Assuming that errors identified by opponents of the regulation balanced out, rather than performing a new cost-benefit analysis using the improved data

The court did *not* perform its own CBA and then use the results of this analysis to evaluate the agency's action. Indeed, the court deferred to the EPA's valuations. The question is whether an ill-motivated EPA could have obtained the result it wanted by tinkering with the valuations while at the same time complying with the standards demanded by the court. Probably not, as EPA has not reintroduced the regulation. Then one must ask whether the court's standards are too strict, and would prevent desirable regulation from being created. We do not see any reason for thinking this is so, but we will not know for sure until we have more experience with judicial enforcement of CBA.

Congress

Cost-benefit analysis has become common over the last two decades mainly because of executive orders issued by presidents Reagan and Clinton, and for that reason scholars associate CBA with the executive branch. The natural treatment of CBA from a positive political theory perspective, then, is the president as principal and the agency as agent. But Congress also has shown an interest in CBA. Several regulatory statutes require agencies to engage in it,[23] and others have been interpreted to permit agencies to use it. And, as noted earlier, there have been efforts to enact bills that require almost all regulatory agencies to use CBA regardless of the language in the authorizing statute.

Who is the principal, then, the president or Congress? Both are, to a degree. On the one hand, Congress has the ultimate authority to delegate regulatory power to the agencies; indeed, one might think of the president as an agent of Congress. On the other hand, the president has an independent political base, and this creates authority to pursue projects through the agencies, whose personnel are members of the executive branch and subordinates of the president. The lines of authority are tangled, and it is plausible to treat the president and Congress as independent principals and any given agency as a joint agent. For clarity, we will discuss (1) Congress as the sole principal and (2) Congress and the president as joint principals.

Congress as the Principal

Assume that Congress has a unitary interest, and that it cannot directly implement its goals legislatively because of the press of time, uncertainty, and lack of specialization. Congress creates an agency and directs it to implement a general authorizing statute. The agency is likely to have interests that diverge from Congress's, just as the agency's interests are likely to diverge from the president's. The reasons are that Congress does not have full control over the personnel of the agency, and Congress's interest will change over time. Congress can sanction the agencies in various ways. For now, consider the bluntest sanction: the ability to reverse an agency project by enacting a new law (with or without the help of the president).[24]

We need not devote much space to the Congress-agency axis because the analysis is the same as the president-agency analysis or the judicial analysis. In the absence of CBA, the agency has two sources of power: its ability to set the agenda and its superior information. If Congress directs agencies to perform and report cost-benefit analyses, and retains the power to impose political sanctions, then the analysis is the same as the president-agency case: Congress learns the location of the status quo and can reverse projects that fail to produce an outcome closer to Congress's ideal point than the status quo.[25] However, if Congress legislatively requires agencies to comply with CBA, and gives *courts* the task of enforcing this requirement, then the analysis is the same as the judicial case.

Congress and the President as Principals

There are different kinds of multiple principal problems. One conflict is between Congress and the president. Another conflict is between members of Congress, or between congressional committees,[26] or between the House and the Senate, or between the parties that control different elements of the executive, legislature, and judiciary. A natural question is whether the existence of conflicting principals increases or reduces the attractiveness of CBA. We will focus on the simplest conflict, between the president and a unitary Congress.

It turns out that CBA has limited value when it is enforced with political sanctions and principals have conflicting ideal points. The reason is that when principals cannot agree, they are in a poorer position to discipline an agency that chooses an extreme project. It seems likely that the reason the quality of regulations has not significantly increased since 1981 (as we discuss later) is that most political sanctions have been ineffective. Agencies know that sometimes presidents acquiesce in cost-unjustified regulations,[27] that sometimes congressional committees will demand cost-unjustified regulations, and perhaps that each branch can be played off against the other.[28]

All of this suggests that good government might require a commitment on the part of both Congress and president to compel agencies to comply with CBA—and such a commitment is best expressed in a statute, rather than in an executive order and through congressional pressure. If courts can resist political pressure and have the capacity to understand and scrutinize cost-benefit analyses, then the statutory route seems most attractive. Alternatively, presidents who care about high-quality regulation may try to staff agencies with political appointees and civil servants who respect and understand CBA. In this way, a culture that favors CBA might gradually evolve.

Interest Groups

Interest groups can influence regulatory practice in many ways. They can influence the design of statutes, so that (for example) an agency charged with reducing pollution is not permitted to target one particular industrial sector responsible for it. They can influence the way the President sets regulatory priorities. They can influence judicial interpretation of regulatory statutes and review of regulations by sponsoring litigation. They can influence agencies by bombarding them with studies, threatening them with litigation, and implicitly promising lucrative positions to agency officials who water down regulations.

It is possible that the influence of interest groups is so great that all talk of CBA and regulatory reform is idle. At the extreme, if powerful interest groups prevent regulatory statutes from being enacted in the first place, then CBA is never an issue. But interest groups have not prevented regulatory statutes from being enacted, agencies issue regulations, and although no doubt interest groups affect them more or less, few people believe that the only effect of regulations is to enrich interest groups.

The interesting question, for our purposes, is whether CBA provides interest groups with an additional tool for influencing or blocking regulations, so that in our world where interest groups have some but not decisive influence, CBA is bad. This view seems to be held by some critics of CBA.[29]

We reject this view. Cost-benefit analysis provides no special advantage to interest groups; on the contrary, by enhancing transparency, CBA should reduce the influence of interest groups on regulatory outcomes. Interest groups do not seek welfare-maximizing regulations, they seek regulations that maximize their own profits. Thus, the goals of interest groups conflict with the results of CBA.

It is true that in recent years interest groups have scored successes by opposing regulations on the ground that they fail cost-benefit tests. But these successes have prevented the issuance of welfare-reducing regulations. The more important point is that there is no reason to think that vaguer regulatory standards would produce better outcomes. Interest groups acting in the shadows would be able to influence agencies to issue regulations that enhance their interests at the expense of the public's. Interest group influence would not disappear if different decision procedures were used; it would manifest itself in a different form.

None of this is to deny that interest groups can use their power to distort

CBA, though their power could be limited by judicial review if the latter were widely available. The point, rather, is to recall that our inquiry is a comparative one: CBA is certainly no worse, and likely much better, than alternative decision procedures for limiting the influence of interest groups.

Additional Structures

Our focus has been on the way that presidents, OMB officials, members of Congress, and judges can more effectively discipline agencies if agencies are required to use CBA. It is worth briefly mentioning some other mechanisms.

First, one can enlist the academic community. Peer review of risk assessments has been discussed a great deal; peer review of cost-benefit analyses would also be beneficial.[30] Agencies might be encouraged or required to submit their cost-benefit analyses to outside experts, who would then report on the quality of the analysis. Peer review would also help educate agency personnel.

Second, one can try to change the culture of agencies. In the past, agencies hired few economists; this has been changing but ought to change more. An EPA that was staffed by economists who sought to enhance welfare, as well as environmentalists who might care more about environmental quality than the public does, might have an ideal point closer to the welfare-maximizing point than it would otherwise. If it does, then the quality of regulations would improve even without external monitoring.

Third, one can invest in improving and standardizing the valuations used in CBA. Agencies should use the same valuations for statistical lives, the same discount rates, the same figures for morbidity risks. They should value environmental amenities in the same way. The government should fund survey and market research so that current valuations can be verified or improved; and, further, Congress or the president should demand that all agencies use consistent valuations.

Fourth, one can try to attack agencies' agenda-setting power, which is the source of their ability to over- or underregulate even when CBA enhances transparency. The key is to prevent agencies from, in effect, presenting the president with a take-it-or-leave-it offer: accept this regulation or you get no regulation at all. Involvement of the OMB earlier in the regulatory process may be part of the answer. Indeed, the OMB has tried to force agencies to announce their regulatory plans well in advance, but little has come of this effort.

Fifth, one can reform the structure of agency incentives. If the trouble is that civil servants do not respond to incentives because of job security and lock-step pay raises, perhaps more of the positions within agencies should be political appointments. If the trouble is that the political appointees are too heavily influenced by interest groups and other constituents, then perhaps more of the positions within agencies should be held by civil servants.

Mistakes

A further point is that CBA is an extremely useful way to exploit the advantages of hierarchy for guarding against error. The introduction of CBA by the Reagan administration was accompanied by centralization of administrative power in the OMB, in the White House. The OMB took it upon itself to monitor agencies, to ensure that they were acting consistently and in a coordinated fashion. When agencies are all using different methods for evaluating and reporting their regulations, hierarchical control is difficult. As agencies gradually became expert in conducting CBA, it became easier for the OMB to monitor their activities. For example, CBA made clear that different agencies made different assumptions about the statistical value of a human life and about the discount rate. There is no reason why agencies should use different values, and over time the OMB has increasingly insisted that uniform values be used.

Because even well-motivated decision-makers make mistakes, the OMB sensibly tried to pool information so that errors could be reduced. It also invited academics and other outsiders to contribute expertise on these issues, and in this way, greater transparency led to more rigorous regulatory analysis. One might liken CBA to the introduction of a uniform system of weights and measures to an unregulated market. By creating a common metric, CBA allows agencies to pool expertise and hierarchical authorities to coordinate the activities of agencies that have disparate missions.

The upshot of this analysis is that although CBA can be technically complicated, so that one might fear that agencies would make more errors using it than using simpler procedures like risk-risk, this fear is surely overstated. The technical difficulties can be minimized through centralization.

Some Evidence

There has been controversy over whether the executive orders mandating CBA for regulatory agencies have actually improved the quality of regulation. Anecdotal evidence provides some reason for hope. Defenders of the executive orders can point to a few controversies where cost-unjustified regulations were withdrawn, apparently because they failed a CBA and not because of political factors. The empirical evidence, however, suggests that the executive orders have not improved regulatory quality.

The graph in Figure 4.2 shows major health and safety regulations issued by government agencies between 1967 and 1991.[31] The x-axis represents the year of promulgation; the y-axis represents the cost per life saved in millions of 1992 dollars. Although cost per life saved is not all that matters for welfare maximization, it is a useful proxy with regard to these regulations because they are directed toward problems of health and safety.[32] The vertical line shows the year of Reagan's executive order, 1981. The horizontal line represents a regulation that assumes a $5 million value for a statistical life, which is the midpoint of the range estimated by empirical studies.[33] The graph shows no noticeable improvement in the quality of regulation after the executive order. (Some post-1981 outliers are omitted to keep the scale within reasonable bounds.) This is confirmed by regressions, but is adequately illustrated in Figure 4.2.[34]

The evidence is bolstered by studies that show that post-1981 cost-benefit analyses are frequently defective. Agencies often provide implausible estimates of costs and benefits, use different discount rates and valuations across

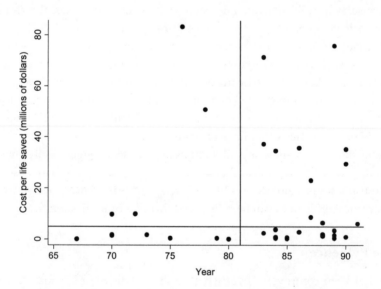

Figure 4.2 Cost per Life Saved by Year in Millions of 1992 Dollars

regulations, and even fail to monetize or quantify all the relevant costs and benefits.[35] One study of forty-eight rules issued between 1996 and 1999 concluded that regulatory impact analyses "typically do not provide enough information to enable the regulatory agencies to make decisions that will maximize the efficiency or effectiveness of a rule."[36]

Most of the rigorous empirical work examines regulations issued before 2000. Some recent scholarship has looked at the use of CBA during the first term of President George W. Bush's administration. Ackerman and Heinzerling argue that the Bush administration used (or misused?) CBA to torpedo socially beneficial regulations, such as a proposed rule to reduce arsenic in drinking water.[37] David Driesen argues that CBA is biased, because when George W. Bush's OMB intervened, it almost always pushed agencies to reduce the stringency of proposed regulations, and very rarely encouraged agencies to increase the stringency of proposed regulations.[38] Therefore, CBA is "biased"; if it were "neutral," then one would have expected the OMB to sometimes encourage greater stringency as well as less stringency. But this neutrality test is flawed: suppose agencies like the EPA tend to overregulate; then it is proper for OMB to push for greater stringency. Because Driesen does not show that agencies' regulations are just as often too weak as too strong, he fails to show that the OMB acted improperly. Similarly, Ackerman and Heinzerling do not show that the regulations squelched by the Bush administration would have advanced overall welfare or some other plausible normative goal.

The authors seem more concerned with political manipulation of CBA than CBA itself, although Ackerman and Heinzerling also criticize it on its own terms. Their work targets the George W. Bush administration and its academic defenders.[39] This raises an interesting possibility: what if the president and the OMB are captured by industry while the agencies themselves are not, but instead seek to maximize overall welfare within their domain? If so, then CBA, by strengthening the president's grip over the agencies, may enable him to reduce overall welfare for the benefit of industry. This strikes us as no more than a theoretical possibility, but it does usefully underline the important point that CBA is not a panacea for our regulatory ills; it can improve regulation only if at least some of the relevant institutional players— the president, Congress, the courts, the agencies, or some combination of them—believe that overall welfare matters.

Do they? The pre-2000 empirical studies are discouraging. The data contradict the natural expectation that the introduction of a CBA requirement would improve the quality of regulations, either directly by constraining agencies or indirectly (in our analysis) by giving the president greater power over agencies. What went wrong? There are two possibilities.

The first is that the political sanctions on which the executive orders depended for their effectiveness were not sufficiently strong. As noted above, courts do not force agencies to comply with executive orders; only the president can do so. A president can try to encourage agencies to comply with his agenda by appointing loyalists, holding up proposed regulations, sending them back for more work, trying to limit agencies' budgets, and so forth, but there are limits on the effectiveness of all these mechanisms. Agencies retain their agenda-setting power, and so can confront presidents with a take-it-or-leave-it offer with respect to a regulation that is slightly better than the status quo, from the president's perspective, but still not cost justified. Agencies also have allies in Congress, and Congress can make life difficult for presidents who attempt to limit the activities of agencies.

The second possibility is that the presidents in question did not care very much about improving the quality of regulation, and so were not willing to expend political capital on constraining agencies. This appears to have been true about Clinton, who was not hostile to regulation;[40] and even Reagan, who was hostile to regulation, could hardly devote his attention exclusively to regulatory reform.[41] When Reagan entered office, the agencies had been controlled by and staffed by a Democratic president and a Democratic Congress, in the latter case for many years, and it was surely the case that the agencies had developed a sense of mission consistent with their Democratic roots. There was probably little that Reagan could do, in the short term, to overcome the entrenched cultures of the agencies, where economics was regarded with skepticism, if not hostility.

The weakness of the executive order as an agent for change suggests that effective regulatory reform must take place through Congress. Congress has, from time to time, shown some interest in requiring agencies to perform cost-benefit analyses—some agencies are already subject to this requirement. But occasional efforts to require all regulatory agencies to use CBA have not borne fruit. As mentioned earlier, a relatively strong bill proposed in 1995 was never passed; nor was a weaker bill proposed in 1999.

Conclusion

Cost-benefit analysis enhances transparency, and in this way can be defended as a partial solution to a principal-agent problem. Congress and the president can accomplish more if they delegate power to agencies, but then they risk the agencies using their power to accomplish ends that Congress and the president do not approve. By forcing agencies to divulge information about their projects, CBA enhances the ability of Congress and the president to control agencies.

Cost-benefit analysis can thus be analogized to more familiar practices in the employment context, where the employer is the principal and the employee is the agent. A simple example is the requirement that employees provide a financial statement that shows that projects they intend to pursue have positive net present value. The employee submits the financial statement to an auditor, who can easily check the math, review the assumptions, and ask for empirical evidence where necessary. Net present value calculations can be manipulated, just as CBA can be; but the degrees of freedom are limited, and so agency costs are reduced.

To be sure, the political setting is significantly more complicated. First, the government's goal is not to make money, but to enhance welfare while respecting rights and other moral considerations. Governments may also be swayed by interest groups and other political actors. For this reason, government may sometimes be uneasy about forcing agencies to comply with CBA. When this uneasiness is based on welfare-irrelevant factors, such as the influence of interest groups, then mandatory CBA should be applauded as a straightforward tool of good government, a tool that enhances transparency and thus reduces rent-seeking and other forms of misbehavior.

Second, even if a government sincerely seeks to maximize welfare, it might be uneasy about CBA because it is only an imperfect decision procedure. As we have stressed repeatedly, CBA does not fully capture the welfare effects of regulations; and the shortfall will be enhanced in complicated cases where welfare effects cannot be reliably monetized. This problem is not unknown in the employment context; a net present value analysis will miss imponderables, such as the effect of the project on the firm's reputation and customer goodwill. But in politics, this problem is exacerbated because of the lack of agreement about ends in so many situations.

Even here, however, we think CBA improves government decision-making by increasing transparency. A cost-benefit analysis, at a minimum, forces agencies to make clear what assumptions they are making about the effects of the regulations on people's well-being. By forcing agencies to use a common metric, CBA allows elected officials, scholars, and the public to get a clear view of the regulatory landscape.

CHAPTER 5

Distorted Preferences

Under the restricted-preference-based account of well-being, a person is made better off by a project if he or she actually prefers the project (or the benefits that it generates), but the preference must not be disinterested, and it must survive idealization. Because a person's CV does not reflect these two conditions, and because it does not reflect the declining marginal utility of money, there may be a gap between a person's actual CV and the CV that would reflect the project's impact on his or her well-being. The actual CV may thus be distorted; or, put differently, the actual CV may be based on distorted preferences relative to the idealized and self-interested preferences that reflect well-being. The distortion may be great or small.

There are several sources of distortion, as follows.

DISINTERESTEDNESS. Suppose that P supports a project that does not benefit him or even costs him on net. He supports it because he believes that the project is morally correct. For example, P supports affirmative action programs even though they put him at a disadvantage because he believes that they are morally required as a corrective for the legacy of slavery. P registers a positive CV for the project, but it does not advance his welfare.

INFORMATION. P prefers the project, a new dam that would reduce the cost of electricity. However, with fuller information about how the noise and commotion from construction of the dam would affect P's vacation home, P would prefer the status quo. Arguably, P is not benefited by the project, or at least not benefited as much as he would be if his fully informed preferences were in favor of the project.

OBJECTIVE GOOD. P prefers the project. However, the status quo is objectively much better for P, in light of objective goods such as friendship, knowledge, aesthetic experience, or accomplishment. For example, the project is a state subsidy for a massive casino development that will incidentally convert P's friendly neighborhood into a red-light district. Arguably, P is not benefited by the project, or at least not benefited as much as he would be if the objective value of the project were greater.

ADAPTATION. P prefers the status quo because that is the world in which his preferences were formed. However, P's preferences are misshapen by various unjust features of the status quo. (Imagine that the status quo is a world in which P lacks wealth, or self-respect, or a basic education, and in which his preferences have been shaped by these deficits.) If the project is implemented, P's preferences may change—such that he now prefers the project, not the status quo—or the preferences may be sufficiently entrenched that they do not change. In either event, there may be good grounds for thinking that P benefits from (or at least is not harmed by) the project even though he prefers or once preferred the status quo.

WEALTH. The distortions described so far result from the divergence between P's well-being and his preferences (or choices). Another type of distortion results from the way CBA reduces the effects of a regulation to a common metric—that of money. Because wealthy people have more money than poor people do, the monetization of effects gives the wealthy a special advantage: because they are willing to pay more for a regulation that affects their well-being to the same extent that it affects the well-being of poor people, CBA overweights the consequences of the regulation for the wealthy.

If preferences are distorted, then regulations that satisfy a cost-benefit analysis that monetizes actual preferences will not necessarily enhance overall welfare. For some skeptics, this may be reason enough to abandon CBA, but we think such a wholesale rejection is unwarranted. One reason it is unwarranted is that in many settings the distortions may be relatively small; or they may wash out. The other reason—the focus of this chapter—is that agencies may be able to accommodate concerns about distorted preferences without abandoning CBA. They may do so by performing CBA using valuations based on "laundered" preferences.[1]

Before discussing the ways preferences can be laundered, we devote some space to agency practice in this area. Agencies do, already, launder preferences to some extent, albeit in crude ways. Our discussion of agency practice has two purposes: to show that distorted preferences are a real phenomenon that cannot be wished away; and to show that ordinary or "textbook" CBA, which relies on undistorted preferences, is therefore not always a realistic approach, as implicitly recognized by the agencies themselves.

Disinterested Preferences: The Problem of Existence Value

Textbook CBA reduces moral commitments to valuations. Consider, for example, the debate over the use of contingent valuation methods to value environmental goods. Textbook CBA, as generally understood, directs agencies to translate people's moral attitudes about the environment into CVs for the existence of environmental goods that they do not directly enjoy, usually called "existence value" or "nonuse value." (Existence value is the value from knowing that some good exists; it is sometimes used interchangeably with nonuse value, but nonuse value also is understood to include the option value of having some good in the future, which we exclude from our analysis.) These CVs are then added to the balance of costs and benefits of a project, like any other CV.

Until recently, agencies did not calculate existence values. The earliest sustained discussion of existence values by an agency that we have found occurred in 1986 and involved the Department of Interior's guidelines on valuing environmental damage caused by discharge of oil or a hazardous substance. But the rule itself did not involve the calculation of an existence value.[2] The first use of existence values in rulemaking was, as far as we have found, by the EPA in 1991, and the practice of measuring existence values has only recently become common.[3] For example, the EPA's recent CBA for effluent regulations included existence values for "benefits to wildlife, threatened or endangered species, and biodiversity benefits."[4] Thus, the use of existence values by government agencies has lagged behind the widespread use of CBA by about a decade.[5]

One reason for hesitation about calculating existence values was no doubt methodological. Existence values cannot be inferred from market behavior, but must be derived from costly and controversial surveys. Another reason for hesitation might have been politics. But it is also likely that agencies have been uncertain about the conceptual soundness of using existence values.

To see why, consider settings in which existence values are *not* used. The FDA does not ask Christian Scientists whether they care about the existence of people using commercial drugs. The USDA does not ask animal rights activists whether they care about the existence of slaughterhouses. The U.S.

Postal Service does not ask individuals whether they care about the existence of pornography in the mail. Funding agencies do not ask people how much they would be willing to pay to prevent those agencies from funding morally controversial research projects involving stem cells. Security agencies such as the Federal Bureau of Investigation (FBI) do not ask people how much they would be willing to pay to prevent those agencies from conducting intrusive and perhaps morally troublesome but legal searches and seizures.

But surely people have preferences about these things, and so there is a puzzle: why do preferences based on moral conviction play a role in some agency evaluations but not others? As we will discuss later in this chapter, we think that the EPA has made an error—it should not have calculated existence values—and that the other agencies we have mentioned correctly did not attempt to monetize people's disinterested preferences.

Uninformed Preferences

Either textbook CBA ignores the problem of uninformed preferences or it recognizes the problem but purports to solve it by conceptualizing information as yet another good. In the first case, people are simply assumed to have informed preferences, so that projects based on their CVs will enhance their well-being. In the second case, the assumptions are a bit more complicated, but the result is the same. Individuals are assumed to know that they lack information and are willing to pay for more information if and only if the expected gain exceeds the cost. So an individual who is partly uninformed about a given project is rationally uninformed, and his CV for the project should be calculated based upon his uninformed preferences.

Government agencies' treatment of uninformed preferences is more complex than the textbook approach. At the outset, it is worth distinguishing between the effect of information on (1) instrumental preferences and (2) intrinsic preferences. In the first case, information has the effect of changing persons' judgments about the causal link between the project and those states of affairs they intrinsically value or disvalue. P opposes a project to fluoridate drinking water because he falsely believes that fluoridation causes cancer and does not help teeth. In the second case, information changes intrinsic valuations. P's CV for an arts project is low because he has not been fully informed about the aesthetic qualities of the project.

Agencies frequently refuse to use CVs that reflect uninformed preferences. Sometimes, agencies supply people with information when asking them for their CVs. Before asking them about air quality over the Grand

Canyon, the EPA showed survey respondents photographs of the site with different levels of pollution.[6] The EPA's goal was presumably to provide information on environmental aesthetics, about which respondent's intrinsic preferences were uninformed. For a regulation involving labeling of meat and poultry products, the USDA relied on CVs for health benefits people would enjoy if they altered their behavior in response to the labels, rather than people's CVs for nutrition disclosure.[7] The agency appeared to take the intrinsic preference (for health) as a given and to circumvent the problem of imperfectly informed instrumental preference (for nutritional disclosure). Instrumental preferences are constructed; people are assumed to have preferences for whichever means will best satisfy their intrinsic preferences, even if they are misinformed about these means—even if, in our example, some people would oppose labeling because they (falsely) think it will confuse them.

The premise of modern workplace regulation is that workers are uninformed about risks.[8] If this premise is false, then wages and workplace safety procedures reflect rational trade-offs made by workers, and regulations simply interfere with the satisfaction of their preferences. It would make no sense, for example, for OSHA to restrict workers' exposure to ethylene dibromide, a carcinogenic chemical used in various industries, because any restrictions sufficiently cheap that workers are willing to pay for them have voluntarily been implemented by employers.[9] More risk-averse workers would move to safer, lower paying jobs; more risk-preferring workers would take the more dangerous, higher paying jobs. In such a labor market, regulations would be costlier than their safety benefits warrant. The denial that this market prevails is implicit in all regulation of contractual relations; agencies occasionally are explicit about it.[10]

In sum, agencies do not always take uninformed preferences as they find them. Instead, they sometimes evaluate projects by using the preferences people would have if they were informed.

Adaptive Preferences

People may psychologically adapt to an unjust or otherwise unfavorable environment, so that their CV for eliminating a risk or irritant is less than what it would be if they did not adapt. The overburdened housewife discussed in Chapter 2 might rationalize her position and so not be willing to pay in order to have her burdens removed.[11] Or a person in a bad environment might feel sour grapes toward someone in a pleasant environment and refuse to pay for an improvement in his own environment because he has convinced himself that the pleasant environment is really worse. Or a person might adapt to the status quo, so while she will oppose any project, if the project were nevertheless implemented, she would oppose a further project that would reverse the first.[12]

Many agency programs assume that people's preferences are distorted by psychological problems. For example, programs to reduce drug use assume that drug addicts would be benefited by restrictions on drugs, not harmed by them, even though their preferences may well be the opposite. In justifying regulations governing antidrug programs for the employees of private air carriers, the Department of Transportation (DOT) did not take into account the preferences of the drug users, even though these people may well be hurt by the regulations on an actual-preference account of well-being.[13] In justifying mandatory drug tests for drivers of commercial vehicles, the DOT did not take account of the cost to drivers who derive pleasure from the use of alcohol and illegal drugs.[14] Yet in the same regulations, the agencies did take account of preferences that are not considered adaptive, such as preferences for time or money.

However, two qualifications are necessary. First, agencies do not generally assume that preferences are defective in these ways unless directed by a statute. Second, it is not clear whether the preferences of drug users are ignored because they are adaptive or because they are considered objectively bad (see below) or distorted in other ways.

Objectively Bad Preferences

Textbook CBA assumes that objectively bad preferences should receive the same weight as morally neutral preferences. An agency should presumably count the preferences of a person who hates children and is willing to pay $1,000 to prevent a children's vaccine program, and it should count the preferences of a person who hates homosexuals and is willing to pay $1,000 to prevent AIDS research.

Agencies routinely ignore sadistic preferences and other preferences for objectively bad outcomes or products. For example, the FDA's cost-benefit analysis of a regulation designed to curb distribution of cigarettes to children did not include as a cost the lost profits to industry, "because most of this profit stems from illegal sales to youths."[15] Nor did it count the children's lost consumer surplus. It is hard to believe that agencies would count a preference that homosexuals not be helped through AIDS research, no matter how widespread that preference may be. And, as we saw above, the DOT's refusal to count the preferences of drug users may reflect an evaluative judgment (on the part of Congress) rather than, or in addition to, a concern that the preferences are adaptive.

As another example, consider a Federal Aviation Administration (FAA) program for airline security, which refused to use profiling on the basis of race, national or ethnic origin, and other possibly relevant but morally suspect factors. Although the FAA performed a cost-benefit analysis, it did not consider the possibility that a discriminatory system might be less costly than the system that it endorsed or that some people (white supremacists, racially biased airline travelers) might have strong tastes for discrimination and therefore have significant, positive CVs for a discriminatory system.[16]

In sum, agencies depart from textbook CBA by refusing to weigh certain kinds of objectively bad preferences. This practice is not as obvious as other adjustments are, because we are not accustomed to thinking that satisfying preferences for discrimination, suffering, and other morally bad outcomes will benefit the holders of the preferences. Thus the agencies' practice seems natural. But that is only because in this significant respect textbook CBA deviates from common moral intuitions.

Wealth Distortions

Textbook CBA does not adjust for distortions caused by the distribution of wealth. A wealthy person is willing to pay more to reduce the risk of death than is a poor person with identical preferences, but it does not follow that the agency maximizes welfare by placing dangerous projects in poor neighborhoods rather than in rich neighborhoods. On the contrary, it seems reasonable to assume that premature death has the same effect upon overall well-being, whether the person who dies prematurely is wealthy or poor. As noted above, this distortion is different from the others. The others arise because of the disjunction between preference satisfaction and well-being. By contrast, the wealth distortion described just now arises because CVs are calculated in terms of dollars, which do not accurately reflect relative well-being when endowments differ.

Agencies correct for wealth distortions in various ways. They use a constant figure for the monetized value of a statistical life.[17] They rely on quality-adjusted or non-quality-adjusted life-years, which is a number that is invariant with wealth.[18] The Department of Health and Human Services, for example, said that the benefit of its organ transplant rule was the saving of 297–1,306 life-years.[19] They quantify other benefits without monetizing them. The EPA, for example, noted that a regulation of certain heavy-duty engines would reduce nitrogen oxide emissions by 593,000 tons, without attaching a value to this amount.[20] In all these cases, the benefits of the regulation are invariant to the wealth of those affected by them. Of course, as the agencies depart farther and farther from the use of CVs, the basis of evaluation becomes increasingly obscure.

Agencies also correct for wealth distortions in more broad-gauged ways. Regulation of pesticides and lead-based paint may have been influenced by a desire to benefit, on distributional grounds, low-income farm workers, in the first case, and low-income inner-city residents, in the second.[21] Agencies also pay attention to whether a regulation will "threaten the existence" of an industry, that is, have substantial, concentrated impacts.[22] Indeed, the executive orders that require consideration of "environmental justice" and equity appear to require attention to the distributional consequences of regulations. President Clinton's executive order directing agencies to use CBA says: "When an agency determines that a regulation is the best available method of achieving the regulatory objective, it shall design its regulations in the most cost-effective manner to achieve the regulatory objective. In doing so, each agency shall consider incentives for innovation, consistency, predictability, the costs of enforcement and compliance (to the government, regulated entities, and the public), flexibility, *distributive impacts, and equity.*"[23]

Distributive justice is not the same as overall welfare, and it is important to note that agencies' sporadic attention to distributional considerations does not necessarily show that they launder preferences by correcting for the variable marginal utility of money. Our examples above do not show that agencies are doing the latter rather than the former; but they do suggest that agencies can, or at least think they can, take account of wealth differences, if in an extremely rough way, when evaluating regulations.

Is Something Else Going On?

Before we turn to our prescriptions, we should address the possibility that agency practice does not reflect moral concerns about the nature of well-being, but that it reflects decision costs, political constraints, or plain sloppiness.

None of these alternatives is plausible. Agencies economize on decision costs in many ways, but what needs to be explained is a more complex pattern of behavior. Often agencies do expend considerable resources to determine what people's CVs are, and often they do not; the question is, why do they expend resources at some times and not at other times? Consider agencies' refusals to determine the CVs of drug users when a project increases the cost of using drugs or their refusals to determine the CVs of racists for a project that involves racial profiling. Calculating these CVs is no more costly than calculating CVs in other contexts—for example, the CV of someone who is harmed by airplane noise or the CV of someone who experiences an increased risk of cancer. When agencies face high decision costs, they are usually quite candid about this problem. They will say that data are unavailable or too costly to acquire. They will make estimates based on a small sample. It is impossible to imagine an agency saying that the only reason it did not calculate the CVs for drug use or racial discrimination is that data were unavailable.

The political argument might be that interest group politics result in the divergences we have discussed. But there are interest groups on both sides of virtually every regulation. A more plausible political account of agency practice is that agencies fear public outrage. Agencies might sometimes hesitate about using wealth-dependent valuations of life, or respecting preferences for drug use, because these practices may produce public outrage. Public outrage may reflect ignorance, herding, or strategic behavior, but we think that it also reflects a conviction that deep moral intuitions are being ignored. If this is the case, the political argument is no different from our moral argument.

Finally, the sloppiness argument is at best incomplete. Agencies are sloppy sometimes, and the ways they handle the problem of distorted preferences—often, by ignoring them—does seem sloppy. But the most plausible explanation here is that agencies know that they are dealing with morally sensitive issues that are not squarely handled either by CBA or by their statutory authorization, and they prefer to duck them or finesse them rather than address them explicitly, lest they provoke public indignation on account of neglect of a moral value. The sloppiness, then, is endogenous, and not a causal factor that explains the practices we have discussed.

Defenders of textbook CBA will more likely regret the divergence between textbook CBA and agency use of CBA than explain it away. But we think that the divergence justifies attention to the problems with textbook CBA and provides support for our view that unrestricted preferences should not always be the basis of agency action.

Nonetheless, the agency practices we have discussed are vulnerable to many objections. First, agencies take an inconsistent approach to distorted preferences, monetizing some (environmental amenities) but not others (drug use). Second, agencies' efforts to handle distorted preferences are ad hoc and unsatisfactory; the problem is that there is no generally accepted means for correcting distortions. Third, agencies' practices raise the danger of lack of transparency: how does one evaluate their implicit claims that certain preferences should be ignored?

Prescription: Disinterested Preferences

Many scholars criticize agencies' use of contingent valuation techniques to measure existence values, but these criticisms are for the most part methodological. Critics argue that contingent valuation techniques do not yield reliable results. Defenders argue that the techniques are adequate or improving. They argue that if surveys were conducted more carefully or with certain controls, then inconsistencies and intransitivities would disappear.[24] However, as several economists have acknowledged, the main problem with contingent valuation of environmental goods is conceptual, not methodological.[25]

When people are asked for existence values, they often respond in strange ways. They refuse to answer surveys on environmental goods or, by way of protest, register a zero valuation or unrealistically high valuations that agencies must ignore. They provide valuations that are invariant across large and small parcels of wilderness or quantities of wildlife or that are inconsistent or intransitive. Their answers depend on the order in which questions are asked and are sensitive to the wording of the questions.

Although one might hope for improvements that will eliminate inconsistencies, it is clear that no amount of methodological refinement will eliminate protest responses in the form of unrealistically high or low valuations or refusals to answer. But these responses must reflect something. When people give valuations of zero or infinity, these responses should be interpreted as an assertion that the question does not make sense, not as an assertion that the respondent would give nothing to save the environmental good (in the first case) or everything (in the second case), or is acting strategically (in either case) since he must know that his response will be disregarded. This is even more clearly true when people refuse to respond to the surveys.

It might seem that when people do respond with "reasonable" valuations to surveys, the valuations they provide are entitled to deference, and ought to be incorporated into cost-benefit analyses. However, when people have no direct experience of environmental goods in question and claim to be willing to pay just for their existence, then (aside from the option value for possible use) this CV cannot reflect the goods' contribution to well-being. The dollar amounts in the survey responses should be interpreted as a valuation of the violation of a moral commitment, not as a valuation of an environmental amenity. To the extent the dollar amounts thus reflect moral commitments, aggregating them does not give one information about the effect of the project upon overall well-being or upon other moral criteria.

Why should agencies not pay attention to valuations people attach to violations of moral commitments? To see why, suppose that P believes that he will gain $100 from the construction of a dam as a result of lower electricity bills, but believes that construction of a dam is immoral. Q would lose $125 as a result of higher fish prices, but believes that construction of a dam is a moral obligation ("the march of progress"). P would pay $50 to see his moral commitment vindicated, and Q would pay $100 to see her moral commitment vindicated. These additional payments are, we suggest, morally irrelevant; they neither change the effect of the project on overall well-being (which is negative) nor change the moral status of the project in some other regard. The project is either moral or immoral or morally controversial; its morality does not depend on how much people are willing to pay to vindicate their moral views. If P receives a large inheritance, and so is willing to pay another $200 to see the project stopped, and this increase reflects his moral values, then it is false to say that the moral status of the project switches back from positive to negative, just because P's inheritance now enables him to outbid Q. Or if R migrates into the relevant jurisdiction, and is willing to pay $200 to stop the project for moral reasons, it would be wrong to say that the project switches back from positive to negative. Now it might be the case that an agency should take account of people's disinterested moral views when it decides whether to implement a project. We discuss this possibility below. The point to understand is that even if an agency should, it should not try to monetize these disinterested preferences, and should not include them as part of a CBA.

How then should environmental commitments (as well as other disinterested preferences) be recognized? There are two possibilities. The first is that agencies should have the minimal task of determining the effect of projects on overall well-being, and different political actors—Congress, the courts—should enforce moral commitments. No one asks agencies to decide whether to implement such "projects" as abortion legalization and capital punishment. In the political arena, controversial issues are resolved not by CBA but instead by political and moral debate through which people find common ground. Congress and the courts can erect constraints that bind agencies. These constraints prevent agencies from approving projects that, among other things, involve racial discrimination, the use of fetal tissue, and experimentation on people who do not give their consent—regardless of the extent to which the benefits of these projects outweigh their costs.

The second possibility is to allow agencies to take into account the full range of moral considerations bearing upon projects and not simply the criterion of overall well-being. We have no objection to this alternative, in theory, as long as it is understood that the agency should not resolve a question of deontological rights or distributive justice—say, the use of fetal tissue in medical research—by engaging in CBA. The use of fetal tissue might be morally correct, or wrong, or morally controversial, but the resolution does not depend on whether one side of the debate is willing to pay more than the other side of the debate in order to see its views embodied in the law.

However, the second approach is probably not practical. Agencies are not generally well positioned to make moral decisions other than decisions regarding welfare maximization. Their expertise is technical and scientific, not moral; that is why a virtue of CBA is that it reduces moral considerations to an algorithm that requires no, or little, moral judgment. Further, moral evaluation would reduce transparency. As we argued in Chapter 4, CBA enhances transparency by forcing agencies to use a common metric for justifying their decisions. If agencies were permitted to rely on moral argument, then they could more easily conceal the true basis of their decisions. Our general point is that CBA is not a superprocedure that accounts for all morally relevant variables.

Finally, it bears emphasis that the case of morally motivated preferences is arguably just the most extreme example of disinterested (non-welfare-relevant) preferences. Consider the case where P prefers the project not because it matters to his own well-being, but also not because he takes it to be morally obligatory; rather, P's preference is motivated by some kind of group loyalty. Or consider the case where P prefers the project out of a sense of obligation to his children. If we had a full and persuasive theory of how preferences should be restricted—of how the distinction between disinterested and welfare-relevant preferences should be drawn—then we might suggest that agencies should ignore *any* kind of disinterested preference or preference-motivating consideration in calculating costs and benefits. But no such theory is yet at hand. The case of morally motivated preferences is, for now, the only case in which it is (1) clear that CVs can be disinterested and therefore can diverge from the effect of a regulation on well-being, and (2) practicable to enjoin agencies that they should adjust CVs so as to eliminate the effect of disinterested preferences.[26]

Prescription: Lack of Information

Suppose that an agency is considering whether to construct a park. A person P has no knowledge about the advantages of parks, so his CV may not reflect the actual welfare impact of the project. Specifically, let us imagine that P's CV is $-\$10$: when asked how much he would pay or require to be paid in the project (park) world so as to be indifferent between the park and the status quo, he answers that he would require to be paid $10.

Further, let us define P's CV-I as his hypothetical willingness to pay, given complete information: the amount that, if P were fully informed, he would pay or require to be paid in the project (park) world so as to be indifferent between the park and the status quo. Assume that CV-I is $100. (Note that CV-I, not CV, is the number an agency elicits when respondents to valuation surveys are provided with detailed information about projects, such as in the Grand Canyon study.) Which number should the agency use in its CBA of the park? Should it be $-\$10$, $100, or something else?

The answer depends on the nature of the project. Let us distinguish several possibilities.

First, people might costlessly and rapidly acquire the relevant information when the project is completed. P's CV is low ($-\$10$) because he thinks that park views are ugly; in fact, they fill him with joy. His belief is wrong because he has never seen a well-maintained park. If P held the correct belief, he would be willing to pay $100, his CV-I; and if the park is implemented, his actual valuation will change to $100. Under these conditions the actual welfare effect is better approximated by CV-I than by CV, and P's valuation should be treated as though it were $100.

Second, people might never acquire the relevant information. P might undervalue the park, because he thinks it is full of common and easily cultivated plants, when in fact they are rare and difficult to grow—something P never learns. So P's actual valuation of the park remains $-\$10$, even after the park is implemented. This is one type of case where correcting for preference distortion by looking to undistorted preferences (CV-I) turns out to be a mistake. Although CV-I is $100, P can't be made better off by the project. It is a necessary condition for a person to benefit from a project that (at some point) she prefer that project to the status quo; actual preferences have at least *that* role on the correct theory of well-being, however idealized.

A harder question is whether the agency should defer to P's CV ($-$10$), or should launder it, setting it at $0, or giving it yet another (negative) value. That question cannot be answered without a particular view as to how uninformed and fully informed preferences interact to produce well-being. On one view, the agency should defer to the CV of $-$10$ because it is P's uninformed preferences that constitute (and continue to constitute) P's view of the world. On another view, both types of preferences have a coequal role in shaping welfare; P cannot be made better off by a project that he never comes to actually prefer, but neither can he be harmed by a project that, if fully informed, he would prefer. Thus he neither truly gains, nor truly loses, and the agency should treat his CV as though it were $0. Without a strong opinion about which view is superior, we suggest that agencies take the pragmatic course and rely on P's actual CV, unless a particular regulatory setting offers a strong reason not to.

Several variations on this second case should be mentioned. One is where CV and CV-I have the same sign but differ in amount. P barely likes the park, and would like it more if he knew about it; or he detests it, and would slightly dislike it if better informed. Note that the premise we invoked above—actual preference is a necessary condition for benefit—does not here help in choosing in the range between CV and CV-I. A different variation on the second case is where information changes P's behavior. For example, a well-informed P would go into the park (and CV-I is based on the prediction that he would thus behave), but in fact P never learns something significant about the park and never goes in. In this particular example, P is not made better off by the park because he does not use it. Generalizing from the example is hazardous, but it at least seems clear that the welfare effect of a project can differ from CV-I by virtue of the behavioral impact of imperfect information.

Finally, the second case can be varied by having the information change instrumental judgments rather than intrinsic valuations. The project is not a park, but an air quality project, which P values (and would value under full information) in light of the effect of air quality on his longevity. He believes, incorrectly, that the cleanser used by the project would actually reduce his longevity, so CV is $-\$10$. In fact, the cleanser improves air quality, so CV-I is $100. Here, the case for using CV-I even if P remains uninformed about the project once implemented seems stronger.

To turn now to a third case: people might acquire the relevant information only if the agency feeds it to them. The agency might have to distribute leaflets describing the benefits of parks or invest in television commercials. These activities are costly and should be included in the cost of the project. If the cost of disseminating information is high enough that the project has negative value once that cost is taken into account, then we have the second case, above. Otherwise, the agency performs an educative function as well as implementing the project.

Prescription: Objectively Bad Preferences

Suppose some people support or oppose projects because their actual as well as fully informed preferences are sadistic.[27] A person might favor a park because he wants to see a neighbor's beloved home demolished in order to make way for the park, or he may oppose the park because he does not want his neighbors to benefit from higher property values. Or a person might oppose AIDS research because he dislikes homosexuals and drug users with whom he is acquainted and does not want to see their suffering relieved. Or, suppose some person prefers a way of life that is clearly worthless. Person P wants to spend his days in an opium-induced haze, rather than working, developing relationships, accomplishing intellectual or practical goals, starting a family, or doing anything else; and this preference is wholehearted, in the sense that it conflicts with no second-order preference of P's and does not change under full information.[28]

The sadism and drug fixation examples show that objective criteria are sometimes plausibly relevant to agency decisions and CBA.[29] The simplistic account of their relevance runs as follows. If the status quo is bad for person P in light of objective criteria, and the project is better for P in light of objective criteria, then the move from the status quo to the project improves P's welfare, regardless of P's actual preferences. But this simplistic account is incorrect, given the role of actual preference as a constituent (if not the sole constituent) of well-being. If the project is objectively better for P than the status quo, but P prefers (and would continue to prefer) the status quo, then the project cannot increase his welfare.

So how should the effect of a project be calculated where criteria of objective welfare value and actual preferences diverge? In theory, we could think of the interaction between preference and value along the following lines. Define a new measure, CV-O, as the amount that P would be willing to pay or be paid for the project if his preferences perfectly tracked considerations of objective value; and then set as an effective CV a number that is a function of the divergence between CV-O and CV. For example, P is willing to pay $10 for a new art museum, but if his preferences tracked objective values, he would be willing to pay $50; the effective CV would be some amount between $10 and $50, depending on how exactly actual preferences and objective values interact under the right theory of well-being.

But this suggestion is not practicable. Calculating CV-O would be a hopelessly difficult task for agencies. Further, instructing agencies to determine CV-O would significantly increase the opacity of CBA and thus the extent to which agencies can pursue their own agendas rather than sincerely attempting to perform CBA. We are less sanguine about integrating considerations of objective value into agency decision-making than we are about integrating the informational considerations discussed above—what P would prefer under full information, as against what he actually prefers—given that claims of objective value are highly contestable and not amenable to empirical testing.

A simpler and more practicable approach would be for objective values to bear upon agency valuations like this: if P is so perverse as to prefer a project that is clearly objectively bad, or to disprefer a project that is clearly objectively good, then P's CV should be taken by the agency to be $0. Otherwise (except in the case of changing preferences, to be considered momentarily), objective values should be ignored. Objective badness would be determined by Congress or the OMB at an abstract level. We could imagine, for example, guidelines holding that preferences that are based on animus against racial minorities, women, and homosexuals would not be counted.

Implementing these guidelines would not always be straightforward. Suppose, for example, that a person's CV for a park is low because he knows that a local racial minority would benefit from the park; it would be extremely difficult for an agency to determine that the CV is distorted in this sense, and even if it could, to separate out that component of the CV that is based on animus. In cases such as these, it would probably be infeasible to launder preferences. But in other cases, laundering preferences should be straightforward. Consider our earlier example of people who would have low CVs for AIDS vaccines because of their animus against homosexuals. The simple solution to this problem is not to take account the CVs of unaffected people, and simply to focus on the medical benefits of those vaccines compared to the cost of research. This is, in fact, agencies' practice. The CVs of unaffected people are properly ignored because they are either based on animus or on moral commitments (pro or con), which also, as we argued earlier, should be ignored.

Prescription: Adaptation

Suppose people are not willing to pay for parks because they have adapted to a world without parks. Or they have persuaded themselves that only rich people need parks because rich people are effete or weak. Merely informing people about the benefits of parks, then, will not change their CVs for parks. Indeed, to keep the analysis as clear as possible, we will assume that people are well informed.

One should distinguish two kinds of adaptation. In the first case, people's adaptive preferences never change. Whether or not the agency creates a park, P will always oppose parks because of his impoverished childhood. For the same reason that agencies should not implement projects that benefit people only if they obtain information that will forever elude them, agencies should not implement projects only because the projects are ranked higher by idealized ("nonadaptive") preferences that will never become actual. Where P prefers and continues to prefer the status quo (given his actual, adaptive preferences), the project cannot be welfare improving for him, even if P's idealized, nonadaptive preferences point in favor of the project.

To see why, imagine that the overburdened housewife discussed by Sen opposes a project to create a well near her home, preferring the long walk to the river (which, let us assume, the well project will make inaccessible to her). If her preferences truly cannot be expected to change in response to the project—if she will use the well with regret, continuing to prefer the world in which she walked to the river—then it is hard to say how the project would make her better off. The project might be supplemented with educational efforts, in the hope that the housewife will develop different preferences as a result of education. But in the limiting case where the housewife's preferences are irrevocably entrenched, by virtue of upbringing, the project cannot benefit her.

As with the information case, the issue remains whether the housewife should be counted as being hurt by the project or instead should be given an effective CV of $0. If the answer is $0, then the housewife is in effect ignored by the agency in its CBA of the well project, even though her actual valuation of that project is negative. If the answer is to use her real CV, then the agency would simply not take account of the fact that the housewife's preferences are adaptive. This might be the right answer, because the third alternative—to choose a number between $0 and the CV that properly reflects the degree of adaptiveness—is unpalatable. The problem with this alternative is its excessive difficulty. The problem here is even more difficult than the problems posed by lack of information. One can more easily imaginatively construct informed preferences out of uninformed preferences than nonadaptive preferences out of adaptive preferences. If the housewife prefers the walk because she was abused as a child, can we imagine what her preferences would be if she had not been abused? If she prefers the walk because she has unconsciously absorbed the views of her neighbors, can we imagine what her preferences would be if she had not unconsciously absorbed these views? We doubt that these questions can be answered, and we are sure that administrative agencies are in a poor position to answer them.

One possible solution to the problem is to use criteria of objective value. This is the solution we tentatively recommend. Sometimes adaptive preferences will also be clearly objectively bad. Perhaps this is true of the well case: perhaps it is clearly objectively better for the housewife to use the well than to walk to the river. If so, our suggested rule for the case of objective value would come into play, and the housewife's CV would be set at $0. Sometimes, however, a person P can have an adaptive preference for the status quo—that preference can be rooted in some injustice or other deficiency of the person's background—even though the status quo is not objectively bad, relative to the project. Imagine that P prefers one kind of recreation to another, that P continues to do so under full information, and that this recreation is not objectively harmful for P, but that P would prefer the second recreation had not the first been the only recreation available to him during an impoverished childhood. In this sort of case, we suggest, P's CV should be used.

In the second variation on the case of adaptive preference, people's preferences change over time. P has an actual preference for the status quo, rooted in some unfortunate feature of his background, while his nonadaptive or idealized preference is in favor of the project. But P's actual preference is not fixed; if the project were implemented, he would come to prefer it. So P's CV based on status quo world preferences is, say, $-$55, while his CV based on project world preferences is, say, $25. In this sort of case, at least in theory, criteria of adaptiveness could be used for choosing between P's conflicting sets of actual preferences, even where the project and the status quo are objectively fine and thus criteria of objective value provide no basis for making the choice. The agency could assign P a laundered CV equal to $25 on the grounds that his actual project world preferences are nonadaptive while his actual status quo preferences are adaptive. But, given the especial malleability of the concept of adaptive preferences (even as compared to the notion of an objectively "good" or "bad" way of life, which seems to have more commonsense resonance), we are skeptical that agencies should be instructed to use adaptiveness as a tiebreaker when status quo and project world preferences are different.

To sum up: adaptiveness is a separate way in which preferences can be distorted, distinct from the lack of information and the lack of objective value. P's preference for the status quo can be adaptive, even if this preference is fully informed and even if the status quo is not clearly objectively worse than the project. Thus, in theory, adaptiveness could be a separate basis for agencies to launder CVs. However, this suggestion strikes us as impracticable. In some cases, P's adaptive preference will also be uninformed, or objectively bad, or both, and in such a case a CV will appropriately be calculated for P based on considerations of full information or objective value. But adaptiveness per se should not, we think, be a component of agency decision-making. If P's preference is distorted solely because it is adaptive, and in no other way, then agencies should stick to textbook CBA and use P's CV as the measure of the project's welfare impact upon him.

Prescription: Wealth Distortions

Cost-benefit analysis is inaccurate, quite apart from the sources of preference distortion discussed so far, by virtue of the fact that it reduces welfare impacts on project winners and losers to dollars—which are, in turn, differentially productive of welfare in different persons. In particular, the marginal utility (strictly, marginal increase in overall well-being) of a dollar expended by a person poor in total wealth is generally larger than the marginal utility of a dollar expended by a rich person. The apparent solution is for agencies to weight CVs by the marginal utility of money. There are technical problems in constructing the right weighting factor; there may also be problems in transparency and reliability. But quite apart from technical and implementation difficulties, the proposal that agencies correct for the distorting effect of endowments by weighting CVs raises the subtler issues of (1) market adjustment (where rich and poor effectively undo the project picked out by weighted CBA, since their behavior is driven by unweighted preferences);[30] (2) the possible welfare superiority of money transfers to agency projects; and (3) the redistributive objection, which points out that weighted CVs would cause agencies to seek out redistributive projects rather than projects that solve market failures. These are the issues we will focus on here.

Suppose that an agency must decide whether to construct a park in a wealthy neighborhood or a poor neighborhood. All people have the same preferences, which include a desire for more park space. More people live in the poor neighborhood than in the wealthy neighborhood, but the wealthy people are willing to pay more for the park because of their lower marginal utility of money. The agency, however, adjusts CVs using the marginal utility of money and relies upon the adjusted CVs to justify placement of the park in the poor neighborhood.

The result of the agency's action is that the property values in the poor neighborhood will rise relative to the property values in the rich neighborhood. If the poor people are renters, landlords might terminate their leases, convert to condominiums, and sell the condominiums to rich people. The rich people move out of the old rich neighborhood, and the poor people move out of the old poor neighborhood. Perhaps they simply switch places. Far from benefiting poor people, the agency's project benefits landlords, who are likely to be relatively wealthy, while causing a large welfare loss as people engage in unnecessary migration. It would be better to give the park to the rich neighborhood.

This is an extreme version of what might happen. Another possibility is that some poor people own their own homes. These people would benefit from the increase in property values. But they would presumably sell to rich people, so the result of the agency decision to place the park in the poor rather than rich neighborhood is a transfer of wealth from rich people and poor people who do not own their homes to poor people who do own their homes. The rich people lose because they must pay to move to a new neighborhood; likewise the poor people without homes. The poor people with homes gain because of the increase in property values.

In this second case, the project of building the park in the poor neighborhood is welfare inferior to the project of building the park in the rich neighborhood plus arranging a lump-sum payment from the rich people to the poor people (or poor people with homes), which would not necessitate the uprooting and migration of large populations. However, agencies do not have the authority to order lump-sum payments. The agency's choice, then, is between benefiting some poor people through a project that diminishes the welfare of other poor people and a few rich people or benefiting a few rich people and some poor people at the expense of other poor people. Both are welfare inferior to the option of building the park in the rich neighborhood plus a transfer.

Suppose finally that people cannot move and that, therefore, property values do not adjust. The rich people will stay in the rich neighborhood and the poor people will stay in the poor neighborhood. Suppose that the rich people's aggregate CV is $1,000 and the poor people's aggregate CV is $500. If the park is placed in the poor people's neighborhood, they will obtain a value of $500. And this is true even of the very poor people who do not own their homes. One might argue that a better project would be the construction of the park in the rich neighborhood with a transfer, of say $600, from rich to poor.[31]

What should the agency do in these three cases? In the first case, by virtue of market adjustment, placing the park in the rich neighborhood turns out to be welfare superior to placing the park in the poor neighborhood. Here, it seems straightforward to us that the park should be placed in the rich neighborhood. In evaluating the project, the agency should take account of market adjustment; if market adjustment undermines the value of a superficially attractive project, the project should not be implemented. Because placing the park in the poor neighborhood does not, after market adjustment, increase overall well-being, the welfare criterion counts against the park's placement there.

The second and third cases are more difficult. The fact that a third project—placing the park in the rich neighborhood and transferring wealth from the rich to the poor—is welfare superior to the projects under consideration hardly seems relevant when that third project is not available to the agency. We know of no agency in the U.S. government that has the authority to order wealth transfers, and there are many good reasons for denying agencies this authority.

Assume that this does not change and that in the second and third cases the only options available to the agency are the simple ones. What should the agency do? There is a plausible case that the agency should just choose the option identified by marginal-utility-weighted CBA, namely, placing the park in the poor neighborhood. After all, this is welfare superior to placing the park in the rich neighborhood; weighted CBA is accurate, to this extent. To be sure, it might be the case that welfare-improving transfers through the tax and welfare system are not made because Congress has other things on its mind, and not because the optimal distribution of wealth has been achieved. But the agency has identified a way of increasing overall well-being and should implement it, and if this result is welfare inferior to an alternative that is politically impossible, that is irrelevant.

One might object to the approach suggested here because it would give agencies a license to search for projects that have differential impacts on rich and poor, and then approve them not because of their public good aspects or because they satisfy other standard market failure rationales for government intervention, but because of their redistributive effects. Agencies will implement projects in poor neighborhoods until people in those neighborhoods are as rich as people in rich neighborhoods. Weighted CBA gives agencies a license to undertake projects that increase overall well-being just by changing the distribution of wealth. This is the redistributive objection to weighted CBA.

The redistributive objection is a cogent one. There may be good, principled reasons against authorizing agencies to approve projects that are welfare increasing merely in virtue of their redistributive effects—because such a practice produces a disincentive to the accumulation of wealth, thereby decreasing overall well-being in the long run; or because, at some point, it invades the property rights of the rich; or perhaps for some other reason. But if this conclusion is correct, then the appropriate response of agencies is not to return to conventional CBA, with unweighted CVs. There is no reason to think that a simple cost-benefit comparison of a project and the status quo that uses unweighted CVs should generally reach the same result as a sophisticated cost-benefit comparison of a project and the status quo that uses weighted CVs and also integrates market adjustment effects and incentive effects into the outcomes being compared.

Rather, we see two possible responses to the redistributive objection. First, as we suggested above, in theory, agencies should count as costs perverse incentives that might result where CVs are weighted to correct for the declining marginal utility of wealth, that is, in inverse proportion to total wealth, thus producing a long-run disincentive to the accumulation of wealth. They should also include costs that would result from market adjustments, like the migration between neighborhoods discussed in the example. Without consideration of market adjustments and perverse incentives, the placement of the park in the poor neighborhood looks better (using weighted CBA) than the placement in the rich neighborhood. With consideration of market adjustments but not perverse incentives, the placement of the park in the poor neighborhood looks better (using weighted CBA) than the placement in the rich neighborhood if rich and poor cannot move (the third case described above) but not necessarily if they can (the first and second cases). Finally, with consideration of both market adjustments and perverse incentives, the placement of the park in the poor neighborhood may not look better (using weighted CBA) than the placement of the park in the rich neighborhood, even in the case where rich and poor cannot move.

To see how perverse incentives might be factored into agency decision-making, consider once more the case of immobile neighbors and assume the following. Rational Rick, in response to the park's placement in the rich neighborhood, will pursue one employment plan, E_1. In response to the park's placement in the poor neighborhood, he will pursue another plan, E_2, that earns him less wealth (because he has less incentive to earn wealth if he thinks that the park agencies and other agencies will weight his CVs in inverse proportion to his wealth). Assume further that Rick's CV for E_1, as against E_2, is $200. Then $200, as weighted for Rick's marginal utility of wealth, could be added to the rich persons' CVs ($1,000, again appropriately weighted) in determining the monetized benefits of placing the park in the rich neighborhood.

A second possible response to the redistributive objection is for agencies to rely upon a rule of thumb. The rule-of-thumb approach would evade the difficulty with the first response, which is that it may be impossible to calculate the ancillary costs—work disincentives, market adjustment—created by a project and by the particular technique that the agency uses to evaluate it. We can imagine three possible rules of thumb: (1) avoid projects that produce large losses for any group; (2) avoid projects that change the distribution of wealth; (3) avoid projects where the distribution of wealth among project winners is different from the distribution among project losers.

Approach (3) is most closely tied to the underlying normative problem that marginal utilities differ across wealth classes, while approach (2) more closely addresses the problem of perverse incentives and the redistributive objection. The choice between these two approaches thus turns on empirical questions such as the sensitivity with which people alter their behavior in response to regulations. Approach (1) is the simplest because it does not require the agency to estimate the effect of the regulation on the distribution of wealth.

Cognitive Biases

In developing our theory of distorted preferences, we have drawn heavily on the philosophy literature, but there is another literature of considerable relevance and significance for our topic, the cognitive psychology literature. This literature is mainly positive in nature, showing the ways human action deviates from the predictions of the rational actor model used in economics. But several scholars have tried to draw normative implications from the cognitive psychology literature, including its implications for CBA.

One such effort is Cass Sunstein's argument that justifies CBA on the ground that it helps dissuade governments from adopting irrational projects in response to cognitive panics.[32] Sunstein argues that certain features of human psychology—its tendency to overestimate the probability that highly salient events will recur, for example—cause people to overreact to environmental disasters and demand overregulation. Cost-benefit requirements may prevent agencies from succumbing to such political pressures.

Sunstein's argument bolsters the view we took in Chapter 4 that CBA might have desirable political characteristics—that, by enhancing transparency, it discourages agencies from adopting socially undesirable regulations. But this can be true only if CBA results in approval of projects that enhance overall welfare. The cognitive psychology literature suggests that it may not do so.

The reason is that cognitive biases drive a wedge between preference satisfaction and well-being. If people overestimate the probability that salient events will be repeated, then people will be willing to pay more to prevent the event's recurrence (supposing the event is bad) than would be desirable from the standpoint of their well-being. If people are myopic, then they will undervalue regulations that benefit them in the long term. If people lack self-control, then their market behavior may similarly suggest valuations for long-term goods that are lower than optimal. If people tend to value goods more if they possess them than if they do not possess them, this will also play havoc with the valuations used in CBA. The list of cognitive biases is lengthy; if taken seriously, then the value of CBA may seem to be thrown into doubt.

However, there are countervailing factors. Cognitive psychology suggests not only that people's valuations are not to be trusted but also that people do not respond sensitively to incentives. If this is so, then laundering preferences will not result in as much offsetting, perverse behavior as our earlier discussion suggested. So, for example, we might determine people's valuation of life by examining their market behavior in settings where cognitive biases do not seem to play too extreme a role (for example, in the workplace, where people have built up experience with certain risks), and then apply them in other settings where people demand extreme measures because their cognitive biases are fired by unusual stimuli (for example, terrorist attacks). Offsetting behavior will not occur, or will not be as bad as it would be under the rational actor model, because cognitive biases blunt people's responses to the new regime.

To be more concrete, suppose that we think that studies that derive valuations of statistical lives (VSLs) from market data are inaccurate because workers underestimate the risk of death, and thus accept wage premiums that are lower than what they would demand if they had an accurate knowledge of the risk of death. Further, suppose that the error is not due to ignorance that could be corrected through education but due to a genuine cognitive bias, such as a tendency to underestimate the probability of bad events. If these suppositions are true, then it may be appropriate for agencies—or, ideally, Congress or the OMB—to adjust VSLs upward. The danger at this point is that people will continue to underestimate the risk, and that the main effect of the tighter regulations based on the higher VSL is to lure into dangerous workplaces people with a somewhat lower risk tolerance than the original workers but who would be better off with a different job even under the new regulatory regime. This is the problem of perverse or offsetting behavior. If this danger is real, then it may be wrong to adjust VSLs upward in the first place. If this danger is not real, because the marginal workers are not sensitive to slight variations in risk, then it is not wrong to adjust VSLs upward. But then again, if people are sufficiently insensitive to incentives, the basis for using workplace data for deriving VSLs becomes obscure.

However, we think that at the current stage of development of the cognitive bias literature, these concerns are more theoretical than real. Although the literature has persuasively established that cognitive biases exist, it has had less success in showing that their magnitude is significant enough to justify an abandonment of CBA (or, for that matter, the free market). Cost-benefit analysis, like the market itself, would remain a crude tool for allocating resources even in a world of perfectly rational actors; our case for it depends on its comparative advantages over the alternatives, which are even cruder. "Wide" intuitive balancing and QALY-based analysis all must obtain valuations from somewhere, and if people's own valuations are not used because they suffer from cognitive biases, then alternative valuations must be used—and there are no good theories or methods for determining these. Because the alternatives to CBA are no more attractive in a world in which people suffer from extreme cognitive biases, the cognitive bias literature provides no reason for abandoning CBA. In the realistic world in which cognitive biases matter on the margin but do not render people's market actions and survey responses utterly useless as evidence of their undistorted preferences, CBA remains the appropriate decision procedure for maximizing overall welfare.

But we do not think that the cognitive bias literature should be ignored. At the retail level, we think that it would be sensible for the OMB to take account of the possibility that well-documented cognitive biases have nontrivial effects on people's valuation of regulatory goods. Further empirical work may establish whether it is proper for agencies to take these effects into account by using multipliers and the like, or to ignore them.

Institutional Considerations

We have mentioned several times that even if preferences are distorted, and ought to be laundered by an epistemically perfect agency, in practice allowing agencies to launder preferences may create more problems than it solves. First, agencies are not epistemically perfect: asking them to monetize the benefits and costs of regulations given actual preferences is demanding enough; asking them to monetize the benefits and costs given laundered preferences may seem overwhelming. Relying on actual preferences allows agencies to use market data and survey results; laundering preferences would require taking these data and results and adjusting them in a manner that cannot be reduced to algorithms or clear rules. It may be true that surveys and other instruments can incorporate various debiasing measures—like informing people before asking them for valuations—but the validity of such methods remains disputed. Thus, CBA based on laundered preferences should be performed cautiously, if at all.

Second, agencies are vulnerable to political manipulation—by their personnel, by interest groups, and by others. As we stressed in Chapter 4, one advantage of CBA is that it increases the transparency of agency decision-making. But this is true for textbook CBA, which forces agencies to rely on (ideally) peer-reviewed, replicable empirical analyses. Cost-benefit analysis that rests on laundered preferences cannot, except in unusual cases, be based directly on empirical analyses. Although an agency might start with market data, its claim that the data must be revised or ignored because preferences are distorted would be hard to evaluate. One might disagree with the agency but have no grounds for arguing that its judgment is wrong.

For these reasons, we have not proposed that agencies launder preferences in the manner that abstract moral theory would suggest. For institutional reasons, the laundering process should be executed by elected officials or possibly bureaucrats who stand outside the agencies, such as the personnel of the OMB. They should provide general guidelines that establish the kind of preferences that should be ignored or adjusted, and, in the latter case, the kind of adjustments that should take place. In extreme cases, it may be appropriate for agencies to act on their own, but then they should report a textbook CBA along with the laundered CBA, and explain why exactly they deviated. As for the guidelines, they are the topic of the next section.

Guidelines for Laundering Preferences

If agencies did not face information and decision costs and were not subject to political constraints, they could maximize overall well-being in several straightforward ways. They would ignore disinterested preferences or else treat widespread moral commitments as (nonmonetized) constraints on projects. They would use informed preferences when persons will become informed as a result of the project or when preferences are instrumental rather than intrinsic; they would otherwise rely, at least to some extent, on uninformed preferences; and they would consider information dissemination a potential supplement to the project, with its own benefits and costs. They would discount adaptive preferences, and rely to some extent on idealized, nonadaptive preferences in performing CBA—if, for example, such preferences will become actual as a result of the project and even, perhaps, if adaptive preferences are entrenched. They would ignore objectively bad preferences. They would adjust for wealth distortions by weighting for marginal utility.

But agencies do face information and decision costs. Such fallible agencies must use whichever decision procedure minimizes the sum of these costs and the cost of error. We propose the following guidelines.

Even fallible agencies can successfully ignore objectively bad preferences when preferences violate widespread, uncontroversial intuitions about valuable and worthless behavior. Moreover, fallible agencies can successfully ignore disinterested preferences in certain situations: they should not use existence values for environmental entities. However, the appropriate response is not always so straightforward. A person might have a high CV for, say, a public commuter train both because of a self-interested preference for convenient transportation and because of a disinterested preference for environmentally sound transportation. A person might have a high CV for a bridge both because it reduces his cost of transportation and because it annoys his neighbors. These CVs would be reflected in market behavior as well as in survey results. In such cases of mixed preferences, the ideal agency would sort them out, but a real agency probably cannot. The real agency might plausibly choose to rely on traditional CVs on the theory that self-interested preferences tend to have much greater influence on CVs, except in domains where it seems likely that disinterested preferences dominate. The most important such domains are ones where the actual CVs are low, because in such cases the direct impact of the project is small and moral feelings are relatively powerful. Environmental regulation is such a domain, and that is why existence values should be ignored.

Agencies are, we suspect, unlikely to be able to distinguish adaptive preferences from nonadaptive preferences. Accordingly, we think that agencies should ignore this category. It is likely that most extreme cases are better handled as objectively bad preferences. For example, preferences of drug addicts, whether or not adaptive, are generally considered objectively bad. Indeed, the fact that agencies would ignore the preferences of nonaddicted drug users suggests that objective value is the more appropriate category.

When preferences are uninformed, agencies should sometimes make adjustments. If projects that are based on informed preferences actually improve well-being, either because people do not need information in order to receive the benefit or because they are likely to obtain information after the project is implemented, then there is a good case for constructing informed preferences. However, when uninformed people do not become informed as a result of the project, it is probably best to use uninformed preferences.

We are more optimistic about restricting preferences on the basis of information than on the basis of adaptation, for two reasons. First, it is easier for agencies to derive informed preferences from uninformed preferences than nonadaptive preferences from adaptive preferences. One can, for example, compare the behavior of people who are informed about nutrition and people who are uninformed about nutrition; one can observe changes in behavior as people obtain information; and one can provide survey participants with information before asking for their valuations. But it is, even as a conceptual matter, hard to distinguish adaptive preferences from nonadaptive preferences. Many influences contribute to the formation of preferences; distinguishing "corrupt" from "pure" influences may be impossible or even meaningless. Second, it is easier to give people information than it is to change their preferences. Indeed, people will seek out information because it can help them satisfy their desires, but people commonly resist efforts to change their preferences. The first requires education; the second requires brainwashing.

Finally, when CVs are distorted because of wealth differences, real agencies might use distributive weights and then make further corrections to deal with the problems of market adjustment and perverse incentives. We have outlined how these corrections could be made. But the more practicable course, we think, is for agencies to rely upon one of the rules of thumb suggested above—in particular, to avoid projects where the distribution of wealth among project winners and losers is substantially different.

Further, it is unclear whether the basic idea of distributive weighting is itself a feasible one. It may be just too complicated for Congress or the OMB to specify a methodology for weighting CVs, in inverse proportion to total wealth or income, that is reasonably accurate (in compensating for the declining marginal utility of wealth) and that agencies can use with reasonable success. The feasibility of distributive weighting has been much debated, without a clear resolution, by welfare economists. If distributive weighting is not feasible, then agencies should probably use unadjusted CVs when the distribution of wealth among the winners does not differ much from the distribution among the losers. When the distributions differ greatly, an agency could refrain from implementing the project. One possible alternative route would be to inform Congress and hierarchical superiors in the executive branch; these officials might be willing to arrange for compensation of the losers or some other politically desirable outcome. Finally, an agency could use a procedure other than CBA for comparing the project and status quo—in effect, a procedure like wide intuitive balancing that reaches the same kind of results as weighted CBA but is more feasible—but this would lead back to the problem of market adjustment and perverse incentives. We are skeptical that agencies can really take account of these.

A comment about this last point should be added. Supporters of CBA have traditionally argued that it avoids distributional judgments and allows agencies to focus on efficiency improvements that their expertise puts them in a position to identify. Critics of CBA have pointed out that distributional judgments cannot be avoided. The efficiency of a project is a function of its distributive effects. Unadjusted CVs are unacceptable because they reward people on the basis of wealth, yet wealthy people are on average likely to value a dollar on the margin less than poor people are. Properly adjusted

CVs would result in possibly massive redistribution to the poor as agencies implemented projects that tax the rich (because their marginal dollars are worth little to them) and benefit the poor (who can then use valuable marginal dollars for other purposes). Our view is that in theory agencies should take account of the costs of market adjustments and work disincentives, and if they could do this, then properly adjusted CBA would not result in a massive redistribution of wealth. In practice, agencies are unlikely to be able to calculate these costs, so certain broad constraints—against projects that have large impacts on the distribution of wealth, for example—might be justified. This may be a rough description of agency practice, but there is much room for improvement.

CHAPTER 6

Objections

This book has reconceptualized CBA. It is an imperfect decision procedure for implementing overall well-being, not a fundamental moral criterion. The moral framework that undergirds CBA is neither a Kaldor-Hicks framework nor utilitarianism, but rather weak welfarism. Weak welfarism rejects the skepticism about interpersonal welfare comparisons that animated classical welfare economics and the development of the Kaldor-Hicks construct. Weak welfarism also rejects the austere focus on total welfare that characterizes utilitarianism. It claims that overall welfare is morally relevant, not necessarily morally decisive. And what, in turn, is welfare? A subject's well-being is not equivalent to the satisfaction of her actual preferences. Rather, we have defended a more nuanced ("restricted") preference-based account of welfare: one that distinguishes between self-interested and disinterested preferences, and that requires preferences to survive some degree of idealization. This more sophisticated view of welfare should influence the actual practice of CBA. As we discussed in the last chapter, agencies should (at least to some extent) adjust CVs to screen out nonideal or disinterested preferences.

CBA, thus reconceptualized, is less vulnerable to the objections that have often been leveled against it. Some of those objections (for example, the irrelevance of Kaldor-Hicks efficiency, or the distortion of CBA in a political environment) have been fully addressed already. In this chapter, we seek to answer the remaining criticisms.

Rights, Distribution, and Nonwelfare Values

Common sense morality believes in the existence of moral rights. Moral rights are "deontological," that is, nonconsequentialist, in that they constrain the maximization of good consequences.[1] For example, it is commonly believed that executing an innocent scapegoat to appease the violent mob that demands his death, or harvesting the organs of an unconsenting donor to save four others who will perish without the organs, or providing untrue information to an adult who would act imprudently if she were told the truth, would be morally wrong even if the net welfare benefits of the execution, the organ-harvesting, or the deception are positive. It is possible that these acts (including their long-run consequences) would reduce overall welfare; but it also seems possible that the actions (even factoring in long-run consequences) are on balance welfare maximizing. The scapegoat's life and welfare would be cut short by his execution, but if he is not executed, many bystanders will have their lives cut short by the rampaging mob. If the organs are not trans-planted, four die; if they are transplanted, only one does, and we can at least imagine a case in which the indirect harms of the involuntary transplant (fear in the general population, incentive effects) would not be large. Finally, it is not hard to envision cases in which lying to someone might make her better off.

But commonsense morality insists that the good consequences that might flow from executing the scapegoat, transferring the organs, or lying to the adult are insufficient to justify these actions.[2] "Deontological" moral phil-osophers have built on these nonconsequentialist lay intuitions.[3] A standard list of moral rights, that is, deontological prohibitions, would include prohi-bitions on killing, injuring, lying, coercing, stealing, and breaking promises.[4] The precise content of these constraints is hotly contested within deonto-logical scholarship; and it is also contested whether the prohibitions are ab-solute or defeasible (in "catastrophe cases") by sufficiently large benefits.[5] But deontological theorists agree that moral rights provide some substantial limitation on the maximization of overall welfare or other sorts of good con-sequences. That is their essential function.

Deontological critics of CBA complain that it ignores moral rights.[6] A dif-ferent criticism comes from egalitarians. Egalitarianism, like deontology, is internally contested. Some egalitarians argue that the equal distribution of welfare is a moral imperative. Within this camp, we can distinguish between those who conceive equality in the "prioritarian" sense and respect the Pareto principle, and those who focus strictly on the dispersion in welfare levels across the population and would countenance Pareto-inferior moves that reduce inequality.[7] A second family of egalitarian views is "resourcist"; it ar-gues that "resources," "capabilities," "primary goods," or other such items, rather than welfare itself, are the things whose equal distribution morality requires. A third kind of egalitarianism, in effect a kind of compromise be-tween the first two types, focuses on equal opportunity for welfare: welfare shortfalls for which the subject is responsible (in the appropriate sense) are not of egalitarian concern.[8] Egalitarians, whatever their specific views, can object—and have objected!—that CBA is insensitive to distribution (be it the distribution of welfare, of opportunities for welfare, or the preconditions for welfare, that is, resources/capabilities/primary goods).[9]

Deontologists and egalitarians do not stray too far from human welfare. Moral rights have special weight, but are ultimately grounded in certain aspects of human well-being: bodily integrity, autonomy, property. Egalitarians care either about the distribution of welfare itself, or about the distribution of things that are fairly closely connected to welfare. But it is possible to believe that morality incorporates some considerations wholly detached from well-being.[10] Let us call these considerations "nonwelfare values." The philosopher G. E. Moore argued a century ago that beautiful art has moral weight transcending its effect on humans.[11] Moore's aestheticism now seems quaint, but aestheticism is not the only kind of nonwelfarism. Some contemporary environmentalists believe in nonwelfare values: they believe that destroying an ecosystem, or taking actions that lead to the extinction of a species, is morally wrong quite apart from whatever utility the ecosystem or species might have for humans.[12]

Contrast nonwelfarist environmentalism with a welfarist environmentalism that grounds its opposition to environmental degradation in a worry about future human generations. So environmentalism need not incorporate nonwelfare values, but it *can* and (in practice) often seems to. Nonwelfarist environmentalists complain that CBA cares only about humans, not about the intrinsic value of the environment;[13] and Moorean aesthetes (if there are still any) could complain that CBA cares only about humans, not about the intrinsic value of art.

What is our response to deontological, egalitarian, and non-welfare-based criticisms of CBA? First, we concede that morality might include deontological, egalitarian, or non-welfare-based considerations. That is the essence of weak welfarism, the view presented in this book. What governmental actors or other individuals should do is, in part, a function of overall welfare; but it may also be a function, in part, of other moral factors $F_1 \ldots F_m$. Deontological, egalitarian, and/or non-welfare-based considerations might be included among the F_i.[14] Weak welfarism does not insist on the existence of moral factors distinct from overall welfare; but, unlike utilitarianism, it does not insist that no such factors exist.

Second, we happily concede that CBA does not track deontological, egalitarian, or non-welfare-based values. Nor do we see how CBA might be rebuilt to do so. The idea of "compensating variation" is at the very core of CBA: it seeks to monetize the welfare effect of a policy on a given individual by asking how much she is willing to pay/accept in return for that policy. CVs can be modified (we have argued) to screen out nonideal or disinterested preferences; but the very point of this modification is to achieve a more accurate money measure of welfare impacts. Modifying CVs to capture moral rights, or non-welfare-based environmental values, would be a much more radical alteration of CBA, and it is *not* an alteration we have proposed or contemplated.

As for egalitarian considerations: we have argued that CBA might incorporate distributive weights to counterbalance the variable marginal utility of money, but it should be stressed that these weighting factors would simply function to help CBA measure overall welfare more accurately. The term "distributive weights," is, admittedly, misleading. "Distributive weights" as we contemplate them, are grounded in overall well-being, *not* egalitarian norms. Whether CBA might be further modified to track egalitarian norms is an interesting question. In the case of prioritarianism, the answer may be yes; but for egalitarian views that focus on the distribution of resources/capabilities/primary goods rather than welfare, or that deny the Pareto principle, it is very hard to see what the modification would be.

In short, *CBA is not a superprocedure.* It implements overall welfare, not the totality of moral considerations. *Egalitarian, deontological, and/or non-welfare-based considerations (to the extent they exist) need to be brought to bear on agency choice through decision rules other than CBA.* What the structure of such decision rules should be is a very complicated matter, which we cannot begin to resolve here. For example, if one is skeptical about the existence of non-welfare-based values, and one believes (as is somewhat plausible) that egalitarian considerations are best implemented through the tax-and-transfer system rather than regulation,[15] then one decision rule sensitive to the totality of moral considerations is "Implement CBA, but do not choose policies that violate moral rights." If the deontological constraints on governmental choice are more or less reflected in constitutional law,[16] then another decision rule sensitive to the totality of moral considerations is "Implement CBA, but do not choose policies that violate constitutional rights." Or "Implement CBA, with your choice subject to review by a constitutional court."

Assume that morality consists of overall welfare W plus other factors $\{F_1 \ldots F_m\}$. One possible implementing rule for the totality of these considerations makes agencies responsible both for W and for the F_i, and tells agencies to use CBA as one step in the overall analysis, the step that determines which choice maximizes W. Another possible implementing rule tells agencies to focus solely on W (using CBA), and makes legislatures, courts, or tax-and-transfer bodies responsible for the F_i. But isn't a third possibility that agencies should be responsible for W and $\{F_1 \ldots F_m\}$, and should implement these considerations using some superprocedure that doesn't incorporate CBA as a separate step? We suppose that that is a theoretical possibility—but we have absolutely no idea what the superprocedure would consist in. None of the competitors to CBA discussed in Chapter 3 seem remotely plausible as this sort of superprocedure.

In any event, the problem of identifying the F_i, and designing decision rules to implement them, is well beyond the scope of this book. The book has tried to show that CBA optimally implements overall welfare. Reciprocally, we have emphasized, in this section, that CBA doesn't implement additional moral factors. Defenders of CBA need to recognize its limits; and critics shouldn't attack an implausibly inflated target.

Incommensurability

In a recent book, Lisa Heinzerling and Frank Ackerman have argued that CBA inappropriately attempts to price goods that are "priceless."

> [T]he benefits [of health and environmental regulation] are, literally, priceless. Herein lies the fatal flaw of cost-benefit analysis: to compare costs and benefits in its rigid framework, they must be expressed in common units. Cancer deaths avoided, wilderness and whales saved, illnesses and anxieties prevented—all these and many other benefits must be reduced to dollar values to ensure that we are spending just enough on them, but not too much . . . [M]ost of what we think is important about human life, health and the environment is lost in this translation. By monetizing the things we hold most dear, economic analysis ends up cheapening and belittling them.[17]

Heinzerling and Ackerman are voicing what might be called the "incommensurability" complaint about CBA—and are simply the latest in a long line of critics to do so. Arguments based on "incommensurability," "nonmarket values," "the plurality of values," "pricelessness, "noncommodification," or "expressive" concerns are a standard weapon deployed against CBA.[18] All of these arguments suggest that CBA runs aground by trying to use a single, monetary scale to measure health, environmental goods, and other things that cannot be, or ought not be, thus commensurated.

But what exactly does the "incommensurability" complaint about CBA assert? In this section we will describe, and seek to deflect, different versions of that challenge. To begin, the complaint might be that health or environmental goods are "priceless" in that their moral importance transcends their impact on overall welfare; they can't be commensurated (on this line of thinking) with commodities, which are morally important only because they advance overall welfare. We have already addressed this version of the incommensurability complaint in the previous section. Cost-benefit analysis is not a superprocedure. It measures the effect of health, environmental, and other changes on overall welfare, nothing more. If there are moral rights to health, or non-welfare-based values implicated by environmental degradation, then agency CBA will need to be combined with other procedures or institutions to reflect those rights or values. Cost-benefit analysis itself will not reflect—and shouldn't be criticized for failing to reflect—those.

The remaining variants of the "incommensurability" critique take as given the goal of maximizing welfare, but argue that—for one or another reason— the monetary scale CBA employs is a poor instrument for doing that. First, "incommensurability" or "pricelessness" might mean the *lexical priority* of some goods vis-à-vis dollars.[19] One welfare dimension is lexically ordered over another if the first dimension takes absolute priority in determining well-being; a positive (negative) change along the first dimension, however small, outweighs a negative (positive) change along the second dimension, however big. The lexical priority of goods vis-à-vis dollars would mean that no amount of money suffices to repair the loss of those goods or, equivalently, that an individual's willingness-to-accept (WTA) amount, in exchange for losing the good, is infinite and that her WTP for the good is equal to her entire stock of wealth. Cost-benefit analysis would break down.

Lexical priority is theoretically possible.[20] But we are skeptical that the environmental and health goods often described by CBA critics as "priceless" are really lexically ordered vis-à-vis dollars. We think it implausible that ecosystem destruction, the loss of an endangered species, or other forms of environmental degradation would have a welfare impact on an ordinary individual so substantial that no amount of money could repair the welfare loss to her. To be sure, individuals do frequently voice infinite WTAs when polled about environmental damage; but those WTAs reflect their *moral* preferences, or their objection to the enterprise of environmental CBA, and not the "restricted" (self-interested, idealized) preferences that are relevant to CBA understood as a welfarist decision procedure.[21] *P* genuinely has an infinite WTA for environmental loss only if P's life history with the environmental goods is better for P than P's life history without the goods, no matter how much money is added to P's stock of assets (and spent in the optimal way for P).

Environmental goods may be collectively very important (that is, the aggregate of WTP/WTA amounts for environmental goods, "laundered" to reflect restricted preferences, may be large, if not infinite), but it is hard for us to see how any given individual's true WTA for environmental loss, tracking her self-interested idealized preferences, would be infinite. Indeed, when pressed, Ackerman and Heinzerling step back from the claim that environmental goods are lexically ordered vis-à-vis dollars. "To say that . . . nature [is] priceless is not to say that we should spend an infinite amount of money to protect [it]."[22]

As for health goods: the fact that no amount of money can compensate for certain death might be seen as a kind of lexical ordering. Absent a "bequest function," WTA for certain death will be infinite, and WTP to avoid certain death will equal the subject's total assets. But this reflects the fact that money postmortem has zero marginal utility. It doesn't reflect the fact there is an infinite *utility* loss in premature death. The utility loss in premature death arises from the loss of additional life-years and all the goods that the subject would enjoy during those life-years. A longer life-history typically has a higher utility than a life-history cut short by premature death; the utility *loss* in premature death is the difference in utility between the two life-histories. The problem, for CBA, is to translate this utility loss into dollars, given that dollars postmortem have zero marginal utility. The solution to that problem is to elicit WTP/WTA for the risk of death. The risk of death is *not* lexically ordered vis-à-vis dollars; people have finite (actually, fairly small) WTA and WTP amounts for small risks. So the special "lexical ordering" problem created by the uselessness of dollars postmortem can be—and has been—circumvented in CBA practice.[23]

More generally, claims that some good is lexically ordered vis-à-vis dollars must confront the fact that money is—as discussed in Chapter 3—what Rawls calls a "primary good," an "all-purpose means" to welfare. Income can be used not merely to purchase commodities for immediate pleasure but also to purchase a huge range of marketed goods and services and thereby to facilitate a wide range of life plans. (This is why egalitarians typically favor the redistribution of income to achieve their goals, and why the "poverty line" is so helpful in identifying those with strong redistributive claims.) If WTA for some loss is really infinite, then none of the numerous ways in which income subserves human flourishing can compensate for the loss. This is possible, but unlikely—and as the example of valuing life shows, even where a good is genuinely lexically ordered vis-à-vis dollars, asking for WTP/WTA for some transformation of the good (for example, a risk of loss) may produce WTP/WTA amounts that are tractable and measure the utility losses reasonably accurately.

So much for the "lexical ordering" variant of the incommensurability argument. A second variant points to the problem of *incomparability*. Economists like to assume that individuals, and society generally, have a "complete" ordering over outcomes: given any two outcomes, either the first is better, or the second is better, or the two are precisely equal.[24] Philosophers, as well as some revisionary economists (most prominently Amartya Sen), have pointed out that outcomes might be incomparable: neither better, nor worse, nor precisely equal.[25] To use a well-known example from the philosopher Joseph Raz: I might have the choice between (1) spending a free hour walking in the park; (2) spending the time enjoying a glass of scotch in my study; or (3) spending the time enjoying a glass of port in my study. Assume I prefer port to scotch. Then (3) is better than (2). But it also seems quite possible that neither (2) nor (3) is better than (1), or vice versa. If so, it follows that (3) and (2) can't be precisely as good as (1).[26] Since drinking scotch or drinking port are neither better than walking in the park, nor worse than walking in the park, nor precisely as good as walking in the park, they must stand in some fourth relation to the walk: they must be *incomparable* with walking in the park.

Incomparability raises a host of issues for welfarism and CBA that one of us has discussed at length elsewhere.[27] To summarize: For various reasons, the criterion of "overall welfare" probably does not provide a complete ordering of outcomes.[28] The ordering is "partial," not complete. There exist pairs of outcomes such that overall welfare is not greater in one outcome than the other, nor is overall welfare precisely equal in the two outcomes. But incomparability with respect to overall welfare is not damaging to weak welfarism. To begin, transitivity still holds (in other words, if one outcome has greater overall welfare than a second, which in turn has greater overall welfare than a third, then the first outcome has greater overall welfare than the third). Further, incomparability doesn't disable choice or justification any more than precise equality does. If one outcome is incomparable—qua overall welfare—with a second, then a government official can choose arbitrarily between them (bracketing the existence of moral rights, and so on), just as she can pick arbitrarily between two outcomes that are precisely equal with respect to overall welfare.

This means that CBA is an accurate welfarist decision procedure as long as it leads officials to choose the policies that are ranked higher by the overall welfare criterion. How CBA chooses between policies that in fact are precisely equal or incomparable in terms of overall welfare is a matter of indifference.

Turning back to the issue of "pricelessness," it *is* possible that certain welfare effects on individual persons are incomparable with dollars. If O is the status quo outcome and $O*$ is the project outcome, then it might be the case that—for some range of dollar payments added to or subtracted from P's assets in $O*$—P is neither better off in $O*$ than O, nor worse off, nor precisely equally well off. This possibility requires a redefinition of the concept of CV—traditionally defined on the assumption that an individual's preferences (and thus that individual's welfare) define a complete, not partial, ordering over outcomes. For example, the CV of a person who gains from a project might be redefined as the largest amount that can be deducted from the individual's resources in the project outcome and still leave her either equally well off or incomparably well off vis-à-vis the status quo.

To put the point another way: Incomparability means that individuals might have "fuzzy" rather than precise money valuations of various welfare changes, and the CV construct needs to be flexible enough to accommodate this fuzziness.[29] But fuzzy valuations don't undermine CBA itself. As long as the sum of CV amounts (now redefined *both* to "launder" nonideal or disinterested preferences *and* to accommodate fuzziness) is better than competing procedures at identifying genuinely welfare-increasing projects (taking into account political context, transparency, and so on), and has decision costs that are not so high as to swamp this accuracy benefit, CBA will be the better welfarist procedure.

Talk of "pricelessness" and "incommensurability" might mean lexical ordering; it might mean incomparability; or, more mundanely, it might mean that money values for the goods involved are difficult to measure, for example because the goods aren't traded on markets. Heinzerling and Ackerman write:

> In comparing monetized benefits to monetized costs, and making this comparison the criterion for judging public policies protecting people and the environment, the analysis also stacks the deck against such policies. In practice, most cost-benefit analyses could more accurately be described as "com-

plete cost–incomplete benefit" studies. Most or all of the costs are readily determined market prices, but many important benefits cannot be meaningfully quantified or priced, and are therefore implicitly given a value of zero.[30]

But CBA emphatically *does not* assume that CVs for nonmarketed goods are zero. Using contingent valuation surveys to estimate money valuations of nonmarketed goods is now a cottage industry in applied economics. Thousands of these surveys have been undertaken; and a large secondary literature has developed sophisticated econometric and debiasing techniques to make the surveys more accurate. A different approach for estimating CVs for nonmarketed goods, also widely employed, is to employ behavioral measures of the goods (for example, variation in housing prices to estimate CVs for noise, visibility, or air quality).[31] On this score, it is often an exaggeration to describe environmental or health and safety goods as wholly "nonmarket." Market transactions may well be aimed at securing the goods, and may thus provide some evidence of valuation. For example, individuals do purchase safety (either in the form of separate safety devices, or in the form of safer items); they do purchase health services; and in their housing and recreational purchases, they do attempt to improve their immediate environment.

In any event, the general problem identified by this variant of the "incommensurability" complaint is the problem of estimation and measurement. Let us place to one side the issues of lexical priority and incomparability, which are really quite different, and assume that individuals have precise, finite CV amounts for a particular good. From the CBA analyst's perspective, these valuations will not be directly observable, and it will be uncertain exactly what the valuations are. (That is true, by the way, even where the good is a quintessential marketed item.) But uncertainty and unobservability are pervasive features of the human situation: for example, we can't see or know each other's minds, or the future, or the past, or indeed what occurs in the present at distant locations. Humans have been pretty creative in evolving techniques for making choices and estimations in the teeth of uncertainty;[32] the "contingent valuation" and "revealed preference" techniques mentioned in the previous paragraph are one example, hardly unique. To insist that an uncertain and unobservable quantity is *always* "unknowable" is silly; nor have the "incommensurability" critics of CBA shown why CVs present an especially deep and intractable kind of uncertainty.

A final version of the incommensurability critique of CBA claims not that environmental, health, or other goods are lexically prior to dollars or incomparable with dollars, or that dollar valuations are uncertain and difficult to estimate, but rather that the very process of dollar valuation cheapens the goods. As Heinzerling and Ackerman put it: "By monetizing the things we hold most dear, economic analysis ends up cheapening and belittling them." This is, once more, a familiar complaint about CBA; opponents of "commodification" often voice it.[33] The idea is that the very effort to attach a money price to certain goods reduces the welfare value of those goods. Joseph Raz calls this "constitutive incommensurability": It is (supposedly) constitutive of the welfare value of certain goods that we not think about them in dollar terms.[34]

What are we to make of the "cheapening"/"constitutive incommensurability" objection to CBA? By exactly what route does CBA cheapen the goods that it prices? To begin, the pricing of environmental, health, or other goods as part of CBA might have negative psychological impacts. It might make people upset. Being upset is certainly a welfare setback (not just on a hedonic view of welfare, but on a restricted preferentialist view, too, since I might well self-interestedly prefer with full information not to be upset).[35]

The psychological distress produced by CBA counts as a kind of decision cost. And this psychological decision cost might, in principle, be large enough to tilt the balance against CBA, in favor of competitor procedures. We believe it would have to be quite large to do that (since we believe that CBA has substantial accuracy advantages vis-à-vis competitors). We are aware of no evidence that agency employment of CBA generally produces substantial psychological distress in the general population, and we are skeptical that it generally does—mainly because citizens ordinarily don't pay much attention to the details of agency decision-making, and also because there are various other contexts (tort law, life insurance) where the value of life, health, and environmental goods are measured on a dollar scale.

It might be objected that agency use of CBA in unusual, salient cases could produce widespread distress even if CBA doesn't generally do that. This is true—and maybe agency officials predicting psychological distress in a particular case would maximize welfare by using a procedure different from CBA in that case. Even with this possibility in mind, the distress-avoidance gains from building a "distress" exception into CBA would have to be weighed against the losses that occur when mistaken or opportunistic officials invoke this exception absent genuine population distress.

Ultimately, the distress question is an empirical one, since no one doubts that distress is a welfare setback. We concede that an accurate and cheap procedure could still be so massively distressing to the population that, on balance, overall welfare would require a different procedure. But the "cheapening" critics of CBA don't frame their critique in these empirical terms. The claim is not (or not just) that CBA bothers and upsets people but that CBA "cheapens" goods in some more abstract way.

We can evaluate *this* claim by bringing to bear our theory of well-being. Is it really true that individuals would self-interestedly prefer, given full information and other idealizing conditions, that certain goods not be subjected to CBA? To be sure, it seems plausible that an individual might prefer with full information that she not consciously monetize certain aspects of her life. (I prefer not to think about how much my friendship with Joe is worth to me in dollars, or about what my CV for my child's life is.)[36] But the question on the table is different: it is whether an individual P would self-interestedly prefer, under ideal conditions, that *government officials* not employ a decision procedure that involves monetizing certain aspects of P's life. Assume that overall well-being does indeed have moral relevance, and that CBA is indeed the best decision procedure for effectuating overall well-being. Why would P, with these truths in hand, still prefer that government not employ a commensurating procedure?

To put the point another way: "incommensurability" critics claim that the very nature of certain welfare goods precludes monetizing them. But our understanding of the "nature" of these welfare goods should cohere with our broader moral views. To say that (1) government is morally required, *ceteris paribus*, to maximize overall well-being, and (2) government can most accurately determine which policies maximize overall well-being through a particular procedure, but (3) some welfare goods are "cheapened" by this very procedure, is to create an incoherence or at least tension within our moral theory.

Note also that it's hard to see why the cheapening claim, if true, would be limited to CBA. Why would it "cheapen" goods to balance them with competing goods using a money scale, but not to employ other forms of balancing? Indeed, why doesn't the "cheapening" objection also apply to narrow procedures? Consider three questions a governmental analyst might ask about a policy that prevents degradation of a pristine ecosystem: (1) what the sum-of-CVs for the ecosystem is; (2) whether, intuitively, the welfare benefits of saving the ecosystem are worth the costs (in higher product prices, lower employment); (3) whether the environmental benefits of saving this ecosystem outweigh any environment losses that might be associated with the policy (for example, if financial or political constraints limit the number of ecosystems that government can protect). Cost-benefit analysis asks the first question; intuitive balancing, the second; a "narrow" procedure of maximizing environmental benefits, the third. "Constitutive incommensurability" critics who claim that CBA, in particular, cheapens environmental goods (for example) need to provide a principled account of why the "nature" of environmental goods precludes the first question, but not the second or third—why individuals under ideal conditions would disprefer government asking the first question, but not the other two.

It should be conceded that the distinction we have drawn here between *governmental* use of CBA and requiring *individuals* to consciously monetize aspects of their own lives is a bit too stark. Government, in conducting CBA, *will* periodically have to ask selected individuals for their money valuations of welfare impacts in their own lives—at least if surveys are used as one source of information for CV amounts. But asking a sample of individuals to spend a relatively short period of time thinking about their CVs is much less costly than asking the entire population to do that, or asking the selected individuals to consciously contemplate the monetary value of their friends, kids, recreation, safety, and so on, on an ongoing basis. Being tapped for inclusion in a contingent valuation survey is a kind of civic duty, perhaps unpleasant and upsetting, but no more costly to the participants (it would seem) than being seated on a tort jury that must adjudicate damages for physical injury, pain and suffering, loss of consortium, or the death of a child.

Willingness-to-Pay versus Willingness-to-Accept

There is a large experimental literature that compares the amounts that individuals are willing to pay in exchange for some good with the amounts that they are willing to accept as compensation for the loss of the same good.[37] This literature finds that WTP and WTA amounts frequently diverge, often substantially. And the existence of these WTP/WTA disparities is routinely described as a problem for CBA.[38] Is it?

Let us start with theory.[39] To begin, we should clarify how WTP and WTA relate to the compensating variation and its mirror image, the so-called equivalent variation. Government is choosing between the status quo and a project. Ignore uncertainty and assume that these are definite outcomes. One individual P is better off with the project. Another individual Q is worse off with the project. These individuals' *compensating variations* are the changes to their wealth *in the project world* that counterbalance its welfare impact on them. In the case of P, that means a reduction in his wealth in the project outcome; in the case of Q, it's an addition to her wealth in the project outcome. By contrast, their *equivalent variations* are the changes to their wealth *in the status quo world* that make them indifferent between that outcome and the project. P's EV is an addition to his wealth in the status quo; Q's EV is a reduction.[40]

The link between CVs, EVs, and WTP/WTA amounts is straightforward. For P, the project winner, his CV is his WTP for the project, and his EV is his WTA for the status quo. Because P is better off in the project world than the status quo, counterbalancing changes in the project world consist in payments from P (WTP in return for the project), while counterbalancing changes in the status quo world consist in payments to P (WTA in return for the status quo). For Q, the project loser, her CV is her WTA for the project, and her EV is her WTP for the status quo.[41]

For most of this book, we have ignored the concept of EV, focusing on CVs instead. Which outcome is designated as the "status quo" and which as the "project" is really arbitrary—a point we'll return to below. An official who is choosing between O and O^* might call O the status quo and O^* the project, or vice versa. If he calls O "status quo," then counterbalancing wealth changes in O^* are CVs, and counterbalancing wealth changes in O are EVs; if he calls O^* "status quo," then counterbalancing wealth changes in O^* are EVs, and counterbalancing wealth changes in O are CVs. The basic methodology of CBA is to sum compensating changes in one outcome, taking the other as baseline. You only need one concept—the concept of a compensating wealth change—to get across that methodology, and that is why we have downplayed the CV/EV distinction to this point. Still, since the distinction is a standard one within the existing literature, and does figure centrally in the literature on WTP/WTA, it bears discussion here.

So much for terminology. The important substantive point is that an individual's WTP and WTA, CV and EV, can be different amounts. WTP and WTA can diverge even if preferences are "well-behaved": even if individuals have fixed preferences, these preferences are complete and transitive (so incomparability is not an issue), and indifference curves have the normal shape, facing out from the origin and curving smoothly. They may diverge because the prices for various goods in the project world are different from the prices in the status quo world. And WTA and WTP can diverge even where prices don't change.

For example, imagine that the project involves the increased provision of some public good, from G to G^*; which benefits P; prices for marketed goods remain the same; and P has wealth M in both the status quo and project worlds. P's WTP in this case is the amount of money, subtracted from M, that just suffices to make him indifferent to an increase in the public good from G to G^*. P's WTA is the amount of money, added to M, that just suffices to make him indifferent to a reduction in the public good from G^* to G. Clearly, if P's marginal utility of money is decreasing, and P's preferences for the public good are separable from his preferences for marketed goods (so that the utility impact of changes to P's wealth is the same regardless of the level of the public good), his WTA amount in this case will exceed his WTP amount. P's WTA is money added to his stock of wealth M, while WTP is money subtracted from P's stock of wealth M. Thus WTA to balance a fixed utility change will be greater than WTP.

This example, and the standard economic analysis of WTP/WTA, focuses on P's actual preferences. Nothing much changes if we switch to "restricted" (idealized, self-interested) preferences, and look at "laundered" WTP/WTA defined in terms of restricted preferences. Money can have variable marginal utility with respect to restricted preferences. So, both in cases where projects involve price changes, and even in cases where they don't, "laundered" WTP can diverge from "laundered" WTA.

The possible divergence of WTP and WTA amounts (ordinary or "laundered") creates a possible indeterminacy in CBA. Because individual WTP/WTA amounts can differ, it follows that CBA can reach different results, depending on whether the project and status quo are compared by summing CVs or summing EVs. If we take the first route, then our decision rule is: subtract aggregate WTA for the project losers (counterbalancing payments to the project losers in the project world) from aggregate WTP for the project winners (counterbalancing payments from the project winners in the project world) and implement the project if this net amount is positive. If we take the second route, then our decision rule is: subtract aggregate WTA for the project winners (counterbalancing payments to the project winners in the *status quo world*) from aggregate WTP for the project losers (counterbalancing payments from the project losers in the *status quo world*) and stick with the status quo if this net amount is positive. It is possible, at least, that the first analysis will tell us to choose the project while the second will tell us to choose the status quo, or vice versa.

To put the point another way, without the terminological decoration:

given the possibility of WTP/WTA disparities, a methodology (CBA) that compares a group of outcomes by first choosing one as the baseline for analysis, and then calculating and summing counterbalancing payments in the other outcomes relative to this baseline, may arrive at different rankings of the outcomes, depending on which one is taken as the baseline.

This interesting fact looks like a deep theoretical difficulty *if* CBA is being evaluated as a bedrock moral criterion and *if* it is insisted that any proper moral criterion must always produce a determinate ranking of outcomes and options. But the latter insistence is misconceived. For example, as discussed in the previous section, overall welfare (which clearly is a genuine moral criterion) can have pockets of incomparability (a kind of indeterminacy). Two outcomes might not be determinately ranked by overall welfare. In any event, CBA itself is a decision procedure, not a moral criterion. The fact that CBA *might* produce an indeterminate result is not a serious problem for CBA, as long as this occurs seldom. Imagine that, in 90 percent of cases where policy options are determinately ranked by overall welfare, CBA is determinate too, and accurate: it ranks the options the same way regardless of which option is taken as baseline, and this ranking is the same as the genuine ranking in light of overall welfare. In 5 percent of these cases, CBA is determinate but inaccurate; and in 5 percent of the cases, CBA fails to produce a ranking at all, requiring the decision-maker to shift to a different procedure to implement overall welfare. If this were the overall pattern, then CBA would generally be a determinate and accurate procedure, and only occasionally would go astray because of indeterminacy or inaccuracy.[42]

So the question becomes: how often, in practice, will WTP/WTA disparities lead to indeterminacies in CBA? Considerable theoretical work suggests that, if preferences are well-behaved, the difference between an individual's WTP and WTA amounts for a given project will usually be small.[43] Although the issue remains somewhat contested, it is quite plausible that "[i]f WTP is only a small fraction of income . . . then for a Hicksian consumer [one with well-behaved preferences], the divergence between WTA and WTP can be expected to be very small—at most, a few percent."[44]

Contingent valuation studies and other experimental work often show a much larger WTP/WTA disparity. WTA is often several multiples of WTP, rather than differing by a few percent—and even in cases where the goods involved represent only a small fraction of the subjects' total income. What is going on? One standard explanation is that subjects are behaving strategically or in a manner that seems to be strategic—voicing WTP amounts that are lower than genuine WTP, and WTA amounts that are larger than genuine WTA, as would be expected in a contracting scenario where the parties attempt to secure a larger share of the surplus by expressing valuations that differ from their true reservation prices.[45] Another explanation is that subjects are stating their moral preferences, or are protesting the monetization exercise. For example, infinite or very high WTA amounts might represent moral objection to a project; zero or very low WTP amounts might represent a moral objection to the additional taxes it would take to fund the project.[46]

Yet another standard explanation for WTP/WTA disparities points to "endowment effects" or "loss aversion." The basic idea here, most fully theorized by Amos Tversky and Daniel Kahneman and collaborators, is that individuals value bundles of goods by starting from arbitrary reference points and seeing the components of the bundle as losses or gains from the reference point.[47] This means that, *pace* traditional economic theory, there is no single set of indifference curves for a given space of possible bundles of goods. Rather, preferences and indifference curves are "reference dependent." Further, losses are valued more than corresponding gains. A given change in the amount of some good is more strongly dispreferred or preferred when seen as a shortfall below the reference level than when seen as an improvement on it. This would explain the large WTP/WTA disparities in experiments where individuals endowed with a low-value item (for example, a coffee mug) demand much more to relinquish it than individuals not thus endowed are willing to pay; the first group of individuals use the endowed state as their reference point and see trading away the item as a loss, while members of the second group see trading for the item as a gain.

Strategic behavior represents a problem of measurement that a well-designed technique for eliciting WTP/WTA amounts should attempt to overcome. Some techniques are "incentive compatible" (respondents, if rational, will state their true preferences), and although respondents may not always understand the incentive-compatibility features of the technique at hand, those can presumably be clarified through further information or practice.[48] WTP or WTA amounts that are substantially colored by moral views about the project, or moral views about CBA itself, represent "disinterested" preferences that are irrelevant to CBA as we conceive it. As we generally discussed in Chapter 5, valuation techniques should, if possible, be designed to screen out "disinterested" preferences.

Finally, the phenomenon variously known as "loss aversion," the "endowment effect," or reference-dependent preferences represents a kind of preference distortion. Fully informed and otherwise idealized subjects would not be "loss averse." They might be subject to diminishing marginal utility, valuing increments of money or goods less as the total amount of money or goods becomes larger; but diminishing marginal utility is not the same as "loss aversion," which (again) involves a totally arbitrary initial choice of reference point that then infects the evaluation of outcomes. As discussed above, also in Chapter 5, CBA analysts should generally try to employ techniques that screen out distorted preferences. And there is some evidence that loss aversion can be screened out—in other words, that individuals can be induced to construct and express WTP/WTA amounts that do not depend, or at least do not depend so heavily, on the choice of reference point. In at least some studies, debiasing measures lead to a reduction in the WTP/WTA disparity.[49]

To sum up: True "laundered" WTP and WTA amounts (WTP and WTA amounts defined in terms of an individual's self-interested and idealized preferences) should not deviate substantially in ordinary cases, where the project's impact is small relative to the individual's total income. Thus, CBA analysts should not simply take large WTP/WTA disparities as given but—ideally—should reduce the disparities by using valuation techniques that are transparently incentive-compatible and that screen out protest votes, loss aversion, and other distortions. Of course, such techniques may be expensive or, to a certain extent, simply unavailable. But, at a minimum, faced with (imperfect) studies producing disparate WTP and WTA amounts for some good, CBA analysts should use that valuation, be it WTP or WTA, that seems less infected by measurement errors and distortions.

In practice, agencies tend to use WTP rather than WTA. This approach is supportable *if* stated or observed WTP amounts are generally better evidence of self-interested, idealized preferences than WTA (for example, if moral preferences tend to be expressed through skewed WTAs rather than skewed WTPs). We will not try to determine here whether WTAs are, in fact, especially distorted.

What if the analyst ends up with no reason to favor WTP versus WTA for some good, and the disparity between WTP and WTA is large enough to result in an indeterminacy in CBA: a project looks good (bad) taking the status quo as baseline and summing CVs, while the status quo looks good (bad) taking the project as baseline and summing EVs? Some proponents of CBA seem to think that there is a "right answer" to the choice between WTP and WTA in this sort of case.[50] Even in a case where true WTP and WTA are known for certain, WTP or WTA is supposedly the natural measure. One thought is that the status quo is the "natural" baseline: this would mean that the analyst should prefer WTP as the valuation measure for project winners and WTA as the valuation measure for project losers. Another thought is that "the appropriate . . . measure can be found by examining the nature of the social transaction that is implied by the policy decision at hand and by the implicit rights to the services of the environment presumed to be held by the various parties to the transaction."[51] Consider an illustrative case where the project involves banning pollution from a factory, to the benefit of nearby residents. If the residents have a right to stop the pollution, then the appropriate valuation of their benefit is WTA. If the factory has a right to pollute, then the appropriate measure of the residents' benefit from the project is WTP—or so it has been suggested.

Both of these suggestions strike us as misconceived. As a matter of overall welfare—the criterion that CBA implements—there is no special priority given to the status quo. We have already suggested that the designation of one outcome as "status quo" and the others as "projects" is actually pretty arbitrary. If there *is* a nonarbitrary way to make the choice, it would, we suppose, be this: the status quo choice is the choice of governmental inaction; "projects" are choices that necessitate some kind of activity on government's part. But the action/inaction distinction has no intrinsic significance whatsoever for purposes of overall welfare. Actions sometimes increase overall welfare, relative to inaction, and sometimes decrease it. Which is true depends on the choice situation at hand, and on the facts; there is no presumption either way. The action/inaction distinction *does* have large significance within certain deontological views (which tend to construe deontological constraints as bars on action rather than inaction),[52] but this point is irrelevant for the overall-welfare criterion and the decision procedures that apply it.

As for using notions of "rights" to choose between WTP and WTA: CBA is not a decision procedure for effectuating rights. Legal rights may limit officials, legally, in following CBA's recommendations; moral rights may do the same, morally; but the question whether the project's welfare benefits outweigh its welfare costs has nothing to do with whether the project winners have a legal or moral right to those benefits.

So the governmental official who (1) confronts a disparity between WTA and WTP for some good that is sufficiently large to affect his evaluation of the policy choice at hand, and (2) has no grounds for preferring one or another valuation as less infected by measurement difficulties, preference distortions, or moral views faces a genuine indeterminacy. In this sort of case, the official must use some procedure other than CBA to decide which policy maximizes welfare—presumably a procedure of intuitive balancing. The possible indeterminacy of CBA in ranking projects is not a deep flaw in the method but does require a supplemental procedure where the indeterminacy actually occurs—something that should occur less and less frequently as preference-estimation techniques improve.

Discounting

At what rate should CBA discount future costs and benefits? This question has great practical significance, and is hotly contested.[53] For instance, the policies that environmental regulators enact or consider frequently produce health and safety benefits in the near or medium term, rather than immediately. An important example is the regulation of carcinogens. Cyanide is toxic right away, but present exposure to a carcinogen may cause death in ten, twenty, or thirty years; and in any event, antipollution policies typically limit future, not just current, pollution. So, typically, much of the health benefit of a carcinogen reduction policy would be realized a decade or decades after adoption of the policy. And sometimes, as in the case of global warming, the policy has its largest impact on "future generations," in the distant future. Given compounding, numerically small differences in the choice of interest rate (say, the use of a 3 percent rather than a 0 percent or 7 percent rate) can produce radically different estimates of project costs and benefits, and radically different evaluation of policy choices (see Table 6.1).

Our aim in this brief section is not to take a position on the appropriate discount rate for CBA, but rather to clarify what the issues are, and in the process to show that the controversy about discounting does not undermine CBA itself. What fuels the controversy is, to begin, the practical impact of

Table 6.1. Discounted Value of a Single Fatality (Undiscounted Value $5 Million)

	Years in the Future When Fatality Occurs		
Discount rate	10	50	100
0%	$5,000,000	$5,000,000	$5,000,000
3%	$3,720,000	$1,140,000	$260,164
7%	$2,540,000	$169,739	$5,762
10%	$1,930,000	$42,593	$363

the choice of discount rate but also contestable questions about the interaction of welfare and time, the meaning of "overall welfare" in the case of policies that affect the size of the population, and distributive justice as between present and future generations, as well as more technical but still difficult questions about how to use the discount rate to fine-tune the accuracy of CBA in tracking overall well-being. That these questions exist, with no definitive resolution in sight, in no way undercuts our basic argument for weak welfarism or for CBA as a welfarist decision procedure.

One aspect of the discounting puzzle is the rationality of *time preference*. Many individuals seem to prefer present enjoyment to future enjoyment, or present consumption to future consumption, simply because of the temporal position of the present benefit—simply because it is "now" or "sooner."[54] Someone with this sort of intrinsic time preference would have a lower present WTP/WTA for a welfare impact that occurs at a later time, as compared to his present WTP/WTA for the very same impact occurring earlier. He cares about the *dates* of his enjoyments or consumption events, just as he may prefer consuming certain kinds of goods, or experiencing certain kinds of hedonic states; and because he less intensely prefers a later benefit, the present money sum required to compensate him for its loss would be smaller.

Some argue that CBA should incorporate a discount rate to reflect the diminished WTP/WTA amounts for future benefits or costs accruing to individuals with an intrinsic time preference. For example, Richard Revesz writes:

> The reason for discounting in the case of latent harms is not that a regulator or some other outsider determines that life in the future is less valuable than life in the present. Instead, discounting simply reflects the fact that the individual who is valuing her own life derives less utility from living a year in the future than in the present. Discounting is therefore necessary to provide an accurate value of the utility that the individual loses in the present as a result of a premature death in the future.[55]

Revesz's argument is unimpeachable on the traditional view of CBA, which equates welfare with the satisfaction of actual preferences and defines WTP/WTA in terms of actual preferences. It is less compelling if preferences are idealized. Philosophers who have written about discounting have tended to view intrinsic time preference as a kind of preference distortion.[56] In effect, their claim is that individuals with full information and full appreciation of the possible effects on their well-being (both current effects and future effects) would not care, per se, about the temporal position of those effects. If these philosophers are correct, then (presumably) "laundered" WTP/WTA amounts would not be sensitive to time per se, and CBA should not incorporate a discount factor to reflect intrinsic time preference—although it still might for other reasons.

So one aspect of the discounting puzzle is whether fully informed and otherwise idealized individuals would retain a time preference regarding their own welfare. This is, at least in substantial part, an empirical question—a question about human psychology. Individuals in full possession of the facts, and in good deliberative conditions, might end up adopting a truly atemporal perspective on welfare impacts; or a preference for present over future pleasures, and future over present pains, might be too entrenched in our nature to wash away. In any event, CBA structured as the sum of "laundered" WTP/WTA amounts can be sensitive to whatever time preference (the analyst believes) suitably idealized individuals would possess.[57]

Even without time preference in the picture, there are a number of plausible reasons for CBA to incorporate some kind of discount factor. One very important reason has to do with investment opportunities. Imagine that an official is choosing between option 1, inaction, and option 2, a project that will impose some costs now, with future benefits at T^*. Assume that intertemporal markets are currently in place, offering a safe interest rate r. A third option (it would seem) is to tax the project losers, invest the proceeds at r until T^*, and distribute the proceeds from the investment to those who would have gained from the project or to the general population. If the project's benefits, discounted at r, are less than current costs, then this third option (if truly available) would be better than option 2. In effect, discounting automatically expands the choice set under consideration, building in a "tax and save" option.

This *opportunity cost* argument for discounting is, we believe, the strongest kind of argument currently in play.[58] Opportunity-cost arguments for discounting are often advanced by economists and have been particularly important in structuring actual agency practice. Note that the argument makes no use of the notion of time preference. Rather, the idea is that decision-makers have options other than the status quo and the current implementation of a regulatory project that produces future benefits: in particular, investing the resources that the project would consume at a positive interest rate, or inducing the individuals affected to invest those resources personally. Discounting alerts the decision-maker to these additional possibilities; if discounted future benefits are less than present costs, then there is some third option available to government that is better for overall welfare than the project.[59]

Note, too, that the "opportunity cost" argument does not invoke notions of intergenerational equity. Rather, discounting functions to increase CBA's accuracy in identifying welfare-improving projects, given the existence of investment opportunities. A different argument in this vein points to *wealth effects*. Future generations will likely be richer. If so, their marginal utility of money will be lower. Discounting can function as a kind of "distributive weight," adjusting WTP/WTA amounts to correct for the intergenerational wealth skew. Finally, discounting is sometimes seen as a way to reflect *uncertainty* about the occurrence of future costs and benefits—although it is unclear why a straightforward uncertainty analysis is not a better way to handle this.

In short, a second set of discounting questions asks: What approach to discounting optimizes CBA's functioning as a welfarist decision procedure? A third set of discounting puzzles involves variable populations. These puzzles arise with future generations.[60] The present generation already exists. No policy option now available will result in the existence or nonexistence of members of the present generation (although policy choices now might, of course, shorten or lengthen their lives). But plenty of policies (indeed, most policies) available and under consideration now will change the membership of future generations. If a particular act of conception would occur in the status quo outcome (resulting in Q's existence), and that act would not occur in the project outcome, then the project itself determines whether Q exists. What overall welfare means in this sort of case is a difficult problem within utilitarian and welfarist theory. Can an individual who has a life in one world, and doesn't exist at all in the second, be worse (or better) off in the second? Answering yes is counterintuitive (since claims about the comparative goodness or badness of outcomes for some subject would seem to presuppose the subject's existence in the various outcomes under comparison). But answering no would have the deeply counterintuitive implication that welfare effects of massive projects that completely change the membership of future generations (for example, massive environmental change) are borne only by the present generation.

The problem, here, is the foundational problem of determining how overall welfare is affected (if at all) by adding or subtracting a member of the population. It is hard to see how discounting future benefits at an exponential rate is the first-best solution to this problem. (After all, a policy can—at least in principle—affect future generations without changing the membership of future generations.) But discounting may be a rough, approximate solution. More generally, the ongoing controversy about the treatment of future generations and, therewith, the choice of discount rate is partly fueled by continuing puzzlement about the meaning of overall welfare in variable-population cases.

Finally, discussion of CBA's discount rate is often linked to questions of distributive justice in relation to future generations. Not discounting seems to be unfair to the present generation. "[R]ejection of discounting would appear to require truly extraordinary sacrifices from the present for the sake of the (infinite) future, as each generation will have to impoverish itself to invest the maximum possible for the benefit of numerous future generations."[61] Discounting seems to be unfair to future generations. As Cass Sunstein and Arden Rowell observe:

> [C]ritics are correct to say that discounting might contribute to serious problems of intergenerational equity. The reason is that with discounting, a cost-benefit analysis can lead the current generation to impose extremely high costs on future generations, and such costs might be imposed without providing compensating benefits to the losers—leading to . . . a serious distributional problem.[62]

The fact that *any* discount rate might produce intertemporal distributive unfairness, shifting too many or too few costs or benefits into the future, is simply a stark illustration of the point that overall welfare and distributive norms are distinct: they can conflict. That fact doesn't undercut weak welfarism (any more than the converse fact that fair intertemporal distribution might reduce overall welfare undercuts the moral force of distributive requirements) or CBA. Moreover, we believe that intertemporal distributive worries shouldn't influence the choice of CBA's discount rate. As we have already emphasized, CBA is not a superprocedure; it is not keyed to distributive norms, or the whole of morality. Cost-benefit analysis should incorporate a discount rate that maximizes its accuracy in tracking overall welfare; if it then ends up recommending policies that threaten to impoverish the present for the future, or vice versa, a *separate* distributive analysis should be undertaken (perhaps by agencies, perhaps by other institutions) to determine whether the policies are on balance morally advisable.

The Value of Life

It is now common practice for regulatory agencies conducting CBA to include lives lost or saved as a cost or benefit, often using a monetary value in the vicinity of $5 million per life.[63] Indeed, "the value of life is easily the single most important number in the economics of health and environmental protection, frequently accounting for the great majority of the benefits in cost-benefit studies."[64] The practice of pricing life is also a flashpoint in the controversy about CBA.[65] Various of the generic objections to CBA are pointedly brought to bear here: its insensitivity to rights, its failure to recognize "incommensurabilities," the WTP/WTA disparity, the difficulty of measuring valuations. We have already addressed all of these objections in a general way, but because the valuation of life has become the "poster child" for CBA's alleged flaws, we briefly address them again in this context.

The valuation of life by CBA does not mean that moral rights to life are dissolved or priced away. Actions that result in premature death reduce overall welfare, *ceteris paribus;* regulatory interventions that prevent those actions increase overall welfare, *ceteris paribus.* By pricing life, CBA attempts to capture these welfare effects. Cost-benefit analysis cannot reflect, and should not be seen as reflecting, deontological constraints against killing/moral rights to life. Some actions that cause premature death will not implicate these constraints. For example, many deontological theorists would deny that causing death by selling an accurately labeled but dangerous product to a competent adult, or by driving nonrecklessly, is a rights violation. Other actions that cause premature death will implicate deontological constraints (if they exist), and if so should be handled by institutions other than CBA—such as the criminal law and its prohibitions on homicide.

Pricing life does not "cheapen life." There are numerous contexts, other than CBA, in which premature death or the risk of premature death is priced: tort judgments for wrongful death, survivors' compensation funds, life insurance, hazard pay for riskier jobs, market prices for safer products. So it would be surprising if (and we are aware of no evidence that) CBA valuation of life generally produces substantial psychological distress, although it might in certain salient cases. Nor does the pricing of life "cheapen life" in a more abstract way. It is implausible that the value of our own longevity is constituted by not thinking about trade-offs between longevity and other goods; any self-conscious life, and any thoughtful procedure for making collective choices that impact longevity, will necessitate consideration of those trade-offs.

Using a number that is too low does constitute a kind of "cheapening." For example, the $200,000 figure used by Ford in the infamous Pinto case "cheapened" life in the sense that it dramatically undervalued the welfare benefit of preventing deaths in auto accidents.[66] The current $5 million number is twenty-five times larger. But the issue here is accuracy, not "incommensurability" in some scarier sense.

John Broome raises a different sort of "incommensurability" objection to CBA's valuation of life, one grounded in the lexical priority of life in relation to money.

> Consider any project in which an unknown person will die. Because whoever it is does not know it will be him, because of his ignorance, he is prepared to accept a ridiculously low compensation for letting the project go forward. The government does not know who will be killed either, but it knows it will be someone, and it knows that, whoever it is, no finite amount of compensation would be adequate for him. The cost of the project must therefore be infinite, and it is only the ignorance of the person destined to die that prevents his demanding an infinite compensation . . . Any other conclusion is a deliberate and unfair use of people's ignorance.[67]

The argument, boiled down, is that (1) the standard practice of determining a valuation of life by aggregating WTP/WTA for small risks of death, the so-called VSL method, is a "deliberate and unfair use of people's ignorance"; and (2) determining a valuation of life by asking about WTA for certain death fails because it produces infinite valuations.

Broome's objection may perhaps show that Kaldor-Hicks efficiency breaks down in the case of projects that cause premature death—the ex post compensation required by the person who ends up dying would indeed be infinite, absent a bequest function—but it doesn't undercut the VSL method within the context of a procedure, CBA, that implements overall welfare. As already explained: the overall-welfare loss in premature death is not infinite, but the *finite* difference in utility between a longer and shorter life history. Let us place to one side the issue of uncertainty about the characteristics of the individuals who die prematurely, and assume that the government is comparing the status quo in which an individual P has life history L_1 (with a determinate consumption history, experiential history, and so on), which is cut short by accident or illness; and the project outcome in which the individual has life history L_2, which is longer than L_1. Then, assuming overall welfare is measurable on a utility scale, the utility cost of premature death here is $U(L_2) - U(L_1) = \Delta U$. That amount is *not* accurately reflected in WTP/WTA for certain death. Absent a bequest function, the dying individual asked about WTP/WTA at the moment before death would pay his entire wealth (above a subsistence level) to avoid death, and would have an infinite WTA—regardless of the size of ΔU.[68] The problem is a wacky cousin of "wealth effects": just as greater wealth typically reduces the marginal utility of money, so death typically reduces it further, to zero.

The VSL method avoids the problem, by translating ΔU into dollars at an ordinary, "premortem" rate rather than the postmortem rate. Imagine P is told that he has a small, 1-in-r risk (say, 1 in 1 million) of life history L_1, and otherwise will receive L_2. He is asked for WTP to avoid that small risk of L_1 and receive L_2 for sure. Assume that P's marginal utility of money, in L_2, is $1/k$. In other words, small changes to P's utility in L_2 are converted to dollars at rate k. P's willingness to pay for a commodity that produces a small increase in his well-being, by ΔU^*, is $k \times \Delta U^*$. What is P's WTP to avoid the 1-in-r risk of the life-history, L_1, in which he dies prematurely? If WTP is calculated here using the axioms of expected utility theory—as it should be, since departures from expected utility theory are one kind of preference distortion that CBA should seek to screen out—then P's WTP to avoid the 1-in-r risk is $k \times \Delta U/r$. Multiplying by r, we arrive at the result that the risk-based dollar valuation of premature death in this case is $k \times \Delta U$: the utility difference between the shorter life L_1 and the longer life L_2 converted into dollars at rate k. K is precisely the rate that would determine P's WTP/WTA for marginal nonlongevity changes to his welfare in L_2 (such as small changes in consumption, in pleasurable or painful experiences, or the provision of some public good), and—assuming that P is not especially wealthy or poor—should not be too distant from the rates at which nonlongevity welfare impacts experienced by other individuals are converted into their WTP/WTA amounts.[69]

So the VSL method is not just an arbitrary device to avoid infinite dollar valuations. Because it translates the utility loss that occurs with an individual's premature death into dollars by using a utility-to-dollar conversion factor proximate to the conversion factor implicit in WTP/WTA for welfare impacts other than premature death, this technique allows CBA to determine with reasonable accuracy whether lifesaving projects really do increase overall welfare, given their additional welfare effects (for example, compliance costs).

Turning to the problem of WTP/WTA disparities: those are, of course, a problem for the valuation of certain death. The WTP amount will necessarily be finite, while the WTA amount may not be. WTP/WTA disparities are, in practice, a difficulty for the VSL method too. "[E]xtreme divergences between WTP and WTA have been found in surveys of attitudes to risk."[70] But (as is generally the case with WTP/WTA disparities) this is a problem of inducing and measuring undistorted valuations. If r is large, and P maximizes expected utility rather than (for example) displaying "loss aversion," the difference between P's WTP to avoid a 1-in-r risk of death and his WTA in return for a 1-in-r risk of death should be small.

To be sure, inducing and measuring undistorted WTP/WTA amounts for small risks of death is a challenging task. There are substantial problems of debiasing and estimation, here, that should not be ignored. Current VSL figures are largely based on wage-risk studies, which look at wage premiums in riskier occupations. These studies have various imperfections: labor market choices may be partly disinterested (for example, workers may take riskier jobs because they feel obliged to support their families); workers may misperceive the risks involved; they may not translate those risks into dollars in accordance with expected utility theory; and WTP/WTA amounts for workers who self-select into risky jobs will be lower than the population average. Contingent-valuation studies may offer a route around these difficulties, but probably need to be supplemented with information about probability theory, or focused on individuals who already grasp it. WTP/WTA amounts, if undistorted, should be sensitive to the magnitude of risk reduction; but valuations voiced in contingent-valuation studies tend to manifest insufficient sensitivity to magnitude.[71]

A different problem with VSL, as currently practiced, involves disaggregation.[72] Agencies almost always employ a single VSL figure, regardless of the number of life-years saved or lost or other individual characteristics. Perfect welfarist measurement would be more disaggregated. It seems very implausible that all life-histories cut short by illness or accident or the other sources of premature death targeted by regulators have the same total utility, and that all comparison life-histories in which individuals die of "natural causes" are similarly identical.

But estimating heterogeneous VSL amounts of the sort that would be useful in welfarist CBA is challenging. Imagine that in one policy situation the utility value of life saving is $\Delta_1 U$; in another situation, it's $\Delta_2 U$; and so on. Then (ideally) our dollar valuations of lifesaving in these cases would be exactly proportionate to the utility changes. The VSL figures need not be exactly proportionate to the utility changes, given variation in the marginal utility of money. One such source of variation—one we have emphasized in this book—is wealth. Richer individuals tend to have higher VSLs; but that may just reflect their lower marginal utility of money, and not the fact that they stand to lose more utility when they die. Older individuals, too, tend to have higher VSLs—and this is also a product, to some extent, of skewed marginal utilities. An older individual asked for WTP to avoid an incremental risk of death tends to be at greater background risk of death, hence at greater risk that current assets will be bequeathed rather than spent on her own welfare, and thus has lower opportunity costs in expending resources to reduce incremental risks.[73]

Much of the economic literature on VSL takes a Kaldor-Hicks perspective, and thus is perfectly comfortable using VSL figures that are inflated by wealth or age. Our recommendation is different. First, CBA should begin to use heterogeneous VSLs; not every premature death has the same impact on overall welfare. Second, if possible, heterogeneity in VSL should mirror those factors (life-years lost or saved) that change the utility loss in premature death, and not the factors (seemingly, age and wealth) that may change WTP/WTA but do not change the utility loss. In effect, this would be a kind of distributive weighting to correct deviations between WTP/WTA and utility. The feasibility of that middle ground, between homogenous VSLs and full heterogeneity, is not something we can pursue here.

Our Response to the Objections: Some Recurring Themes

This chapter has considered a number of standard criticisms to CBA: its insensitivity to rights, distribution, and nonwelfare values; various objections that go under the heading of "incommensurability" (lexical priority, incomparability, measurement difficulties, the cheapening effect of CBA itself); the disparity between WTP and WTA; the fact that CBA discounts future costs and benefits; and its ascription of a money value to life.

Our responses to these criticisms have been diverse, and are hard to summarize neatly. Still, certain themes emerge. To begin, CBA is not a superprocedure. It should be seen as a decision procedure implementing overall well-being, not the totality of moral considerations. This handles the general objection from rights, distribution, and nonwelfare values; the claim that CBA ignores moral rights to life; and, less obviously, part of the concern about discounting. The discount rate incorporated in CBA should be chosen to maximize its accuracy in tracking overall welfare, and any resultant unfairness as between current and future generations should be considered in a separate, distributive analysis.

Further, CVs should be laundered to some extent, as described in detail in Chapter 5, to wash out disinterested and nonideal preferences. Moral preferences account for some of the lexical priorities that emerge when individuals are asked for their valuations, for example, when they voice infinite WTAs for environmental goods. Loss aversion is a distortion of self-interested preferences that accounts for much of the WTP/WTA disparity, and well-designed valuation studies should try to eliminate it. Laundering preferences may also partly eliminate individual time preference, one of the bases for discounting (although, we stress, not the only one; opportunity costs is a distinct basis).

In addition, the fact that overall welfare fails to produce a complete ordering of outcomes (some outcomes are incomparable with each other), and CBA also may fail to produce a complete ordering (for example, because of WTP/WTA disparities that persist after "laundering"), is not a deep objection to weak welfarism or CBA. Moral criteria have pockets of incomparability. And the possibility that CBA itself may fail to rank the policy choices presented to the decision-maker—an eventuality that would require her to employ a different procedure, such as intuitive balancing—in no way shows that she should eschew CBA in other situations, where it does give determinate guidance.

It should also be recognized that CBA is a flexible and practicable set of techniques for attaching money values to welfare impacts (as was emphasized in Chapter 3) and not a single, rigid, formula. Although a monetizing procedure that relied solely on market prices to arrive at its valuations would understate the welfare importance of nonmarket goods (thus one of the "incommensurability" objections), CBA is not this procedure. Contingent valuation surveys and nonprice behavioral evidence of valuations are now widely used by cost-benefit analysts. In discussing the pricing of life, we pointed to a different way in which CBA has been responsive to valuation difficulties. Although life itself is lexically ordered in relation to money (in the sense that self-interested WTA for instant death would be infinite, absent a bequest function), the utility impact of death can be reasonably measured by eliciting and aggregating WTP/WTA for small risks of death, which is not infinite.

Finally, we are unpersuaded by the claim that the very act of using CBA to measure the welfare impact of certain goods cheapens those goods. This claim might be an empirical claim that CBA produces psychological distress.

But we are aware of no evidence that it generally does. Or it could be a more evaluative claim that the very nature of certain goods precludes government from thinking about them in money terms. In effect, fully informed individuals would disprefer monetization. But that version of the claim fails to grapple with the fact that CBA itself is a morally justified procedure; that asking government to price goods is not the same as asking individuals to do so on an ongoing basis; and that the most attractive competitor procedures to CBA would also require explicit governmental judgments about the welfare significance of policy effects.

Conclusion

We have argued that the conventional economic defense of cost-benefit analysis is not satisfactory (Chapter 1). The largely technical literature has failed to ground CBA in the Pareto standard—which is normatively attractive but very limited in scope, since it provides no guidance for governmental choices that have both winners and losers—or even in the Kaldor-Hicks standard, which in any event is extremely dubious as a moral principle. Nonetheless, CBA, or at least a suitably modified version of it, can be rescued from welfare economics.

In Chapters 2–4 we argued that CBA can be defended as a decision procedure that generates outcomes that are desirable against the standards of a plausible moral theory, while also enhancing transparency so that elected officials and the public can monitor agency action. The plausible moral theory we have in mind ("weak welfarism") holds that government is morally obliged to advance the overall welfare of its citizens. This may not be government's sole moral obligation, since, for example, rights and distributive considerations may also be part of the moral picture. But it is plausible to think that overall welfare is one of the fundamental moral criteria that ought to structure governmental choice and, concomitantly, that interpersonal welfare comparisons are possible. "Overall welfare" is a meaningful notion, even in choice situations where the Pareto standard is inapplicable. By welfare, we mean the satisfaction of preferences, with the caveats that the preferences must be self-interested and survive idealization. This view of welfare builds on the insights of both economic and philosophical scholarship, and has important implications for the actual practice of CBA (Chapter 5).

Agencies are institutions that play a role within government: their role is not necessarily the same as government's; indeed, the institutional division of labor suggests otherwise. Each agency's mission is not to advance overall

185

welfare; it is to play its proper role in a government that advances overall welfare. Agencies are created and limited by statutes that define their legal purposes and limit their powers and procedures. Agencies should advance overall welfare only to the extent that doing so involves a particular agency's mission and expertise. The EPA should advance overall welfare by regulating industries that pollute the environment, the USDA by regulating farmers, and the Federal Emergency Management Agency by administering responses to disasters. Further, agencies should expend resources to perform cost-benefit analyses, and should rely on a cost-benefit standard for evaluating projects, only to the extent that doing so is legally permissible. In point of fact, many statutes do permit administrative CBA—either explicitly, by setting forth a cost-benefit standard, or implicitly, by using words such as "reasonable" or "appropriate," which instruct the agency to be sensitive to the diverse welfare impacts of its choices rather than focusing narrowly on one particular aspect of welfare. And our argument suggests that statutes that currently prohibit CBA should be amended to allow it.

Cost-benefit analysis can be expensive. We therefore have recommended (Chapter 3) that agencies employ relatively full-blown CBA only where the project satisfies some threshold test of size (for example, appearing likely to have annual costs exceeding $100 million). This has been the approach of the presidential cost-benefit orders since their inception in 1981. Smaller projects demand less expensive decision procedures: either abbreviated forms of CBA, or yet cheaper procedures. It is beyond the scope of this book to attempt to specify these procedures.

Cost-benefit analysis is not a superprocedure (Chapter 6). It tracks overall well-being, not rights, distributive considerations, or putative moral factors that entirely transcend human well-being (for example, putative intrinsic environmental factors). Some of these considerations may prove to be illusory. Others may be best addressed by nonadministrative bodies, for example, courts that protect moral rights using the apparatus of constitutional law, or the tax system in the case of distributive goals. We find it reasonably plausible that, just as there is an institutional division of labor within the administrative state—different agencies address types of market failures, or regulate different types of activities, or draw on different types of expertise—so there is an institutional division of labor between the administrative state and the rest of government. Administrative bodies, collectively, focus on overall welfare (with the exception of agencies that are part of the tax-and-transfer system, such as the Internal Revenue Service or welfare agencies); legislatures and courts balance overall welfare with other moral considerations, either ex ante by structuring agency choice or ex post by overturning particular agency decisions.

But the latter division-of-labor thesis is controversial, raising contentious issues about the content of moral rights, the role of constitutional courts, and the optimality of income transfer as the mechanism for redistribution. These issues are beyond the scope of this book. We do not, in fact, defend the division-of-labor thesis in this book, or indeed argue for any specific view about how moral considerations other than overall well-being should be allocated between agencies and other governmental bodies. What we *have* argued is this: to the extent that agencies should attend to rights, distributive considerations, and so on, CBA is not the vehicle for doing so. Cost-benefit analysis tracks overall well-being, nothing more. Rights are not the same thing as preferences about rights; fair distribution is not the same thing as preferences about distribution. "Incorporating" rights and distribution into CBA by monetizing corresponding preferences would be doubly mistaken: first, because these preferences are disinterested; and second, because claims about rights and what a fair distribution would be need to be resolved through argument, not by aggregating CVs. Compensating variations are proxies for interpersonal utility numbers; but the whole point of any moral view that invokes rights or distribution is to introduce moral considerations that are distinct from overall utility.

How, then, should CBA, as we see it—as a decision procedure implementing overall welfare—be structured?

Textbook CBA is not the appropriate algorithm, nor are the implicit algorithms of actual agency practice, which deviate from textbook CBA in various ways. But textbook CBA provides the right starting point. Cost-benefit analysis needs to be further refined, so that it more clearly advances overall welfare rather than simple preference satisfaction.

We have argued that under certain circumstances, CBA should be based on laundered rather than actual preferences (Chapter 5). For example, it is already uncontroversial, at least in agency practice, that sadistic and other morally objectionable preferences should receive no weight. Uninformed preferences can be dealt with in various ways, and here complexities emerge. When the preferences are instrumental—for example, people want to be healthier but believe that fluoride in water makes them ill—then agencies may be able to finesse the information problem by using people's valuations for health rather than their valuations for fluoride-in-water, the actual project. Further regulation may be needed to deter offsetting behavior or to educate people (people switch to expensive bottled water unless they are educated), but this will not always be necessary because people do not always learn about the regulation. When the preferences are intrinsic—for example, people fail to appreciate parks because of lack of information about nature—it may be inappropriate for the agency to launder the preference.

More controversially, we have argued that agencies should stop using existence values and should otherwise refuse, as much as possible, to use valuations based on disinterested preferences. Just as agencies do not ask people to price their moral discomfort from stem cell research, they should not ask people to price their moral discomfort from environmental degradation that they never experience.

Absent concerns about transparency and decision costs, we might suggest that agencies engage in further laundering, for example, discounting preferences that are an adaptation to unjust circumstances. But it is hard to imagine reasonably clear guidelines for distinguishing between adaptive and nonadaptive preferences, and in many of the most troubling cases, adaptive preferences are also uninformed, or clearly objectively bad, and so will be filtered out using the screens we have recommended.

Distributive weighting raises difficult issues. To be clear: the issue here is not how to make CBA an instrument of redistributive policy. We have argued, emphatically, that CBA is not a procedure for determining what a fair or unfair distribution of welfare would be. Rather, the problem to be addressed is the diminishing marginal utility of money, and the effect that has in diminishing the accuracy of CBA as a proxy for overall welfare. Individuals with greater income and greater wealth will tend to have larger CVs—not because projects tend to have larger welfare or utility impacts on them, but because that impact is being measured using a scale (CVs) that is inflated by their large money endowments.

Cost-benefit analysis should be a good proxy for overall welfare where the distribution of wealth or income among project winners is not dramatically different from its distribution among project losers. But what to do when these wealth distributions, and therewith the distribution of marginal utilities among project winners as compared to project losers, are very different? One possibility is for the agency to use CBA adjusted using distributive weights. A second is for the agency to shift from CBA to a nonmonetized procedure for estimating overall welfare—the procedure we have termed intuitive balancing (Chapter 3). One problem with the first option is that economists have as yet failed to develop readily implementable schemes for distributive weighting. A different problem, here for both options, is that agencies that deviate from ordinary, unweighted CBA may run afoul of market adjustment and create perverse incentives (Chapter 5). A third option is for the agency to use ordinary CBA but report to Congress and the president that project winners and losers have substantially different wealth distributions, calling into question the accuracy of CBA in tracking overall well-being. A fourth is to refrain from implementing projects in this sort of case. We are inclined to think that the fourth approach is the best, but our recommendation here is tentative. How to adjust CBA for the variable marginal utility of wealth merits intensive study. Economists and policy analysis will, we hope, continue to tackle this problem unfettered by the traditional linkage of CBA to Kaldor-Hicks efficiency and traditional worries about the interpersonal comparability of well-being.

Agencies have not always shown much enthusiasm for CBA. The major form of enforcement currently in place is political: the president directs agencies to use CBA, and if they fail to do so, or do so improperly, the president has various instruments for disciplining agencies—firing officials, reducing the budget, and so forth. This approach has been, at best, only partially successful. Agencies conduct and report cost-benefit analyses more often than in the past, and the quality of CBA has improved, but the overall quality of regulation does not seem to have improved. There are many possible reasons: lack of attention by the president and his staff; the limited value of the political sanctions at his disposal; congressional interference; bureaucratic resistance; and so forth. All of this suggests that judicial enforcement of CBA should be expanded, albeit perhaps on an experimental basis. A statute that banned agencies from issuing regulations that fail a cost-benefit test would allow courts to police agencies. As long as courts can adequately review cost-benefit analyses, this is an attractive route to take. However, we do not know whether courts have this capacity.

Another approach that we recommend is to try to improve the culture of agencies, to make their staffs more friendly to economic analysis and CBA. Requiring agencies to hire more economists and statisticians and to give them administrative authority may help improve agency culture in this way. Training of existing staff would also be desirable. The OMB could further assist this process by providing financial and technical support to agencies. To a large extent, this has already been done; but more along these lines is called for.

Two final recommendations to increase the quality and impact of agency cost-benefit analyses are that they be subjected to some form of external peer review, and that agencies use standard valuations. To be sure, peer review must be structured with a keen sensitivity to possible delay costs. And standardization must be sensitive to the point that some degree of heterogeneity is optimal. For example, it would be silly for agencies to value every project that improves environmental quality (whether by improving visibility, or reducing noise or smells, or enhancing stocks of fish and wildlife) by using a single CV for environmental quality. One of the advantages of CBA, as compared to intuitive balancing, is that CBA is better at reflecting the heterogeneity of projects' utility impacts, an upshot of the heterogeneity of individual preferences (Chapter 3). On the other hand, the OMB can give agencies clearer guidance about the degree to which CVs should be standardized (given the huge decision costs that a cost-benefit procedure fully sensitive to the heterogeneity of preferences would have) and, if so, what the standardized values should be.

We have no illusions that our book will quiet or even much diminish the controversy about CBA. Our basic moral framework, weak welfarism, should be reasonably uncontroversial. But some economists and some philosophers will take issue with it: the former because of continuing worries about interpersonal welfare comparisons, the latter because of philosophical views that give overall welfare zero weight (Chapter 2). Others will accept the moral importance of overall welfare, but insist that some other decision procedure—feasibility analysis? intuitive balancing? a "narrow" procedure such as safety maximization?—is the best way to maximize welfare. The welfare-maximizing decision procedure must be reasonably accurate, must not have excessive decision costs, and must be structured for a political context where agencies and their overseers are often opportunistic. It is at bottom an empirical question whether CBA fulfills these desiderata; some will quarrel with our analysis, and more evidence gathering and theorizing about the optimal procedure is vitally important.

Yet others will continue to argue that CBA runs afoul of the problem of "incommensurability": environmental, health, safety, and other nonconsumption components of well-being shouldn't be, or can't be, measured on a money scale along with marketed commodities. This objection, we believe, is quite mistaken (Chapter 6), and our arguments against the variety of challenges to CBA that cluster under the heading "incommensurability" are not particularly empirical or tentative. But here, too, debate ought to continue, and, in any event, debate undoubtedly will.

Notes

Introduction

1. United States v. Carroll Towing Co., 159 F.2d 169 (2d Cir. 1947).
2. AEI-Brookings Joint Center, www.aei.brookings.org.
3. For example, Frank Ackerman and Lisa Heinzerling, *Priceless: On Knowing the Price of Everything and the Value of Nothing* (New York: New Press, 2004). The outlines of the critique of CBA were first laid down by Steven Kelman, "Cost-Benefit Analysis: An Ethical Critique," *AEI Journal on Government and Society Regulation* 5 (1981): 33–40.
4. Examples of such defenders include Stephen Breyer, *Regulation and Its Reform* (Cambridge, Mass.: Harvard University Press, 1982); and Cass Sunstein, *Risk and Reason: Safety, Law, and the Environment* (Cambridge: Cambridge University Press, 2004).
5. Some exceptions are David Copp, "The Justice and Rationale of Cost-Benefit Analysis," *Theory and Decision* 23 (1987): 65–87; Donald C. Hubin, "The Moral Justification of Benefit/Cost Analysis," *Economics and Philosophy* 10 (1994): 169–194; and Peter Railton, "Benefit-Cost Analysis as a Source of Information about Welfare," in P. Brett Hammond and Rob Coppock, eds., *Valuing Health Risks, Costs, and Benefits for Environmental Decision Making: Report of a Conference* (Washington, D.C.: National Academy Press, 1990).
6. We will fill in the details and supply citations in Chapter 1.

1. The Traditional View

1. See Lionel Robbins, *An Essay on the Nature and Significance of Economic Science* (London: Macmillan, 1932).
2. See, e.g., J. R. Hicks, "The Foundations of Welfare Economics," *Economic Journal* 49 (1939): 696; Harold Hotelling, "The General Welfare in Relation to Problems of Taxation and of Railway and Utility Rates," *Econometrica* 6 (1938): 242; Nicholas Kaldor, "Welfare Propositions of Economics and Interpersonal Comparisons of Utility," *Economic Journal* 49 (1939): 549. A useful discussion of these tests can be found in Ian Malcolm David Little, *A Critique of Welfare Economics*, 2nd ed. (Oxford: Clarendon Press, 1957), 88–96.

3. See J. de V. Graaff, *Theoretical Welfare Economics* (Cambridge: Cambridge University Press, 1957), 169–171.

4. See, e.g., John S. Chipman and James C. Moore, "The New Welfare Economics 1939–1974," *International Economic Review* 19 (1978): 547–548. This view is briefly discussed in Ajit K. Dasgupta and D. W. Pearce, *Cost Benefit Analysis: Theory and Practice* (London: Macmillan, 1972), 15.

5. See D. W. Pearce and C. A. Nash, *The Social Appraisal of Projects: A Text in Cost-Benefit Analysis* (London: Macmillan, 1981), 3–4; R. Shep Melnick, "The Politics of Benefit-Cost Analysis," in P. Brett Hammond and Rob Coppock, eds., *Valuing Health Risks, Costs, and Benefits for Environmental Decision Making: Report of a Conference* (Washington, D.C.: National Academy Press, 1990), 23.

6. A large legal literature addresses the related question whether legal rules in general, and the common law in particular, do or should reflect efficiency concerns. See, e.g., "Symposium on Efficiency as a Legal Concern," *Hofstra Law Review* 8 (1980): 485. This literature is of limited usefulness for our purposes. It does not address cost-benefit analysis, for the most part, and much of it is concerned about the role of common-law judges. Otherwise it resembles earlier discussions in the economics literature. More recent treatments in the legal literature include Mark Kelman, *A Guide to Critical Legal Studies* (Cambridge, Mass.: Harvard University Press, 1987), 114–150; David M. Driesen, "The Societal Cost of Environmental Regulation: Beyond Administrative Cost-Benefit Analysis," *Ecology Law Quarterly* 24 (1997): 545; Lewis A. Kornhauser, "Wealth Maximization," in Peter Newman, ed., *The New Palgrave Dictionary of Economics and the Law* (New York: Stockton Press, 1998); and Richard S. Markovits, "Duncan's Do Nots: Cost-Benefit Analysis and the Determination of Legal Entitlements," *Stanford Law Review* 36 (1984): 1169.

7. It is possible that if *P* radically changes endowments, this price effect will not occur.

8. Because CV is defined in terms of preference satisfaction, it is the same as the amount a person is willing to pay (WTP) for a project that benefits him, or willing to accept (WTA) in exchange for a project that hurts him.

9. See C. Edwin Baker, "The Ideology of the Economic Analysis of Law," *Philosophy and Public Affairs* 5 (1975): 3, 47–48.

10. This is also the source of certain paradoxes and intransitivies discussed in the economics literature, such as the Boadway paradox. The basic problem is that if a project shifts the distribution of wealth, it will also shift people's valuations, and thus could result in an outcome that—given people's new endowments, hence valuations—would lead to the (original) status quo being socially preferable on the basis of CBA.

11. Notable exceptions include Sen and Harsanyi. See Amartya Sen, *Choice, Welfare and Measurement* (Oxford: Blackwell, 1982), 84–106; John C. Harsanyi, "Game and Decision Theoretic Models in Ethics," in Robert J. Aumann and Sergiu Hart, eds., *Handbook of Game Theory with Economic Applications*, vol. 1 (New York: North Holland, 1992), 669, 703–704. Although both scholars appear to support CBA, at

least under certain conditions, neither of them has attempted to reconcile his views with the traditional approach to cost-benefit analysis.

12. This view is implicit in Kaldor, "Welfare Propositions," which argues that economists should not concern themselves with the distributive consequences of projects, since distribution is essentially a political issue. The implication is that if an "efficient" policy produces Losers, the government can compensate them if the outcome is distributively objectionable.

13. See A. Mitchell Polinsky, "Probabilistic Compensation Criteria," *Quarterly Journal of Economics* 86 (1972): 407.

14. One path around this objection might be to conceptualize individuals as choosing ex ante between CBA and other procedures under a veil of ignorance—without knowing what their wealth, preferences, and welfare-affecting characteristics will turn out to be. But it is hardly clear that the rational choice, ex ante, under broad uncertainty, is to choose the world where government uses CBA. Harsanyi has argued famously that the rational choice, under such circumstances, is to choose the world where overall well-being is higher. See Harsanyi, "Game," 694–696. Insofar as CBA and overall well-being diverge—as we argue they do—the introduction of uncertainty into an ex ante perspective does not secure the Pareto defense of CBA.

15. See, e.g., E. J. Mishan, *Cost-Benefit Analysis* (New York: Praeger, 1976), 382–402; Arnold C. Harberger, "Three Basic Postulates for Applied Welfare Economics: An Interpretive Essay," *Journal of Economic Literature* 9 (1971): 785. A textbook discussion can be found in Dasgupta and Pearce, *Cost-Benefit Analysis*, 57.

16. See Robin W. Boadway, "The Welfare Foundations of Cost-Benefit Analysis," *Economic Journal* 84 (1974): 926.

17. We are not persuaded by the argument that Kaldor-Hicks is justified on the basis of hypothetical consent. See Richard A. Posner, "The Ethical and Political Basis of the Efficiency Norm in Common Law Adjudication," *Hofstra Law Review* 8 (1980): 487. But see, e.g., Jules L. Coleman, "Efficiency, Utility, and Wealth Maximization," *Hofstra Law Review* 8 (1980): 509. Nor are we persuaded that it is consistent with people's moral intuitions. See Richard A. Posner, "Utilitarianism, Economics, and Legal Theory," *Journal of Legal Studies* 8 (1979): 103. But see, e.g., Ronald M. Dworkin, "Is Wealth a Value?" *Journal of Legal Studies* 9 (1980): 191. Other contributions to this debate can be found in "Symposium on Efficiency as a Legal Concern," *Hofstra Law Review.*

18. See, e.g., Pearce and Nash, *Social Appraisal*, 26–27. Pearce and Nash do not themselves accept this approach.

2. The Moral Foundations of Cost-Benefit Analysis

1. See, e.g., A. J. Ayer, *Language, Truth, and Logic*, 2nd ed. (London: Gollancz, 1946); Charles Stevenson, *Ethics and Language* (New Haven: Yale University Press, 1944); R. M. Hare, *The Language of Morals* (Oxford: Oxford University Press, 1952).

2. Hicks elegantly summarizes the moral skepticism fueling the new welfare

economics in his "Foundations of Welfare Economics" (and then proceeds to present a compensation principle that, he believes, is not vulnerable to the skeptical challenge): It is "widely accepted," he writes, that "[s]o long as economics is concerned with explanation, it can hope to reach conclusions which will command universal acceptance . . . but once it goes beyond that point, and endeavours to prescribe principles of policy, then [many economists believe] its conclusions must depend upon the scale of social values held by the particular investigator . . . Positive economics can be . . . the same for all men; one's welfare economics will inevitably be different according as one is a liberal or a socialist, a nationalist or an internationalist, a christian or a pagan." J. R. Hicks, "The Foundations of Welfare Economics," *Economic Journal* 49 (1939): 696. The leading contemporary textbook in welfare economics exudes a similar skepticism about the truth-content or objectivity of moral statements.

> The ranking of social states is inevitably a normative procedure; that is, it involves making *value judgments.* For each set of value judgments adopted, a different social ordering results. Therefore there is no objective or unique way to order social states. This does not imply that nothing useful can be said. On the contrary, some value judgments might, in fact, command widespread support . . . Much of the welfare economic analysis underlying policy prescriptions is based on a certain set of value judgments which are widely accepted among economists, including ourselves.

Robin Boadway and Neil Bruce, *Welfare Economics* (Oxford: Blackwell, 1984), 2.

3. See generally, Alexander Miller, *An Introduction to Contemporary Metaethics* (Cambridge: Blackwell, 2003).

4. See Michael Smith, *The Moral Problem* (Oxford: Blackwell, 1994).

5. For an overview of social choice theory, see Boadway and Bruce, *Welfare Economics* 137–179.

6. See, e.g., David B. Spence, "A Public Choice Progressivism, Continued," *Cornell Law Review* 87 (2002): 397; Jonathan Baron, "Value Analysis of Political Behavior—Self-Interested : Moralistic :: Altruistic : Moral," *University of Pennsylvania Law Review* 151 (2003): 1135. For a general discussion of the importance of moral commitments in helping to explain behavior, see, e.g., Daniel M. Hausman and Michael S. McPherson, *Economic Analysis and Moral Philosophy* (Cambridge: Cambridge University Press, 1996).

7. See H. L. A. Hart, *The Concept of Law,* 2nd ed. (Oxford: Oxford University Press, 1994), 124–136.

8. See Cass R. Sunstein, "Cost-Benefit Default Principles," *Michigan Law Review* 99 (2001): 1651, 1666–1667.

9. For good overviews of the philosophical literature on well-being, see James Griffin, *Well-Being* (Oxford: Oxford University Press, 1986), 7–72; Derek Parfit, *Reasons and Persons* (Oxford: Oxford University Press, 1984), 493–502; T. M. Scanlon, *What We Owe to Each Other* (Cambridge, Mass.: Harvard University Press, 1998), 108–143; L. W. Sumner, *Welfare, Happiness, and Ethics* (Oxford: Oxford University Press, 1996), 45–137; Moazaffar Qizilbash, "The Concept of Well-Being," *Economics and Philosophy* 14 (1998): 51.

10. The development of mental-state views of well-being by Bentham, Mill, and Sidgwick is described by Sumner, *Welfare, Happiness, and Ethics*, 83–92.

11. See, e.g., Fred Feldman, *Pleasure and the Good Life: Concerning the Nature, Varieties, and Plausibility of Hedonism* (Oxford: Oxford University Press, 2004); Mark H. Bernstein, *On Moral Considerability: An Essay on Who Morally Matters* (New York: Oxford University Press, 1998).

12. This literature is reviewed in Bruno S. Frey and Alois Stutzer, *Happiness and Economics: How The Economy and Institutions Affect Human Well-Being* (Princeton: Princeton University Press, 2002).

13. See Daniel Kahneman, "Experienced Utility and Objective Happiness: A Moment Based Approach," in Daniel Kahneman and Amos Tversky, eds., *Choices, Values, and Frames* (Cambridge: Cambridge University Press, 2000), 673; Daniel Kahneman, "Objective Happiness," in Daniel Kahneman et al., eds., *Well-Being: The Foundations of Hedonic Psychology* (New York: Russell Sage Foundation, 1999), 3; Daniel Kahneman et al., "Back to Bentham? Explorations of Experienced Utility," *Quarterly Journal of Economics* 112 (1997): 375.

14. Sumner, *Welfare, Happiness, and Ethics*, 106.

15. See Griffin, *Well-Being*, 8.

16. Robert Nozick, *Anarchy, State, and Utopia* (New York: Basic Books, 1974), 42–43.

17. Nozick, *Anarchy, State, and Utopia*, 44.

18. For an overview of research on the determinants of well-being, see Ed Diener et al., "Subjective Well-Being: Three Decades of Progress," *Psychological Bulletin* 125 (1999): 276. The famous study finding adaptation by lottery winners and quadriplegics and paraplegics is Philip Brickman et al., "Lottery Winners and Accident Victims: Is Happiness Relative?" *Journal of Personality and Social Psychology* 36 (1978): 917.

19. See John Finnis, *Natural Law and Natural Rights* (Oxford: Oxford University Press, 1980), 59–99; James Griffin, *Value Judgment: Improving Our Ethical Beliefs* (Oxford: Oxford University Press, 1996), 19–36; Thomas Hurka, *Perfectionism* (New York: Oxford University Press, 1993), 9–143; Martha Nussbaum, *Women and Human Development: The Capabilities Approach* (Cambridge: Cambridge University Press, 2000), 34–110; George Sher, *Beyond Neutrality: Perfectionism and Politics* (Cambridge: Cambridge University Press, 1997), 199–244.

20. See Finnis, *Natural Law and Natural Rights*, 85–90; Nussbaum, *Women and Human Development*, 78–80; Parfit, *Reasons and Persons*, 499; Griffin, *Value Judgment*, 29–30.

21. See Hurka, *Perfectionism*, 9–51.

22. Sher, *Beyond Neutrality*, 229.

23. See Qizilbash, "The Concept of Well-Being," 63.

24. Objectivism is more plausible in the case of individuals who lack preferences—for example, the comatose—but in the case of ordinary adults we believe that preference-satisfaction is a necessary if not sufficient condition for well-being.

25. Ronald Dworkin, *Foundations of Liberal Equality*, Tanner Lectures on Human Values, vol. 11 (Salt Lake City: University of Utah Press, 1990), 75–76.

26. Dworkin, *Foundations of Liberal Equality*, 77.

27. See Sumner, *Welfare, Happiness, and Ethics*, 20–21.

28. Our view is therefore a kind of preferentialism about well-being. For the philosophical literature concerning preferentialist accounts of well-being, see, e.g., Griffin, *Well-Being*, 10–19; Parfit, *Reasons and Persons*, 494–499; Scanlon, *What We Owe to Each Other*, 113–123; Sumner, *Welfare, Happiness, and Ethics*, 113–137; Qizilbash, "The Concept of Well-Being," 58–63.

29. For critical discussion of the economic view of well-being, see Daniel M. Hausman and Michael S. McPherson, *Economic Analysis and Moral Philosophy* (Cambridge: Cambridge University Press, 1996), 71–83; Scanlon, *What We Owe to Each Other*, 113–123; Sumner, *Welfare, Happiness, and Ethics*, 113–137; Tyler Cowen, "The Scope and Limits of Preference Sovereignty," *Economics and Philosophy* 9 (1993): 253.

30. Amartya Sen, *On Ethics and Economics* (Oxford: Blackwell, 1987), 45.

31. Parfit, *Reasons and Persons*, 494. Many other scholars have pointed to this problem, the problem of disinterested preferences, for a preferentialist account of well-being. See Sumner, *Welfare, Happiness, and Ethics*, 134–135; John Broome, "Choice and Value in Economics," *Oxford Economic Papers* 30 (1978): 313; Allan Gibbard, "Interpersonal Comparisons: Preference, Good, and the Intrinsic Reward of a Life," in Jon Elster and Aanund Hylland, eds., *Foundations of Social Choice Theory* (Cambridge: Cambridge University Press, 1986), 165, 173–175; Mark Carl Overvold, "Self-Interest and the Concept of Self-Sacrifice," *Canadian Journal of Philosophy* 10 (1980): 105; Amartya Sen, "Rational Fools: A Critique of the Behavioral Foundations of Economic Theory," *Philosophy and Public Affairs* 6 (1977): 317; David Sobel, "On the Subjectivity of Welfare," *Ethics* 107 (1997): 501.

32. On the nature of preferences, see S. L. Hurley, *Natural Reasons* (New York: Oxford University Press, 1989), 55–83; Christoph Fehige and Ulla Wessels, eds., *Preferences* (Berlin: de Gruyter, 1998); Richard Arneson, "Liberalism, Distributive Subjectivism, and Equal Opportunity for Welfare," *Philosophy and Public Affairs* 19 (1990): 158, 161–164; Arthur Ripstein, "Preference," in R. G. Frey and Christopher W. Morris, eds., *Value, Welfare, and Morality* (Cambridge: Cambridge University Press, 1993), 93, 93–111.

33. On posthumous preferences, see, e.g., Sumner, *Welfare, Happiness, and Ethics*, 126–127.

34. Yet another reason to carve out a category of disinterested preferences is that seeing all preferences as self-interested forces a counterintuitive change in our conceptual framework. The concept of "self-sacrifice" and cognate concepts, e.g., "altruism," become incoherent. It becomes impossible for an individual to deliberately and knowingly reduce his own well-being for the sake of others. See Overvold, "Self-Interest and the Concept of Self-Sacrifice."

35. See, e.g., Jon Elster, *Ulysses and the Sirens: Studies in Rationality and Irrationality* (Cambridge: Cambridge University Press, 1979), 65–76.

36. On second-order preferences, see Harry G. Frankfurt, "Freedom of the Will and the Concept of a Person," *Journal of Philosophy* 68 (1971): 5.

37. See Don Loeb, "Full Information Theories of Individual Good," *Social Theory and Practice* 21 (1995): 1; Connie S. Rosati, "Persons, Perspectives, and Full Information Accounts of the Good," *Ethics* 105 (1995): 296; David Sobel, "Full Information Accounts of Well-Being," *Ethics* 104 (1994): 784.

38. See Sumner, *Welfare, Happiness, and Ethics*, 162–171.

39. See Shelly Kagan, "The Limits of Well-Being," *Social Philosophy and Policy* 9 (1992): 169.

40. See Mark Carl Overvold, "Morality, Self-Interest, and Reasons for Being Moral," *Philosophy and Phenomenological Research* 44 (1984): 493, 499–501; Mark Carl Overvold, "Self-Interest and Getting What You Want," in Harlan B. Miller and William H. Williams, eds., *The Limits of Utilitarianism* (Minneapolis: University of Minnesota Press, 1982), 186. For criticism of Overvold's account, see David Sobel, "Well-Being as the Object of Moral Consideration," *Economics and Philosophy* 14 (1998): 249, 266–269.

41. On the problem of interpersonal welfare comparisons, see generally Jon Elster and John E. Roemer, eds., *Interpersonal Comparisons of Well-Being* (Cambridge: Cambridge University Press, 1991); Daniel M. Hausman, "The Impossibility of Interpersonal Utility Comparisons," *Mind* 104 (1995): 473; Ken Binmore, *Game Theory and the Social Contract*, vol. 1, *Playing Fair* (Cambridge, Mass.: MIT Press, 1994), 282–296.

42. The term "Pareto-superior" is ambiguous. It might mean (1) an outcome that at least one person *prefers* to an alternative, and no one disprefers; or (2) an outcome in which at least one person is *better off* than an alternative, and no one is worse off. On a simple preference-based account of welfare, this ambiguity is harmless. On other accounts, the ambiguity is more significant. For example, on our restricted preference-based view, an individual can prefer an outcome without benefiting from it. So let us clarify: for the remainder of this book, "Pareto-superior" means an outcome that benefits at least one person and makes no one worse off.

43. Lionel Robbins, *An Essay on the Nature and Significance of Economic Science* (London: Macmillan, 1932).

44. See, e.g., Robert A. Pollak, "Welfare Comparisons and Situation Comparisons," *Journal of Econometrics* 50 (1991): 31, 31; Yew-Kwang Ng, "A Case for Happiness, Cardinalism, and Interpersonal Comparability," *Economic Journal* 107 (1997): 1848.

45. See Norman Daniels, *Justice and Justification: Reflective Equilibrium in Theory and Practice* (New York: Cambridge University Press, 1996).

46. Hausman, "Impossibility of Interpersonal Utility Comparisons," 489. Or as Harsanyi put it: "In everyday life we make, or at least attempt to make, interpersonal utility comparisons all the time." John Harsanyi, "Morality and the Theory of Rational Behaviour," in Amartya Sen and Bernard Williams, eds., *Utilitarianism and Beyond* (Cambridge: Cambridge University Press, 1982), 39, 49.

47. For a discussion of the extent to which different types of social welfare function require interpersonal comparisons, see Boadway and Bruce, *Welfare Economics*, 137–169; Claude d'Aspremont and Louis Gevers, "Social Welfare Functionals

and Interpersonal Comparability," in Kenneth J. Arrow et al., eds., *Handbook of Social Choice and Welfare*, vol. 1 (Amsterdam: Elsevier, 2002), 459.

48. Utilitarianism and weak welfarism are indifferent to a positive linear transformation of utilities (where each person's utility U_i is transformed to $a \times U_i + b$, and a is positive). The sum of the original utilities will order outcomes one particular way, and the sum of a positive linear transformation of the original utilities will order outcomes the same way.

It is therefore sufficient, for purposes of utilitarianism and weak welfarism, to have a methodology for interpersonal comparisons that leads to utility numbers that are unique only up to a positive linear transformation (as does, for example, the Harsanyi construct for interpersonal comparisons, discussed below). That is not true for prioritarianism. Consider, for example, the prioritarian view that sums the square root of individual utilities. Replacing the original assignment of utilities with a positive linear transformation, then taking square roots and summing, may lead to a different ranking of outcomes than if the square roots of the original utilities are taken and summed.

49. See, e.g., d'Aspremont and Gevers, "Social Welfare Functionals," 469–470; Amartya Sen, "Social Choice Theory," in Kenneth J. Arrow and Michael Intriligator, eds., *Handbook of Mathematical Economics*, vol. 3 (Amsterdam: North-Holland, 1986), 1073, 1115–1121; Philippe Mongin and Claude d'Aspremont, "Utility Theory and Ethics," in Salvador Barberà et al., eds., *Handbook of Utility Theory*, vol. 1 (Dordrecht: Kluwer, 1998), 371, 415–419.

50. See Larry S. Temkin, *Inequality* (New York: Oxford University Press, 1993).

51. Kahneman, the chief contemporary proponent of interpersonal hedonic comparisons, points to Bentham and Edgeworth as precursors. See Kahneman, "Objective Happiness," 4–5.

52. Ng, "A Case for Happiness," 1852.

53. See Kahneman, "Experienced Utility"; Kahneman, "Objective Happiness"; Kahneman, "Back to Bentham?"

54. By "cardinal," we mean that the array of numbers assigned to a set of momentary experiences is sufficiently unique that the numbers can be seen as representing the differences between the experiences—not just the ordering of the experiences themselves. The method for assigning numbers to the experiences may permit the numbers to be transformed in various ways—for example, multiplying all by a positive number, or adding a constant—but any permissible transformation of the array will preserve both the ordering of the experiences, and the ordering of the differences between the experiences. Kahneman's method, in fact, measures momentary experiences on a ratio scale. See Kahneman, "Objective Happiness," 6. These numbers can only be multiplied by a positive constant, and are therefore "cardinal" in the sense we are using that term.

55. Kahneman, "Objective Happiness," 5–6.

56. Kahneman, "Experienced Utility," 684.

57. Griffin, *Well-Being*, 116–117.

58. If life-histories can be "incomparable" with respect to one welfare dimension, or

the totality of dimensions, then a more complicated numbering scheme would be needed to represent objectivist interpersonal comparisons. For example, it is sometimes suggested that an incomplete ordering of items can be represented by a plurality of precise assignments of numbers to the items; the incomplete ordering is then the "intersection" of these precise orderings. See Amartya Sen, *Inequality Reexamined* (Cambridge, Mass.: Harvard University Press, 1992), 46–49. On incomparability, see Chapter 6.

59. A good review focusing on preferentialist approaches to interpersonal comparisons is Peter J. Hammond, "Interpersonal Comparisons of Utility: Why and How They Are and Should Be Made," in Elster and Roemer, *Interpersonal Comparisons of Well-Being*, 200.

60. See John von Neumann and Oskar Morgenstern, *Theory of Games and Economic Behavior*, 3rd ed. (Princeton: Princeton University Press, 1953), 15–31, 617–632. Expected utility theory has, of course, been hugely important for decision theory and economics. For reviews, see, e.g., David M. Kreps, *A Course in Microeconomic Theory* (Princeton: Princeton University Press, 1990), 71–131; Michael D. Resnik, *Choices: An Introduction to Decision Theory* (Minneapolis: University of Minnesota Press, 1987), 81–120.

61. See J. R. Isbell, "Absolute Games," in A. W. Tucker and R. D. Luce, eds., *Contributions to the Theory of Games*, vol. 4 (Princeton: Princeton University Press, 1959), 357. The approach is discussed at length in Hausman, "The Impossibility of Interpersonal Utility Comparisons."

62. A number of philosophers and economists have criticized the zero-one rule on these grounds, as summarized in Hausman, "The Impossibility of Interpersonal Utility Comparisons," 483–485.

63. Harsanyi developed and presented his approach to interpersonal comparisons in a number of different publications. One accessible summary is Harsanyi, "Morality and the Theory of Rational Behavior." The approach is discussed at length by John A. Weymark, "A Reconsideration of the Harsanyi-Sen Debate on Utilitarianism," in Elster and Roemer, *Interpersonal Comparisons of Well-Being*, 255.

64. See James Griffin, "Against the Taste Model," in Elster and Roemer, *Interpersonal Comparisons of Well-Being*, 45, 52.

65. This analysis of overall welfare assumes a constant population. We will not engage the difficult problem of determining overall welfare in a case where the individuals who exist in the two outcomes being compared are not the same.

66. See, e.g., Griffin, "Against the Taste Model," 53–54; Hausman, "The Impossibility of Interpersonal Utility Comparisons," 477–478.

67. This suggestion builds on work by Michael Smith, who argues that moral reasons are determined by convergent fully informed preferences. See Michael Smith, *The Moral Problem*.

68. On utilitarianism, see, e.g., Geoffrey Scarre, *Utilitarianism* (London: Routledge, 1996); Sen and Williams, *Utilitarianism and Beyond*; J. J. C. Smart and Bernard Williams, *Utilitarianism: For and Against* (Cambridge: Cambridge University Press, 1973).

69. Shelly Kagan describes the view we call weak welfarism in *Normative Ethics*

(Boulder, Colo: Westview Press, 1998), 25–186, which we have found very helpful.

70. See, e.g., Andrew Moore and Roger Crisp, "Welfarism in Moral Theory," *Australasian Journal of Philosophy* 74 (1996): 598; Louis Kaplow and Steven Shavell, *Fairness versus Welfare* (Cambridge, Mass.: Harvard University Press, 2002).

71. Dennis McKerlie, "Equality and Priority," *Utilitas* 6 (1994): 25, 26. Derek Parfit makes a similar observation: "If we cared only about equality, we would be *Pure* Egalitarians. If we cared only about utility, we would be Pure Utilitarians—or what are normally just called Utilitarians. But most of us accept a *pluralist* view . . . We believe that it would be better both if there was more equality, and if there was more utility." Derek Parfit, "Equality or Priority?" in Matthew Clayton and Andrew Williams, eds., *The Ideal of Equality* (Basingstoke, England: Palgrave, 2000), 81, 85. Even Larry Temkin, the leading proponent of the view that moral principles, paradigmatically equality, need not be Pareto-respecting, is not a pure egalitarian. "[D]o I *really* think that there is some respect in which a world where only some are blind is worse than one where all are? Yes. Does this mean I think it would be better if we blinded everyone? No. Equality is not all that matters." Larry Temkin, "Equality, Priority, and the Levelling Down Objection," in Clayton and Williams, *The Ideal of Equality,* 126, 155.

72. Shelly Kagan, *The Limits of Morality* (Oxford: Oxford University Press, 1989), 16–17.

73. On the centrality of the Pareto principle to welfare economics, see, e.g., Boadway and Bruce, *Welfare Economics,* 137–169; Bertil Tungodden, "The Value of Equality," *Economics and Philosophy* 19 (2003): 1, 8 ("The Pareto Principle is the core of normative economics"). For philosophical discussion of the Pareto principle, see the recent literature on egalitarianism and prioritarianism, e.g., Larry Temkin, *Inequality;* Clayton and Williams, *The Ideal of Equality;* and the articles in *Economics and Philosophy* 19: 1–134 (2003).

74. On prioritarianism, see, e.g., Larry Temkin, *Inequality;* McKerlie, "Equality and Priority"; the articles in Clayton and Williams, *The Ideal of Equality;* the articles in *Economics and Philosophy* 19: 1–134 (2003); Paul Weirich, "Utility Tempered with Equality," *Nous* 17 (1983): 423. On leximin, see, e.g., d'Aspremont and Gevers, "Social Welfare Functionals," 469–470; Sen, "Social Choice Theory," 1115–1121; Mongin and d'Aspremont, "Utility Theory and Ethics," 415–419.

75. McKerlie, "Equality and Priority," 28. For similar complaints about leximin, see Weirich, "Utility Tempered with Equality," 429–430; Parfit, "Equality or Priority?" 121.

76. Weirich, "Utility Tempered with Equality," 430.

77. Parfit, "Equality or Priority?" 105.

78. The problem is that equality is a comparative fact: a matter of how one person's welfare compares to another's. But prioritarianism is noncomparative in structure. Imagine two outcomes O and $O*$ such that P and Q each have different welfare levels in the two outcomes, but a third person, Z, has the same welfare in both outcomes. Then, necessarily, because prioritarians maximize a function $\Sigma g(U_i)$, the level of Z's welfare in the two outcomes is irrelevant. Prioritarians must rank

O and O^* the same way, regardless of whether Z is very well off, very badly off, or just as well off as P or Q in one or the other outcome. To put the point technically, prioritarian social welfare functions are "separable" in individual welfares, while genuinely egalitarian functions (arguably) are not. Cf. Tungodden, "The Value of Equality." It is hard to see why merging a moral factor that is "separable" in this sense (overall welfare) with one that is not (equality) would yield one that is (prioritarianism).

79. Thomas Nagel, "Autonomy and Deontology," in Samuel Scheffler, ed., *Consequentialism and Its Critics* (Oxford: Oxford University Press, 1988), 142, 145–146.

80. For similar criticisms of Nagel's sort of view, see Griffin, *Well-Being,* 45; Kagan, *The Limits of Morality,* 51–55. Cf. Parfit, "Equality or Priority?" 101–103.

81. It has been suggested that morality might require the maximization of desert- or responsibility-adjusted welfare rather than welfare simpliciter. See Fred Feldman, *Utilitarianism, Hedonism and Desert* (Cambridge: Cambridge University Press, 1997), 151–192; Richard Arneson, "Liberalism, Distributive Subjectivism, and Equal Opportunity for Welfare," *Philosophy and Public Affairs* 19 (1990): 158, 159. Our response to these suggestions runs along the same lines as our response to Nagel.

82. John Rawls, *A Theory of Justice* (Cambridge, Mass.: Harvard University Press, 1971), 92.

83. See Ronald Dworkin, "What Is Equality? Part 1: Equality of Welfare," *Philosophy and Public Affairs* 10 (1981): 185; Ronald Dworkin, "What Is Equality? Part 2: Equality of Resources," *Philosophy and Public Affairs* 10 (1981): 283.

84. See Amartya Sen, *Inequality Reexamined,* 39–55; Amartya Sen, "Capability and Well-Being," in Martha Nussbaum and Amartya Sen, eds., *The Quality of Life* (Oxford: Oxford University Press, 1993), 30; G. A. Cohen, "Equality of What? On Welfare, Goods, and Capabilities," in Nussbaum and Sen, *The Quality of Life,* 9. Nagel and Scanlon might also be seen as adopting variants of resourcism. See Nagel, "Autonomy and Deontology," 145–150; Thomas M. Scanlon, "The Moral Basis of Interpersonal Comparisons," in Jon Elster and John E. Roemer, eds., *Interpersonal Comparisons of Well-Being* (Cambridge: Cambridge University Press, 1991), 39–44.

85. Richard J. Arneson, "Welfare Should Be the Currency of Justice," *Canadian Journal of Philosophy* 30 (2000): 497.

86. On this issue see, e.g., Samuel Scheffler, *The Rejection of Consequentialism,* rev. ed. (Oxford: Oxford University Press, 1994); Kagan, *The Limits of Morality;* Kagan, *Normative Ethics,* 161–170.

87. Robert E. Goodin, *Utilitarianism as a Public Philosophy* (Cambridge: Cambridge University Press, 1995), 8–9. See also pp. 65–68.

3. Cost-Benefit Analysis as a Decision Procedure

1. We are not the first to argue that CBA is a morally justified decision procedure rather than a moral criterion. That view is also suggested by Donald Hubin, "The Moral Justification of Benefit/Cost Analysis," *Economics and Philosophy* 10 (1994): 169.

2. See Shelly Kagan, *Normative Ethics* (Boulder, Colo: Westview Press, 1998), 1–186.

3. We are not aware of any counterexample.

4. This distinction is familiar to philosophers. See, e.g., David O. Brink, *Moral Realism and the Foundations of Ethics* (Cambridge: Cambridge University Press, 1989), 216–217; R. Eugene Bales, "Act-Utilitarianism: Account of Right-Making Characteristics or Decision-Making Procedure?" *American Philosophical Quarterly* 8 (1971): 257; Robert L. Frazier, "Act Utilitarianism and Decision Procedures," *Utilitas* 6 (1994): 43.

5. See, e.g., Frederick E. Schauer, *Playing by the Rules: A Philosophical Examination of Rule-Based Decisionmaking in Law and in Life* (Oxford: Clarendon Press, 1991); Louis Kaplow, "Rules versus Standards: An Economic Analysis," *Duke Law Journal* 42 (1992): 557; Colin S. Diver, "The Optimal Precision of Administrative Rules," *Yale Law Journal* 93 (1983): 65.

6. Actually, in the simplified case where the legislator's goal is just safety maximization, rather than safety maximization plus other goals—for example, preserving the liberty to engage in harmless activities—the extent to which different legal provisions are overinclusive relative to the safety goal should not matter to her. In this case, only underinclusion is relevant. But even with a single-minded focus on underinclusion, the point remains that the safety-maximizing choice for the legislator could well be to enact a provision that says "motorists must not drive faster than 55 miles per hour" rather than one that says "drive safely."

7. On value-of-information analysis, see, e.g., Maxine E. Dakins, "The Value of the Value of Information," *Human and Ecological Risk Assessment* 5 (1999): 281; Jack Hirshleifer and John G. Riley, *The Analytics of Uncertainty and Information* (Cambridge: Cambridge University Press, 1992), 167–208.

8. The *locus classicus* for discussions of bounded rationality is, of course, Herbert Simon's scholarship. See Herbert Simon, *Models of Bounded Rationality: Economic Analysis and Public Policy*, vols. 1 and 2 (Cambridge, Mass.: MIT Press, 1982); Herbert Simon, *Models of Bounded Rationality*, vol. 3 (Cambridge, Mass.: MIT Press, 1997). For more recent work, see, e.g., Ariel Rubenstein, *Modeling Bounded Rationality* (Cambridge, Mass.: MIT Press, 1998); Gerd Gigerenzer et al., *Simple Heuristics That Make Us Smart* (New York: Oxford University Press, 1999).

9. On expected utility theory, see, e.g., David M. Kreps, *A Course in Microeconomic Theory* (Princeton: Princeton University Press, 1990), 71–131; and Michael D. Resnik, *Choices: An Introduction to Decision Theory* (Minneapolis: University of Minnesota Press, 1987), 81–120.

10. The problem of specifying the choice set to which CBA or other policy-analytic procedures are then applied is discussed at length by Matthew D. Adler, "Rational Choice, Rational Agenda-Setting, and Constitutional Law: Does the Constitution Require Basic or Strengthened Public Rationality?" in Christoph Engel and Adrienne Heritier, eds., *Linking Politics and Law* (Baden-Baden: Nomos Verlagsgesellschaft, 2003), 109.

11. See Robert W. Hahn and Patrick Dudley, "How Well Does the Government Do

Cost-Benefit Analysis?" AEI-Brookings Joint Center for Regulatory Analysis working paper, April 2005, 15–16, www.aei-brookings.org; Robert W. Hahn et al., "Assessing Regulatory Impact Analyses: The Failure of Agencies to Comply with Executive Order 12,866," *Harvard Journal of Law and Public Policy* 23 (2000): 859, 874–885.

12. Office of Management and Budget, "Circular A-4, September 17, 2003," p. 7 at www.whitehouse.gov/omb.

13. For discussions of how the construct of CV should be refined to account for uncertainty about the outcomes of policy choice, see, e.g., A. Myrick Freeman III, *The Measurement of Environmental and Resource Values: Theory and Methods*, 2nd ed. (Washington, D.C.: Resources for the Future, 2003), 209–257; Richard C. Ready, "Environmental Valuation under Uncertainty," in Daniel W. Bromley, ed., *Handbook of Environmental Economics* (Oxford: Blackwell, 1995), 568–593; Lewis A. Kornhauser, "On Justifying Cost-Benefit Analysis," in Matthew D. Adler and Eric A. Posner, eds., *Cost-Benefit Analysis: Legal, Economic, and Philosophical Perspectives* (Chicago: University of Chicago Press, 2001), 201, 205–209.

14. On the use of market prices to estimate valuations, see Richard E. Just et al., *The Welfare Economics of Public Policy: A Practical Approach to Project and Policy Evaluation* (Cheltenham, England: Edward Elgar, 2004). On other revealed preference techniques, see Freeman, *The Measurement of Environmental and Resource Values*, 95–136, 353–452; Nancy E. Bockstael, "Travel Cost Models," in Bromley, *Handbook of Environmental Economics*, 655–671; A. Myrick Freeman III, "Hedonic Pricing Methods," in Bromley, *Handbook of Environmental Economics*, 672–686.

15. On stated preference techniques, see Freeman, *The Measurement of Environmental and Resource Values*, 161–187; Ian J. Bateman et al., *Economic Valuation with Stated Preference Techniques: A Manual* (Cheltenham, England: Edward Elgar, 2002).

16. See Ian J. Bateman and Kenneth G. Willis, eds., *Valuing Environmental Preferences: Theory and Practice of the Contingent Valuation Method in the US, EU, and Developing Countries* (Oxford: Oxford University Press, 1999); Jerry A. Hausman, ed., *Contingent Valuation: A Critical Assessment* (Amsterdam: North-Holland, 1993).

17. See Matthew D. Adler, "Against 'Individual Risk': A Sympathetic Critique of Risk Assessment," *University of Pennsylvania Law Review* 153 (2005): 1121, 1193–1197. On possible worlds, see Michael J. Loux, *Metaphysics: A Contemporary Introduction* (London: Routledge, 2002), 176–214.

18. We discuss the valuation of lifesaving at greater length in Chapter 6. Governmental use of risk assessment techniques is discussed by Adler, "Against 'Individual Risk.'"

19. Cf. Matthew D. Adler, "Fear Assessment: Cost-Benefit Analysis and the Pricing of Fear and Anxiety," *Chicago-Kent Law Review* 79 (2004): 977.

20. See Cass R. Sunstein, "Valuing Life: A Plea for Disaggregation," *Duke Law Journal* 54 (2004): 385.

21. See, e.g., Freeman, *The Measurement of Environmental and Resource Values*, 453–456.

22. For example, Robert Hahn, who systematically studies actual agency policy-analytic practice, finds that the regulatory impact documents submitted to the

OMB frequently fail to monetize or fully monetize policy effects. See, e.g., Hahn et al., "Assessing Regulatory Impact Analyses," 868–870; Hahn and Dudley, "How Well Does the Government Do Cost-Benefit Analysis?" 12–15.

23. See, e.g., Matthew D. Adler, "Risk, Death and Harm: The Normative Foundations of Risk Regulation," *Minnesota Law Review* 87 (2003): 1293, 1414–1417; Cass R. Sunstein, "Cost-Benefit Default Principles," *Michigan Law Review* 99 (2001): 1663–1666.

24. 21 United States Code §348(c)(3)(A) (2000).

25. 42 United States Code §7409(b)(1) (2000).

26. See David M. Driesen, "Distributing the Costs of Environmental, Health, and Safety Protection: The Feasibility Principle, Cost-Benefit Analysis, and Regulatory Reform," *Boston College Environmental Affairs Law Review* 32 (2005): 1.

27. 33 United States Code §1316(a)(1) (2000).

28. 29 United States Code §655(b)(5) (2000).

29. See Martha C. Nussbaum, *Women and Human Development: The Capabilities Approach* (Cambridge: Cambridge University Press, 2000), 78–80.

30. In actuality, many "feasibility" provisions in environmental law take account of "economic" as well as technological feasibility—meaning that regulations cannot be so costly as to bankrupt firms. See Driesen, "Distributing the Costs," 8–20. In other words, these provisions combine a technological feasibility requirement with a cost cutoff. Our discussion will focus on the simpler case of a pure technological feasibility requirement without a cost cutoff.

31. See, e.g., Richard A. Epstein, "The Path to *The T. J. Hooper:* The Theory and History of Custom in the Law of Tort," *Journal of Legal Studies* 21 (1992): 1; Steven Hetcher, "The Jury's Out: Social Norms' Misunderstood Role in Negligence Law," *Georgetown Law Journal* 91 (2003): 633.

32. On agency use of de minimis risk thresholds, see Adler, "Against 'Individual Risk,'" 1149–1179. On longevity maximization and the use of QALY adjustments, see 1220–1223. On QALYs, see generally Matthew D. Adler, "QALYs and Policy Evaluation: A New Perspective," *Yale Journal of Health Policy, Law and Ethics* 6 (2006): 1.

　　A procedure that focuses the agency on safety but incorporates a de minimis risk threshold might be classified either as a safety-maximization procedure or as a kind of hybrid decision procedure. Since the threshold here is defined by a function of safety (e.g., regulate the hazard up to the point where the fatality risk to the maximally exposed individual is below 1 in 1 million), rather than by costs or feasibility, we place it in the safety-maximization category. However, like a cost or feasibility threshold, the de minimis threshold can be seen as an attempt to screen out projects whose welfare benefits, in improving safety, are not likely to justify their costs, along other dimensions of welfare.

33. Education is an aspect of Nussbaum's "senses, imagination, and thought" value. Environmental quality—in the sense of ecosystem preservation rather than human safety—as well as species preservation are aspects of her "other species"

value. The arts is an aspect of the "senses, imagination, and thought" value. Protecting individuals from discrimination is an aspect of the "affiliation" value. Finally, religious freedom is an aspect of the "practical reason" value and the "senses, imagination, and thought" value. See Nussbaum, *Women and Human Development*, 78–80, for a summary description of the content of each value.

34. Robert W. Hahn and Cass R. Sunstein, "The Precautionary Principle as a Basis for Decision Making," *Economists' Voice* 2 (2005): 1 (quoting Wingspread Declaration), at www.bepress.com/ev/vol2/iss2/art8.

35. For a survey, see Bruno S. Frey and Alois Stutzer, *Happiness and Economics: How The Economy and Institutions Affect Human Well-Being* (Princeton: Princeton University Press, 2002).

36. Frey and Stutzer, *Happiness and Economics*, 176.

37. See Nussbaum, *Women and Human Development*, 79.

38. Cost-effectiveness analysis in the classic sense, as described in the text, maximizes some goal given a fixed budget. A different kind of cost-effectiveness analysis, used in the health policy field, employs cost-effectiveness ratios to identify recommended choices, and is (in effect) a variant of cost-benefit analysis that makes certain assumptions about the homogeneity of valuations. See Adler, "QALYs and Policy Evaluation."

39. See Adler, "Risk, Death and Harm," 1391–1392.

40. This may even be true of statutes that explicitly require CBA. As already mentioned, Robert Hahn finds that many putative cost-benefit analyses submitted to OMB under the presidential cost-benefit orders fail to monetize, or fully monetize, welfare effects.

41. Richard H. Pildes and Cass R. Sunstein, "Reinventing the Regulatory State," *University of Chicago Law Review* 62 (1995): 1, 65. Intuitive balancing also seems to be the approach recommended by Frank Ackerman and Lisa Hezinerling, who are vocal critics of monetized cost-benefit analysis. See Frank Ackerman and Lisa Heinzerling, *Priceless: On Knowing the Price of Everything and the Value of Nothing* (New York: New Press, 2004), 213–215.

42. James Griffin, *Well-Being: Its Meaning, Measurement and Moral Importance* (Oxford: Oxford University Press, 1986), 122–123. For Scanlon's suggestion, see Thomas M. Scanlon, "The Moral Basis of Interpersonal Comparisons," in Jon Elster and John E. Roemer, eds., *Interpersonal Comparisons of Well-Being* (Cambridge: Cambridge University Press, 1991), 17, 41.

43. See, e.g., David M. Driesen, "The Societal Cost of Environmental Regulation: Beyond Administrative Cost-Benefit Analysis," *Ecology Law Quarterly* 24 (1997): 545, 601–605; Thomas O. McGarity, "A Cost-Benefit State," *Administrative Law Review* 50 (1998): 7, 50; Sidney A. Shapiro and Robert L. Glicksman, *Risk Regulation at Risk: Restoring a Pragmatic Approach* (Stanford: Stanford University Press, 2003), 120–146.

44. See Richard D. Morgenstern and Marc K. Landy, "Economic Analysis: Benefits, Costs, Implications," in Richard D. Morgenstern, ed., *Economic Analyses at EPA:*

Assessing Regulatory Impact (Washington, D.C.: Resources for the Future, 1997), 455, 461–462.

45. Risk assessment requires sophisticated data gathering and modeling. See generally, Dennis J. Paustenbach, ed., *Human and Ecological Risk Assessment: Theory and Practice* (New York: Wiley, 2002). As for feasibility requirements, David Driesen documents that "courts have frequently reversed and remanded agencies' determinations that their regulations are feasible, usually on the ground that the agency has run afoul of the technology constraint." Driesen, "Distributing the Costs," 13–14. These reversals presumably result from uncertainty about the meaning of feasibility; were that a bright-line rule, the reversals would be surprising.

46. Morgenstern and Landy, "Economic Analysis," 463.

47. Executive Order 12,291 required agencies to submit regulatory impact analyses to the OMB for all "major" rules, defined as "any regulation that is likely to result in: (1) An annual effect on the economy of $100 million or more; (2) A major increase in costs or prices for consumers, individual industries, Federal, State, or local government agencies, or geographic regions; or (3) Significant adverse effects on competition, employment, investment, productivity, innovation, or on the ability of United States–based enterprises to compete with foreign-based enterprises in domestic or export markets." Executive Order 12,291 secs. 1(b), 3, in *Code of Federal Regulations* 3 (1981): 127.

   Executive Order 12,866 requires agencies to submit cost-benefit analyses for all "significant" rules, but demands a full-blown analysis only for so-called economically significant rules, namely those that "may . . . [h]ave an annual effect on the economy of $100 million or more or adversely affect in a material way the economy, a sector of the economy, productivity, competition, jobs, the environment, public health or safety, or State, local, or tribal governments or communities." Executive Order 12,866 secs. 3(f), 6(a), in *Code of Federal Regulations* 3 (1993): 638. By using the language of "may" and "likely," the orders make clear that agencies should apply the $100 million threshold by doing a quick and preliminary estimate of the rule's effects, not by doing a full-blown CBA—since the very point of the threshold is to determine whether that full-blown analysis is to be undertaken.

48. This practice is known as "benefits transfer." See, e.g., Freeman, *The Measurement of Environmental and Resource Values*, 453–456.

49. McGarity, "A Cost-Benefit State," 50.

50. See, e.g., Driesen, "The Societal Cost of Environmental Regulation," 601–605; Shapiro and Glicksman, *Risk Regulation at Risk*, 134–136.

51. For citations to the literature about ossification, see William S. Jordan III, "Ossification Revisited: Does Arbitrary and Capricious Review Significantly Interfere with Agency Ability to Achieve Regulatory Goals through Informal Rulemaking?" *Northwestern University Law Review* 94 (2000): 393, 393–394 nn. 1, 4.

52. See Thomas O. McGarity, "Some Thoughts on 'Deossifying' the Rulemaking Process," *Duke Law Journal* 41 (1992): 1385; Thomas O. McGarity, "The Courts

and the Ossification of Rulemaking: A Response to Professor Seidenfeld," *Texas Law Review* 75 (1997): 525.

53. McGarity, "The Courts and the Ossification of Rulemaking," 528.

54. See Cary Coglianese, "Empirical Analysis and Administrative Law," *University of Illinois Law Review* 2002: 1111, 1127.

55. Jordan, "Ossification Revisited," 440.

56. Cornelius M. Kerwin and Scott R. Furlong, "Time and Rulemaking: An Empirical Test of Theory," *Journal of Public Administration Research and Theory* 2 (1992): 113, 126–129.

57. Stuart Shapiro, "Speed Bumps and Roadblocks: Procedural Controls and Regulatory Change," *Journal of Public Administration Research and Theory* 12 (2002): 29, 40.

58. See, e.g., John D. Graham, "Legislative Approaches to Achieving More Protection against Risk at Less Cost," *University of Chicago Legal Forum* 1997: 13, 50.

59. The OMB recently issued a peer review guidance document that instructs agencies to subject certain scientific information to peer review, including some of the scientific information used in the preparation of cost-benefit analyses. However, the guidance does not require the cost-benefit analyses themselves to be peer reviewed. See "Final Information Quality Bulletin for Peer Review," *Federal Register* 70 (January 14, 2005): 2664.

60. Executive Order 12,291 did state that absent any OMB response within a certain period of time after submission of a regulatory impact analysis, review would be deemed concluded; but OMB could also choose to notify the agency that review would take longer. See Executive Order 12,291 §§3(e), (f). By contrast, Executive Order 12,866 sets a real deadline for OMB review. See Executive Order 12,866 §6(b).

61. See McGarity, "A Cost-Benefit State," 26, 50, which argues that risk assessment, like cost-benefit analysis, has substantial delay costs.

62. Coglianese, "Empirical Analysis and Administrative Law," 1127–1128.

63. As already explained in the notes above, the presidential cost-benefit orders have required full-blown cost-benefit analyses, with OMB review, for "major" (Executive Order 12,291) or economically "significant" (Executive Order 12,866) rules. The OMB review is triggered by the size of the agency's choice, not by the agency's decision to evaluate the choice using monetized as opposed to intuitive balancing, and, indeed, many of the analyses submitted to OMB incompletely monetize impacts.

64. We also assume, for simplicity, that the probability distribution of project utility effects for any given choice situation in the set is independent of the policies chosen in the other situations. The implementing agency will confront situation 1, then situation 2, and so on. The independence assumption means that the distribution for situation 2 is the same whether the agency ends up choosing the project or status quo in situation 1 (and so on).

65. In other words, the distribution of utility effects, conditional on the coin coming up heads, is the same as the unconditional distribution in figure 3.1.

66. See, e.g., Stephen Breyer, *Regulation and Its Reform* (Cambridge, Mass.: Harvard

University Press, 1982), 15–35. Anthony Ogus, *Regulation: Legal Form and Economic Theory* (Oxford: Oxford University Press, 1994), 29–54.

67. See Robert Ellickson, *Order without Law: How Neighbors Settle Disputes* (Cambridge, Mass.: Harvard University Press, 1991), 167.

68. See Eric A. Posner, "Law, Economics, and Inefficient Norms," *University of Pennsylvania Law Review* 144 (1996): 1697.

69. This analysis, for simplicity, assumes that the targeted dimension and the background dimensions make additively separable contributions to overall welfare. We can assign utility numbers to a project's effects along the targeted and background dimensions and determine its overall utility by summing the two numbers. As discussed below, additive separability may not in fact hold true. However, the basic point of the analysis is robust: that narrow procedures ignore project effects on background dimensions, and can be expected to be increasingly inaccurate the larger these effects are expected to be.

The analysis also assumes that regulators implement the narrow procedure by measuring the project's utility along the targeted dimension. This is a simplification that is too generous to narrow procedures; in fact, regulators may measure project impacts in natural units (e.g., years of life saved), and the natural units might have a variable rather than constant marginal utility. Adding an incremental year to the life of an eighty-year-old may not have the same impact on overall welfare as adding an incremental year to the life of a twenty-year old.

70. This point is illustrated by the history of the Clean Air Act. Section 112 governs "hazardous air pollutants," mainly certain carcinogens. As initially drafted, it put in place a safety-maximization criterion: the EPA was instructed to list pollutants and then issue standards for pollutants that would "protect the public health" with "an ample margin of safety." But safety maximization would have involved huge economic costs, and so the EPA instead interpreted the original version of section 112 using a feasibility approach. The D.C. Circuit invalidated that approach, and the statute was then explicitly amended to incorporate considerations of feasibility and de minimis risk, rather than simply telling the EPA to maximize safety. See Adler, "Against 'Individual Risk,'" 1150–1152; John P. Dwyer, "The Pathology of Symbolic Legislation," *Ecology Law Quarterly* 17 (1990): 233. Section 109, which applies to certain widespread noncarcinogenic ("criteria") pollutants, still uses safety-focused language. See Whitman v. American Trucking Associations, 531 U.S. 457, 464–471 (2001), which holds that section 109 precludes the EPA from considering costs. In practice, the EPA has resisted issuing standards for criteria pollutants that would truly reduce the risk of harm to zero. See Cary Coglianese and Gary E. Marchant, "Shifting Sands: The Limits of Science in Setting Risk Standards," *University of Pennsylvania Law Review* 152 (2004): 1255.

Another example of a safety-maximization provision is the Delaney Clause, which flatly bars carcinogenic food additives. For a critical discussion, see, e.g.,

Richard A. Merrill, "FDA's Implementation of the Delaney Clause: Repudiation of Congressional Choice or Reasoned Adaptation to Scientific Progress?" *Yale Journal on Regulation* 5 (1998): 1, 74–76. The FDA has evaded the Delaney Clause, at least partly, through creative interpretations, and it was amended in 1996 so as to be inapplicable to carcinogenic pesticides that enter the food chain. See Adler, "Against 'Individual Risk,'" 1158–1159, 1164–1167.

71. For descriptions of health and safety programs, showing the various ways that these programs often depart from the narrowest sort of safety-maximization exemplified by the Delaney Clause (for example, by using de minimis cutoffs) or depart from safety-maximization entirely (by incorporating feasibility requirements or simply moving to straight cost-benefit analysis), see Adler, "'Against Individual Risk,'" 1147–1183; Adler, "Risk, Death, and Harm," 1389– 1423; Sunstein, "Cost-Benefit Default Principles,"1663–1667.

72. Amy Sinden, "In Defense of Absolutes: Combating the Politics of Power in Environmental Law," *Iowa Law Review* 90 (2005): 1405, 1493, quoting Tennessee Valley Authority v. Hill, 437 U.S. 153, 173, 184 (1978).

73. See Sinden, "In Defense of Absolutes," 1491–1510.

74. The Delaney Clause does not contain a de minimis threshold, let alone contemplate procedures that balance the fatalities or health effects resulting from the prohibition of a food additive against the fatalities or diseases caused by the additive. See Public Citizen v. Young, 831 F.2d 1108 (1987). The Supreme Court in the *American Trucking* case made clear that section 109 of the Clean Air Act precludes risk-risk analysis and other procedures that balance the health costs of regulation against the health costs of a pollutant, as well as procedures that consider straight economic costs. See 531 U.S. at 466–468. Section 109 and the old version of section 112 do not explicitly include a de minimis threshold but, plausibly, can be interpreted to contain one. See Natural Resources Defense Council, Inc. v. EPA, 824 F.2d 1146, 1164–1165 (D.C. Circuit 1987) (en banc). The Supreme Court did not address this issue in *American Trucking.*

75. For a detailed discussion of QALYs, see Adler, "QALYs and Policy Evaluation."

76. More precisely, let $f(x)$ represent the distribution of project utility conditional on it having net money benefits, $g(x)$ the distribution conditional on the project not having net money benefits, and p the probability of the project having net money benefits. Then $-p\int_{-\infty}^{0} xf(x)\,dx + (1-p)\int_{0}^{\infty} xg(x)\,dx$ is the loss of CBA relative to a perfect procedure.

77. This model is developed in more detail in Adler, "QALYs and Policy Evaluation."

78. We discussed "primary goods" and "resources" in Chapter 2. Rawls discusses "primary goods" at pp. 90–95 of *A Theory of Justice* (Cambridge, Mass.: Harvard University Press, 1971). Ronald Dworkin presents his resourcism in "What Is Equality? Part 1: Equality of Welfare," *Philosophy and Public Affairs* 10 (1981): 185; and "What Is Equality? Part 2: Equality of Resources," *Philosophy and Public Affairs* 10 (1981): 283.

4. Political Oversight

1. Steve Croley, "Theories of Regulation: Incorporating the Administrative Process," *Columbia Law Review* 98 (1998): 1.
2. For an overview of this research, see David Epstein and Sharyn O'Halloran, *Delegating Powers: A Transaction Cost Politics Approach to Policy Making under Separate Powers* (New York: Cambridge University Press, 1999), 18–29.
3. A critical review by a legal scholar can be found in Jerry L. Mashaw, *Greed, Chaos, and Governance: Using Public Choice to Improve Public Law* (New Haven: Yale University Press, 1997), 118–130.
4. David Epstein and Sharyn O'Halloran, "A Theory of Strategic Oversight: Congress, Lobbyists, and the Bureaucracy," *Journal of Law, Economics, and Organization* 11 (1995): 227, 232–246. An alternative, equally plausible approach would hold that the principal can audit the agent at some cost. See Jeffrey S. Banks and Barry R. Weingast, "The Political Control of Bureaucracies under Asymmetric Information," *American Journal of Political Science* 36 (1992): 509, 512–515. But this would require a more complex model, and does not yield different insights.
5. The president does not always have the legal authority to reject a regulation proposed by an agency. Viscusi notes that the OMB has been unable to block regulations that are based on valuations of statistical lives that are significantly above the accepted range. See W. Kip Viscusi, "Risk Equity," *Journal of Legal Studies* 29 (2000): 843, 854. But the White House can almost always hold up the regulation for a period of time. See W. Kip Viscusi, *Fatal Tradeoffs: Public and Private Responsibilities for Risk* (New York: Oxford University Press, 1992), 265–270 (giving examples drawn mostly from automobile regulations in the 1980s); Thomas O. McGarity, *Reinventing Rationality: The Role of Regulatory Analysis in the Federal Bureaucracy* (New York: Cambridge University Press, 1991), 282–288. And, as we discuss below, the president may have other ways of punishing an agency that proposes an undesired regulation.
6. The value w is uniformly distributed with mean equal to 0. However, the value of w is fixed once the game has begun.
7. Formally, President's utility is $U_P = -(r + w)^2$. Agency's utility is $U_A = -(r + w - A)^2$, where President's ideal point is $P = 0$, and Agency's ideal point is $A > P$. Squaring the expressions ensures that parties do not attach special importance to whether the policy outcome is negative or positive; it also creates risk aversion.
8. For details, see Eric Posner, "Controlling Agencies with Cost-Benefit Analysis: A Positive Political Theory Perspective," *University of Chicago Law Review* 68 (2001): 1137.
9. Technically, a cost-benefit analysis will usually determine only whether the project is an improvement, not whether it is optimal.
10. The description of the complete information equilibrium is taken from Epstein and O'Halloran, "A Theory of Strategic Oversight," 234–236; it was derived originally by Thomas Romer and Howard Rosenthal, "Political Resource Allocation, Controlled Agendas, and the Status Quo," *Public Choice* 33 (1978): 27, 29–35.

11. See also, W. Kip Viscusi, "Risk Equity," 843; and Shi-Ling Hsu, "Fairness versus Efficiency in Environmental Law," *Ecology Law Quarterly* 31 (2004): 303, on equity and fairness.

12. *Comprehensive Regulatory Reform Act of 1995,* S 343, 104th Cong. §623 (1995).

13. *Comprehensive Regulatory Reform Act of 1995,* §624(d).

14. *Regulatory Improvement Act of 1999,* S 746, 106th Cong. §623(d)(2) (1999).

15. *Regulatory Improvement Act of 1999,* §627(d).

16. For models that explore the influence of judicial ideology on political outcomes, see Richard L. Revesz, "Environmental Regulation, Ideology, and the D.C. Circuit," *Virginia Law Review* 83 (1997): 1717; Pablo T. Spiller and Matthew L. Spitzer, "Where Is the Sin in Sincere? Sophisticated Manipulation of Sincere Judicial Voters (with Applications to Other Voting Environments)," *Journal of Law, Economics, and Organization* 11 (1995): 32, 36–51. See also Pablo T. Spiller and Emerson H. Tiller, "Decision Costs and the Strategic Design of Administrative Process and Judicial Review," *Journal of Legal Studies* 26 (1997): 348–359.

17. See Jason Scott Johnston, "A Game Theoretic Analysis of Alternative Institutions for Regulatory Cost-Benefit Analysis," *University of Pennsylvania Law Review* 150 (2002): 1343.

18. See Matthew D. Adler and Eric A. Posner, "Implementing Cost-Benefit Analysis When Preferences Are Distorted," *Journal of Legal Studies* 29 (2000): 1116–1120.

19. See, for example, Matt Spitzer and Eric Talley, "Judicial Auditing," *Journal of Legal Studies* 29 (2000): 679.

20. The third and fourth implications are subject to a complication, which is whether the court should consider the existing Congress or the original coalition.

21. 947 F2d 1201 (5th Cir 1991).

22. 947 F2d at 1229–1230.

23. See, for example, *Federal Insecticide, Fungicide, and Rodenticide Act,* 7 USC §136(bb) (2005); *Toxic Substances Control Act,* 15 USC §2605(c); *Unfunded Mandates Reform Act,* 2 USC §§1532, 1571 (2005).

24. This is not at all uncommon. One recent example, chosen at random, is Congress's reversal of the Federal Communications Commission's low-power FM radio rules. For a discussion, see Stuart Benjamin, Douglas Lichtman, and Howard Shelanski, *Telecommunications Law and Policy* (Durham, N.C.: Carolina Academic Press, 2001), 325–332. However, legislative rejection is not exactly the same as presidential rejection (in the model). It requires collective action, rather than unilateral action, of course, and a supermajority, unless the president cooperates. And if it does not occur before the final rule is issued, Congress must decide whether to make the override prospective or retroactive, and in the latter case, various judicial constraints may come into play.

25. Congress will need a two-thirds majority if, as seems likely, the president will not go along with reversal of the agency. See U.S. Constitution, art. 1, sec. 7, cl. 2.

26. Much work focuses on congressional committees, treating them as the relevant principals in the relationship with agencies. In Epstein and O'Halloran's recent book, for example, the committee has partial information about w, and reports a bill to the floor. The floor, which has no information about w, then decides on the

content of the bill and whether to delegate to an agency. In the latter case, the president sets the agency's ideal point, and then the agency observes w and sets policy. See Epstein and O'Halloran, *Delegating Powers*, 182–187.

27. See Elena Kagan, "Presidential Administration," *Harvard Law Review* 114 (2001): 2245.

28. In reality the conflict between president and Congress has taken two forms: sporadic efforts by Congress to reduce the power of the Office of Information and Regulatory Affairs, and new substantive legislation that imposed greater constraints directly on agencies, so that they could not comply with cost-benefit analyses without violating the law. See Terry M. Moe and Scott A. Wilson, "Presidents and the Politics of Structure," *Law and Contemporary Problems* 57 (spring 1994): 1, 37–40.

29. See, for example, Johnston, "A Game Theoretic Analysis," 1343; Amy Sinden, "In Defense of Absolutes: Combating the Politics of Power in Environmental Law," *Iowa Law Review* 90 (2005): 1405.

30. The OMB already requires agencies to subject certain scientific information to peer review. See Office of Management and Budget, "Final Information Quality Bulletin for Peer Review," *Federal Register* 70 (January 14, 2005): 2664. It does not require peer review of cost-benefit analyses, however.

31. The data are taken from Scott Farrow, "Improving Regulatory Performance: Does Executive Office Oversight Matter?" unpublished manuscript, July 26, 2000.

32. A $6 million environmental regulation that saves one statistical life and also enhances the recreational value of a wilderness by $2 million is a welfare-maximizing regulation even though the cost per life saved is $6 million. A more accurate accounting would accordingly include benefits other than reduced mortality. But it seems unlikely that the post-1981 regulations have a larger nonmortality component than the pre-1981 regulations.

33. See W. Kip Viscusi, "The Value of Risks to Life and Health," *Journal of Economic Literature* 31 (1993): 1912, 1930. Viscusi used 1990 dollars, but the figures are rough anyway.

34. See Farrow, "Improving Regulatory Performance," table 4; Robert W. Hahn, "Regulatory Reform: Assessing the Government's Numbers," working paper, 99-6 AEI-Brookings Joint Center for Regulatory Studies (July 1999), 28 table 7. Both authors examined health and safety regulations issued before and after 1981, and found no statistically significant relationship between their cost-effectiveness and a dummy variable representing whether the regulation was issued before or after 1981. (Although the authors name this dummy variable OIRA because their studies focus on that institution, one cannot separate out the effect of OIRA and the cost-benefit executive order.)

35. Hahn's review of all 168 final and proposed rules issued from 1981 through mid-1996 found that only 26 percent of the rules were accompanied by an estimate of monetized benefits (Hahn, "Regulatory Reform," 6 table 1) and that 23 percent of the rules were accompanied by a statement that the benefits exceed the costs

(41 table 9). Hahn's own calculations indicate that about 43 percent of the rules would pass a cost-benefit test, depending on various assumptions. See 43 table 10. Hahn and his coauthors also reviewed forty-eight regulatory impact assessments (which contain the cost-benefit analysis) published from 1996 to 1999, and found that agencies presented monetized costs and benefits for only 19 percent of the rules. See Robert W. Hahn et al., "Assessing Regulatory Impact Analyses: The Failure of Agencies to Comply with Executive Order 12,866," *Harvard Journal of Law and Public Policy* 23 (2000): 859, 871. See also Office of Information and Regulatory Affairs, Office of Management and Budget, *Report to Congress on the Costs and Benefits of Federal Regulations* (Washington, D.C.: September 30, 1997), chap. 3 (reporting that of twenty-one economically significant rules issued in the past year, agencies supplied monetized costs in eight cases and monetized benefits in sixteen cases); W. Norton Grubb, Dale Whittington, and Michael Humphries, "The Ambiguities of Benefit-Cost Analysis: An Evaluation of Regulatory Impact Analysis under Executive Order 12,291," in V. Kerry Smith, ed., *Environmental Policy under Reagan's Executive Order: The Role of Benefit-Cost Analysis* (Chapel Hill: University of North Carolina Press, 1984), 154 (finding that individuals in the Department of Agriculture performed "perfunctory" cost-benefit analyses using "incomprehensible" numbers both before and after the Reagan executive order); Winston Harrington, Richard D. Morgenstern, and Peter Nelson, "On the Accuracy of Regulatory Cost Estimates," Resources for the Future discussion paper 99–18, January 1999, at www.rff.org, accessed September 27, 2001 (finding in a study of twenty-five regulations that agencies tend to overestimate the costs of complying with regulations); Robert W. Hahn, "Regulatory Reform: What Do the Government's Numbers Tell Us?" in Robert W. Hahn, ed., *Risks, Costs and Lives Saved* (New York: Oxford University Press, 1996) 208, 218 (finding that thirty-eight of eighty-three rules proposed or issued from 1990 to 1995 passed a cost-benefit test); Arthur Fraas, "The Role of Economic Analysis in Shaping Environmental Policy," *Law and Contemporary Problems* 54 (1991): 114, 124 (pointing out errors in regulatory impact analyses for lead phasedown and asbestos regulations); Maureen L. Cropper et al., "The Determinants of Pesticide Regulation: A Statistical Analysis of EPA Decision Making," in Roger D. Congleton, ed., *The Political Economy of Environmental Protection: Analysis and Evidence* (Ann Arbor: University of Michigan Press, 1996), 140 (finding that EPA's pesticide regulations implicitly value statistical lives in a range between $60,000 and $35 million); Adler and Posner, "Implementing Cost-Benefit Analysis," 1146 (finding that agencies use a wide range of valuations of life); Edward R. Morrison, "Judicial Review of Discount Rates Used in Regulatory Cost-Benefit Analysis," *University of Chicago Law Review* 65 (1998): 1333, 1364–1369 (finding that agencies use a wide range of discount rates). This literature is large, and this is just a sample.

36. Hahn et al., "Assessing Regulatory Impact Analyses," 861.
37. Frank Ackerman and Lisa Heinzerling, *Priceless: On Knowing the Price of Everything and the Value of Nothing* (New York: New Press, 2004). For a contrasting view on

the arsenic regulation, see Cass R. Sunstein, "The Arithmetic of Arsenic," *Georgetown Law Journal* 90 (2002): 2255.

38. David M. Driesen, "Is Cost-Benefit Analysis Neutral?" unpublished manuscript, 2005.

39. See also Richard W. Parker, "Grading the Government," *University of Chicago Law Review* 70 (2003): 1345.

40. Kagan, "Presidential Administration," 2245.

41. See Harold Seidman and Robert Gilmour, *Politics, Position, and Power: From the Positive to the Regulatory State*, 4th ed. (New York: Oxford University Press, 1986), 130–131.

5. Distorted Preferences

1. Robert Goodin, "Laundering Preferences," in Jon Elster and Aanund Hylland, eds., *Foundations of Social Choice Theory* (New York: Cambridge University Press, 1986).

2. See Department of the Interior, Natural Resource Damage Assessments, 51 Fed. Reg. 27,674 (August 1, 1986).

3. See Environmental Protection Agency, Approval and Promulgation of Implementation Plans: Revision of the Visibility FIP for Arizona, 56 Fed. Reg. 5173 (February 8, 1991).

4. Environmental Protection Agency, Effluent Limitations Guidelines, Pretreatment Standards, and New Source Performance Standards for the Transportation Equipment Cleaning Point Source Category, 63 Fed. Reg. 34,686, 34,724 (June 25, 1998).

5. See also Environmental Protection Agency, Lead Fishing Sinkers: Response to Citizens' Petition and Proposed Ban, 59 Fed. Reg. 11,122, 11,135 (March 9, 1994) (endorsing use of existence values). The use of the methodology has been approved by the D.C. Circuit; see Ohio v. U.S. Dep't Interior, 880 F.2d 432, 474–81 (D.C. Cir. 1989).

6. See Leland B. Deck, "Visibility at the Grand Canyon and the Navajo Generating Station," in Richard D. Morgenstern, ed., *Economic Analyses at EPA: Assessing Regulatory Impact* (Washington, D.C.: Resources for the Future, 1997), 267.

7. Department of Agriculture, Nutrition Labeling of Meat and Poultry Products, 56 Fed. Reg. 60,302 (November 27, 1991).

8. It has been suggested to us that OSHA and advocates of workplace regulation see workplace regulation as a form of in-kind transfer to workers. If so, there is no point in evaluating workplace regulation from the perspective of CBA; instead, the question is whether it is a cost-effective form of transfer. See Eric A. Posner, "Transfer Regulations and Cost-Effectiveness Analysis," *Duke Law Journal* 53 (2003): 1067.

9. See Department of Labor, Occupational Exposure to Ethylene Dibromide, 48 Fed. Reg. 45,956 (October 7, 1983).

10. See, for example, Department of Labor, Occupational Exposure to Bloodborne Pathogens, 56 Fed. Reg. 64,004, 64,087 (December 6, 1991) (arguing that

workers do not know about many risks and are unable to analyze them correctly).

11. Amartya Sen, *On Ethics and Economics* (New York: Blackwell, 1987), 45.

12. Cass R. Sunstein, *Free Markets and Social Justice* (New York: Oxford University Press, 1997), 252–253, 256–258; Jon Elster, *Sour Grapes: Studies in the Subversion of Rationality* (New York: Cambridge University Press, 1983).

13. Department of Transportation, Anti-Drug Program for Personnel Engaged in Specified Aviation Activities, 53 Fed. Reg. 47,024 (November 21, 1988).

14. See Department of Transportation, Federal Motor Carrier Safety Regulations; Controlled Substances and Alcohol Use and Testing; Commercial Driver's License Standards, Requirements and Penalties; Hours of Service of Drivers, 57 Fed. Reg. 59,567 (December 15, 1992).

15. Food and Drug Administration, Regulations Restricting the Sale and Distribution of Cigarettes and Smokeless Tobacco to Protect Children and Adolescents, 61 Fed. Reg. 44,396, 44,593 (Aug. 28, 1996).

16. Department of Transportation, Security of Checked Baggage on Flights within the United States, 64 Fed. Reg. 19,220 (April 19, 1999).

17. See U.S. General Accounting Office, *Regulatory Reform: Agencies Could Improve Development, Documentation, and Clarity of Regulatory Analysis*, GAO/RCED 98-142, (May 26, 1998, Washington, D.C.) at 26–27. More precisely, they use a range, but they do not make their choice within the range depend on the wealth of the victims.

18. See Department of Health and Human Services, Regulatory Impact Analysis of the Proposed Rules to Amend the Food Labeling Regulations, 56 Fed. Reg. 60,856, 60,871 (November 27, 1991) ("dying of a heart attack at age 80 is posited to be of less societal concern than dying in a car accident at age 35"). Yet the eighty-year-old might have a higher CV than the thirty-five-year-old.

19. Office of Management and Budget, Draft Report to Congress on the Costs and Benefits of Federal Regulations, 63 Fed. Reg. 44,034, 44,048 (August 17, 1998); see also at 44,052–44,053, on the FDA and other agencies.

20. OMB, Draft Report, at 44,048.

21. Louis P. True, Jr., "Agricultural Pesticides and Worker Protection," in Morgenstern, *Economic Analyses at EPA*. Environmental Protection Agency, Lead: Identification of Dangerous Levels of Lead, 63 Fed. Reg. 30,302, 30,305 (June 3, 1998); Department of Housing and Urban Development, Office of Lead-Based Paint Abatement and Poisoning Prevention; Requirements for Notification, Evaluation and Reduction of Lead-Based Paint Hazards in Federally Owned Residential Property and Housing Receiving Federal Assistance, 61 Fed. Reg. 29,170, 29,202 (June 7, 1996).

22. See, for example, Department of Labor, Occupational Exposure to Bloodborne Pathogens, 64,082.

23. Executive Order 12,866, Regulatory Planning and Review, 58 Fed. Reg. 51, 735 (September 30, 1993) (emphasis added). Guidelines issued by the OMB say: "Your regulatory analysis should provide a separate description of distributional

effects (i.e., how both benefits and costs are distributed among sub-populations of particular concern), so that decision makers can properly consider them along with the effects on economic efficiency." Office of Management and Budget, Circular A-4, September 17, 2003 p. 14, available at www.whitehouse.gov/omb. The environmental justice order is Executive Order 12,898, Federal Actions to Address Environmental in Minority Populations and Low-Income Populations, 56 Fed. Reg. 7629 (February 11, 1994).

24. See the essays in Ian J. Bateman and Kenneth G. Willis, eds., *Valuing Environmental Preferences: Theory and Practice of Contingent Valuation in the US, EU, and Developing Countries* (New York: Oxford University Press, 1999); Robert Cameron Mitchell and Richard T. Carson, eds., *Using Surveys to Value Public Goods: The Contingent Valuation Method* (Washington, D.C.: Resources for the Future, 1989).

25. See, for example, Charles R. Plott, "Contingent Valuation: A View of the Conference and Associated Research," in Jerry A. Hausman, ed., *Contingent Valuation: A Critical Assessment* (New York: North Holland, 1993) 470–473; Donald H. Rosenthal and Robert H. Nelson, "Why Existence Values Should *Not* Be Used in Cost-Benefit Analysis," *Journal of Policy Analysis and Management* 11 (1992): 116. But compare Gardner M. Brown, Jr., "Economics of Natural Resource Damage Assessment: A Critique," in Raymond J. Kopp and V. Kerry Smith, eds., *Valuing Natural Assets: The Economics of Natural Resource Damage Assessment* (Washington, D.C.: Resources for the Future, 1993).

26. Compare David Sobel, "Well-Being as the Object of Moral Consideration," *Economics and Philosophy* 14 (1998): 249, which provides a critical overview of philosophical attempts to distinguish between disinterested and welfare-relevant preferences.

27. In Chapter 2 we distinguished two views about objective goods. One view is that objective goods would be desired by people who are fully informed; the other view is that even people who are fully informed may fail to choose objective goods. As the first view is close to identical to the lack of information problem, which we discussed above, for the purposes of this section we will assume that the second view is correct.

28. Harry G. Frankfurt, "Freedom of the Will and the Concept of a Person," *Journal of Philosophy* 68 (1971): 5.

29. For arguments to the effect that objective values are a component of welfare, see, for example, John Finnis, *Natural Law and Natural Rights* (New York: Oxford University Press, 1980); Martha C. Nussbaum, "Nature, Function, and Capability: Aristotle on Political Distribution," in Julia Annas and Robert Grimm, eds., *Oxford Studies in Ancient Philosophy,* supp. vol. (New York: Oxford University Press, 1988), 145; George Sher, *Beyond Neutrality: Perfectionism and Politics* (New York: Cambridge University Press, 1997).

30. Similar phenomena are widespread and much discussed—for example, the possibility that safety regulations cause consumers to take less care. See, for example, W. Kip Viscusi, *Fatal Tradeoffs: Public and Private Responsibilities for Risk* (New York: Oxford University Press, 1992), 223–227.

31. See Louis Kaplow and Steven Shavell, "Why the Legal System Is Less Efficient Than the Income Tax in Redistributing Income," *Journal of Legal Studies* 23 (1994): 667. Note, however, that an even better project than that might be constructing the park in the poor neighborhood and transferring some amount of money from rich to poor.

32. Cass Sunstein, "Cognition and Cost-Benefit Analysis," *Journal of Legal Studies* 29 (2000): 1059.

6. Objections

1. On the distinction between consequentialist and deontological moral views, with particular reference to the feature of deontological views emphasized here—the existence of deontological prohibitions or "constraints," which we are calling "rights"—see Shelly Kagan, *Normative Ethics* (Boulder, Colo: Westview Press, 1998), 70–78; Shelly Kagan, *The Limits of Morality* (Oxford: Oxford University Press, 1989), 1–182; Robert Nozick, *Anarchy, State, and Utopia* (New York: Basic Books, 1974), 26–53; Thomas Nagel, "Autonomy and Deontology," in Samuel Scheffler, ed., *Consequentialism and Its Critics* (Oxford: Oxford University Press, 1988), 142, 156–172; and Samuel Scheffler, *The Rejection of Consequentialism,* rev. ed. (Oxford: Oxford University Press, 1994), 80–114.

2. See Kagan, *The Limits of Morality,* 1–46.

3. Jeffrey Brand-Ballard, "Contractualism and Deontic Restrictions," *Ethics* 114 (2004): 269, 270–271, cites much of the recent philosophical work that defends deontological constraints, including work by Thomas Nagel, Frances Kamm, and others. One name that should be added to Brand-Ballard's list is Judith Thomson. See, e.g., Judith Jarvis Thomson, *The Realm of Rights* (Cambridge, Mass.: Harvard University Press, 1990).

4. See, e.g., Nagel, "Autonomy and Deontology," 157; Kagan, *Normative Ethics,* 70–152.

5. See Kagan, *Normative Ethics,* 78–84.

6. See, e.g., Steven Kelman, "Cost-Benefit Analysis: An Ethical Critique," *Regulation,* January/February 1981, 33, 33–36; Lester B. Lave, "Benefit-Cost Analysis: Do the Benefits Exceed the Costs?" in Robert Hahn, ed., *Risks, Costs, and Lives Saved: Getting Better Results from Regulation* (Oxford: Oxford University Press, 1996), 104, 112–113.

7. We discussed prioritarianism at some length in Chapter 2. On the debate between prioritarians and those who think that an equality principle might require Pareto-inferior moves, see Matthew Clayton and Andrew Williams, eds., *The Ideal of Equality* (Basingstoke, England: Palgrave, 2000), and the articles in *Economics and Philosophy* 19: 1–134 (2003).

8. We also discussed resourcism, with citations, in Chapter 2. Equal opportunity for welfare is defended in Richard J. Arneson, "Equality and Equal Opportunity for Welfare," *Philosophical Studies* 56 (1989): 77.

9. For complaints that CBA is insensitive to distribution, see, e.g., Frank Ackerman

and Lisa Heinzerling, *Priceless: On Knowing the Price of Everything and the Value of Nothing* (New York: New Press, 2004), 149–151; Thomas O. McGarity, "A Cost-Benefit State," *Administrative Law Review* 50 (1998): 7, 72–73; and Amy Sinden, "In Defense of Absolutes: Combating the Politics of Power in Environmental Law," *Iowa Law Review* 90 (2005): 1405, 1453.

10. See, e.g., L. W. Sumner, *Welfare, Happiness, and Ethics* (Oxford: Oxford University Press, 1996), 20–25, 200–217.

11. Sumner, *Welfare, Happiness, and Ethics*, 50, discusses Moore's view.

12. See Robin Attfield, *The Ethics of Environmental Concern* (Oxford: Blackwell, 1983); Holmes Rolston III, *Environmental Ethics: Duties to and Values in the Natural World* (Philadelphia: Temple University Press, 1988); Paul W. Taylor, *Respect for Nature* (Princeton: Princeton University Press, 1986).

13. See, e.g., Elizabeth Anderson, *Value in Ethics and Economics* (Cambridge, Mass.: Harvard University Press, 1993), 203–210; Mark Sagoff, *The Economy of the Earth: Philosophy, Law, and the Environment* (Cambridge: Cambridge University Press, 1988), 153–238; Cass Sunstein, "Incommensurability and Valuation in Law," *Michigan Law Review* 92 (1994): 779, 839–840.

14. Chapter 2 ruled out "pure" egalitarian, rights-centric, or environmental views that have no place for overall welfare. Chapter 2 did not criticize pluralistic moral views recognizing *both* egalitarian, deontological, or non-welfare-based factors *and* overall welfare as morally relevant considerations. By contrast with the "pure" views, these pluralistic views fall under the rubric of weak welfarism.

15. See, e.g., Louis Kaplow and Steven Shavell, "Why the Legal System Is Less Efficient Than the Income Tax in Redistributing Income," *Journal of Legal Studies* 23 (1994): 667; Aanund Hylland and Richard Zeckhauser, "Distributional Objectives Should Affect Taxes but Not Program Choice or Design," *Scandinavian Journal of Economics* 81 (1979): 264. For a different view, see Chris William Sanchirico, "Deconstructing the New Efficiency Rationale," *Cornell Law Review* 86 (2001): 1003.

16. This possibility is discussed in Matthew D. Adler, "Beyond Efficiency and Procedure: A Welfarist Theory of Regulation," *Florida State University Law Review* 28 (2000): 314–315.

17. Ackerman and Heinzerling, *Priceless*, 39–40.

18. See, e.g., Anderson, *Value in Ethics and Economics*, 190–216; Lave, "Benefit-Cost Analysis: Do the Benefits Exceed the Costs?" 113–114; Kelman, "Cost-Benefit Analysis: An Ethical Critique," 38–40; Richard H. Pildes and Cass R. Sunstein, "Reinventing the Regulatory State," *University of Chicago Law Review* 62 (1995): 1, 64–72; Margaret Jane Radin, *Contested Commodities: The Trouble with Trade in Sex, Children, Body Parts, and Other Things* (Cambridge, Mass.: Harvard University Press, 1996), 115–122; Sinden, "In Defense of Absolutes," 1423–1445; Sunstein, "Incommensurability and Valuation in Law," 786–787, 840–843; Laurence Tribe, "Policy Science: Analysis or Ideology," *Philosophy and Public Affairs* 2 (1972): 66, 84–94. Martha Nussbaum criticizes CBA for obscuring the "tragic" nature of

certain choices. Martha C. Nussbaum, "The Costs of Tragedy: Some Moral Limits of Cost-Benefit Analysis," in Matthew D. Adler and Eric A. Posner, eds., *Cost-Benefit Analysis: Legal, Economic, and Philosophical Perspectives* (Chicago: University of Chicago Press, 2001), 169. This criticism seems to be related to the issue of value pluralism, which fuels much of the incommensurability literature; however, Nussbaum declines to style herself an incommensurabilist. See 194–195.

19. See Donald H. Regan, "Authority and Value: Reflection on Raz's *Morality of Freedom*," *Southern California Law Review* 62 (1989): 995, 1056–1074.

20. There is in fact a substantial economic literature on lexicographic preferences. For a good summary, with citations, see Clive L. Spash and Nick Hanley, "Preferences, Information and Biodiversity Preservation," *Ecological Economics* 12 (1995): 191.

21. See, e.g., Jonathan Baron, "Biases in the Quantitative Measurement of Values for Public Decisions," *Psychological Bulletin* 122 (1997): 72.

22. Ackerman and Heinzerling, *Priceless*, 9. For a similar denial of the lexical ordering of health and environmental goods over money, see Sagoff, *The Economy of the Earth*, 80. For a qualified defense of lexical ordering, see Tribe, "Policy Science," 90–91.

23. The analysis in this paragraph is fleshed out in the section on the valuation of life, at the end of this chapter. The existing literature on the valuation of life, cited there, documents the now widespread practice by empirical economists of eliciting, or using market evidence to ascertain, WTP/WTA for small risks of death.

24. See, e.g., Robin Boadway and Neil Bruce, *Welfare Economics* (Oxford: Blackwell, 1984), 137–138.

25. There is a large philosophical literature on incommensurability, much of which focuses on incomparability or closely related phenomena ("rough equality," "parity"). See Ruth Chang, "The Possibility of Parity," *Ethics* 112 (2002): 659; Ruth Chang, ed., *Incommensurability, Incomparability, and Practical Reason* (Cambridge, Mass.: Harvard University Press, 1997); Ruth Chang, *Making Comparisons Count* (New York: Routledge, 2002); James Griffin, *Well-Being: Its Meaning, Measurement, and Moral Importance* (Oxford: Oxford University Press, 1986), 75–92; S. L. Hurley, *Natural Reasons* (New York: Oxford University Press, 1989), 254–270; John Kekes, *The Morality of Pluralism* (Princeton: Princeton University Press 1993) 53–75; Isaac Levi, *Hard Choices: Decision Making under Unresolved Conflict* (New York: Cambridge University Press, 1986); Joseph Raz, *The Morality of Freedom* (Oxford: Oxford University Press, 1986), 321–366; Henry Richardson, *Practical Reasoning about Final Ends* (Cambridge: Cambridge University Press, 1997), 89–118; Michael Stocker, *Plural and Conflicting Values* (Oxford: Oxford University Press, 1990), 211–240; David Wiggins, *Needs, Values, Truth* (Oxford: Blackwell, 1987), 239–262. Sen has argued for the possibility of incomparability in many places. See, e.g., Amartya Sen, *Inequality Reexamined* (Cambridge, Mass.: Harvard University Press, 1992), 46–49; Amartya Sen, "Interpersonal Aggregation and Partial Comparability," in *Choice, Welfare and Measurement* (Cambridge, Mass.: Harvard University Press, 1982), 203; Amartya Sen, "The

Discipline of Cost-Benefit Analysis," in Adler and Posner, *Cost-Benefit Analysis,* 103–105.

Finally, legal scholars have begun to focus on the problem of incomparability. See the articles in the symposium "Law and Incommensurability," *University of Pennsylvania Law Review* 146 (1998): 1169, particularly those by Kornhauser, Craswell, and Katz, as well as Adler and Posner.

26. See Raz, *The Morality of Freedom,* 328. The premises are that (3) is better than (2), that (2) is neither better nor worse than (1), and that (3) is neither better nor worse than (1). If (2) were precisely as good as (1), then from the first premise it would follow that (3) is better than (1), which contradicts the third premise. Similar reasoning shows that (3) cannot be precisely as good as (1), given the premises.

27. See Matthew Adler, "Incommensurability and Cost-Benefit Analysis," *University of Pennsylvania Law Review* 146 (1998): 137, 1401–1408.

28. One important reason has to do with nonconvergence in extended preferences. It is plausible, as we argued in Chapter 2, that overall welfare is determined by the extended self-interested preferences of idealized observers, contemplating each outcome as an equiprobability lottery over the life-histories that occur in that outcome. But even if each observer's extended self-interested preferences define a complete ordering over outcomes, the different observers' preferences need not fully converge; and this would lead to some incompleteness in the overall-welfare ranking of outcomes.

29. See Maurice Salles, "Fuzzy Utility," in Salvador Barberà et al., eds., *Handbook of Utility Theory,* vol. 1, *Principles* (Dordrecht: Kluwer, 1998), 321, 322.

30. Ackerman and Heinzerling, *Priceless,* 40. This recapitulates the longstanding complaint that CBA "dwarfs soft variables." See, e.g., Tribe, "Policy Science," 97; Lave, "Benefit-Cost Analysis: Do the Benefits Exceed the Costs?" 114; McGarity, "A Cost-Benefit State," 58–59.

31. On contingent valuation surveys, see A. Myrick Freeman III, *The Measurement of Environmental and Resource Values: Theory and Methods,* 2nd ed. (Washington, D.C.: Resources for the Future, 2003), 161–187; Ian J. Bateman et al., *Economic Valuation with Stated Preference Techniques: A Manual* (Cheltenham: Edward Elgar, 2002). On revealed preference techniques for measuring valuations of nonmarket goods, see Freeman, *The Measurement of Environmental and Resource Values,* 95–136, 353–452; Nancy E. Bockstael, "Travel Cost Models," in Daniel W. Bromely, ed., *Handbook of Environmental Economics* (Oxford: Blackwell, 1995), 655–671; A. Myrick Freeman III, "Hedonic Pricing Methods," in Bromely, *Handbook of Environmental Economics,* 672–686.

32. See, e.g., M. Granger Morgan and Max Henrion, *Uncertainty: A Guide to Dealing with Uncertainty in Quantitative Risk and Policy Analysis* (Cambridge: Cambridge University Press, 1990).

33. See, e.g., Kelman, "Cost-Benefit Analysis: An Ethical Critique," 38–39; Sunstein, "Incommensurability and Valuation in Law," 805; Radin, *Contested Commodities,* 115–122.

34. See Raz, *The Morality of Freedom*, 345–356. For a critical analysis of Raz's arguments, see Regan, "Authority and Value," 1067–1075; Chang, *Making Comparisons Count*, 95–119. The argument for "constitutive incommensurability" is related to the claim that utilitarian or consequentialist deliberation imperils friendships and other relationships. The substantial philosophical literature discussing that claim is cited in Adler, "Incommensurability and Cost-Benefit Analysis," nn. 60, 116.

35. See Matthew D. Adler, "Fear Assessment: Cost-Benefit Analysis and the Pricing of Fear and Anxiety," *Chicago-Kent Law Review* 79 (2004): 977, which argues at length that fear and anxiety, a different sort of negative mental state, should (at least sometimes) be counted as a cost for CBA purposes.

36. Lester Lave puts the point vividly. "In theory, there are circumstances under which I would have sold the sexual services of my adolescent daughter and son, but I do not regard thinking through those circumstances as uplifting, calming, or enlightening. Few if any of us will ever face those circumstances; I see no value in torturing myself to sketch the offer curve." Lave, "Benefit-Cost Analysis: Do the Benefits Exceed the Costs?" 113. We have no doubt that many people (including us) prefer not to sketch this sort of offer curve, and it seems very plausible that this preference survives idealization.

37. This empirical literature is reviewed in John K. Horowitz and Kenneth E. McConnell, "A Review of WTA/WTP Studies," *Journal of Environmental Economics and Management* 44 (2002): 426.

38. The critics of CBA standardly rely on the fact of WTP/WTA disparities. See, e.g., Driesen, "The Societal Cost of Environmental Regulation," 589–592; Kelman, "Cost-Benefit Analysis: An Ethical Critique," 37–38; Shapiro and Glicksman, *Risk Regulation at Risk*, 97–98; Duncan Kennedy, "Cost-Benefit Analysis of Entitlement Problems: A Critique," *Stanford Law Review* 33 (1981): 387, 401–421; Sinden, "In Defense of Absolutes," 1425–1427; McGarity, "A Cost-Benefit State," 67–69. Another line of argument, less critical, is that WTP/WTA disparities argue for a change in the current practice of CBA. See, e.g., Jack L. Knetsch, "Environmental Policy Implications of Disparities between Willingness to Pay and Compensation Demanded Measures of Values," *Journal of Environmental Economics and Management* 18 (1990): 227, 230.

39. The theoretical literature on the WTP/WTA disparity, like the empirical literature, is large. Helpful overviews include: W. Michael Hanemann, "The Economic Theory of WTP and WTA," in Ian J. Bateman and Kenneth G. Willis, eds., *Valuing Environmental Preferences: Theory and Practice of the Contingent Valuation Method in the US, EU, and Developing Countries* (Oxford: Oxford University Press, 1999), 42; Robert Sugden, "Alternatives to the Neo-Classical Theory of Choice," in Bateman and Willis, *Valuing Environmental Preferences*, 152; Jonathan Baron, "Biases in the Quantitative Measurement of Values for Public Decisions"; Freeman, *The Measurement of Environmental and Resource Values*, 43–94; Bateman et al., *Economic Valuation with Stated Preference Techniques*, 385–391.

40. On CVs and EVs, see, e.g., Freeman, *The Measurement of Environmental and Resource Values,* 49–63; Boadway and Bruce, *Welfare Economics,* 195–206.

41. More precisely, WTP and WTA are always positive; CVs and EVs can be positive or negative. The sum-of-CVs decision rule says to pick the project if the sum of CVs is positive. In other words, CVs for project winners are positive, and CVs for project losers are negative. A project winner's CV is, therefore, his WTP for the project, while the project loser's CV is the negative of his WTA for the project. By contrast, the sum-of-EVs decision rule says to pick the project if the sum of EVs is negative. So EVs for project winners are negative, and EVs for project losers are positive. A project winner's EV is, therefore, the negative of his WTA for the status quo, while a project loser's EV is his WTP for the status quo.

42. What about cases where overall welfare fails to produce a determinate ranking of policy options? In some of these cases, CBA might "incorrectly" produce a determinate ranking, but that "error" is not practically significant, since in such cases the official is free (as a matter of overall welfare) to choose any one of the options. None is better than any other. In other cases, CBA itself will end up failing to produce a ranking. That result, too, is not a deficit of CBA that should lead agency overseers to require a different procedure. Rather, CBA's indeterminacy here will prompt the decision-making official to employ some supplemental technique for picking one of the options, any one of which is permissible as a matter of overall welfare.

43. The classic articles here are Robert Willig, "Consumer's Surplus without Apology," *American Economic Review* 66 (1976): 589; and Alan Randall and John R. Stoll, "Consumer's Surplus in Commodity Space," *American Economic Review* 70 (1980): 449. W. Michael Hanemann challenges the claim that WTP and WTA should not normally differ substantially in "Willingness to Pay and Willingness to Accept: How Much Can They Differ?" *American Economic Review* 81 (1991): 635. The literature on how much WTP and WTA can diverge given well-behaved preferences is reviewed in Freeman, *The Measurement of Environmental and Resource Values,* 63–87; and Sugden, "Alternatives to the Neo-Classical Theory of Choice," 155–159.

44. Sugden, "Alternatives to the Neo-Classical Theory of Choice," 159.

45. See, e.g., Sugden, "Alternatives to the Neo-Classical Theory of Choice," 160–163; Bateman et al., *Economic Valuation with Stated Preference Techniques,* 386–387.

46. See, e.g., Baron, "Biases in the Quantitative Measurement of Values for Public Decisions"; Bateman et al., *Economic Valuation with Stated Preference Techniques,* 387.

47. Amos Tversky and Daniel Kahneman, "Loss Aversion in Riskless Choice: A Reference-Dependent Model," *Quarterly Journal of Economics* 106 (1991): 1039. The theory is reviewed in Sugden, "Alternatives to the Neo-Classical Theory of Choice," 163–166; Bateman et al., *Economic Valuation with Stated Preference Techniques,* 389–391; and Hanemann, "The Economic Theory of WTP and WTA," 73–78.

48. See Sugden, "Alternatives to the Neo-Classical Theory of Choice," 160–163.
49. Don L. Coursey et al., "The Disparity Between Willingness to Accept and Willingness to Pay Measures of Value," *Quarterly Journal of Economics* 102 (1987): 679, employed repeated elicitation of WTP or WTA valuations and a Vickrey auction format to reduce the WTP/WTA disparity. For a review of the evidence about the generalizability of this result, and more generally about the effect of experimental design on WTP/WTA differences, see Sugden, "Alternatives to the Neo-Classical Theory of Choice," 171–175; Horowitz and McConnell, "A Review of WTA/WTA Studies," 437–442.
50. See, e.g., Knetsch, "Environmental Policy Implications"; Freeman, *The Measurement of Environmental and Resource Values*, 60–61, 90–91.
51. Freeman, *The Measurement of Environmental and Resource Values*, 91.
52. See, e.g., Kagan, *Normative Ethics*, 94–105.
53. For legal scholarship on CBA and discounting, which in turn cites the economic and philosophical literatures, see Ackerman and Heinzerling, *Priceless*, 179–205; John J. Donohue, "Why We Should Discount the Views of Those Who Discount Discounting," *Yale Law Journal* 108 (1999): 1901; Daniel A. Farber, "From Here to Eternity: Environmental Law and Future Generations," *University of Illinois Law Review* 2003: 289; Lisa Heinzerling, "Discounting Our Future," *Land and Water Review* 34 (1999): 39; Edward Morrison, comment, "Judicial Review of Discount Rates used in Regulatory Cost-Benefit Analysis," *University of Chicago Law Review* 65 (1998): 1333; Richard L. Revesz, "Environmental Regulation, Cost-Benefit Analysis, and the Discounting of Human Lives," *Columbia Law Review* 99 (1999): 941; Dexter Samida and David A. Weisbach, "Paretian Intergenerational Discounting," University of Chicago Law and Economics, Olin working paper no. 255, August 2005, at www.ssrn.com; Cass Sunstein and Arden Rowell, "On Discounting Regulatory Benefits: Risk, Money, and Intergenerational Equity," AEI-Brookings Joint Center for Regulatory Studies, working paper no. 05-08, May 2005, at www.aei-brookings.org.
54. See George Loewenstein et al., eds., *Time and Decision: Economic and Psychological Perspectives on Intertemporal Choice* (New York: Russell Sage Foundation, 2003).
55. Revesz, "Environmental Regulation," 983.
56. See, e.g., David O. Brink, "Prudence and Authenticity: Intrapersonal Conflicts of Value," *Philosophical Review* 112 (2003): 215; John Broome, "Discounting the Future," in *Ethics out of Economics* (Cambridge: Cambridge University Press, 1999), 44–48. But see Derek Parfit, *Reasons and Persons* (Oxford: Oxford University Press, 1984), 317–318.
57. A possible objection to this position is that, even if present individuals under idealized conditions do retain a time preference that gives greater weight to present over future welfare effects, governmental officials should ignore this preference. An official who seeks to maximize overall welfare has no reason to weight differently the well-being of person P and person Q; on what grounds, then, should the official weight differently the well-being of person P at time 1

and person P at time 2? True, P at time 1 cares more about his welfare than he does about the welfare of his future self, but this seems no more relevant than P's preference for increasing his own welfare at the expense of person Q. See Parfit, *Reasons and Persons*, 318–320.

58. For a presentation of opportunity cost arguments for discounting, see, e.g., Donohue, "Why We Should Discount"; Morrison, "Judicial Review of Discount Rates"; Samida and Weisbach, "Paretian Intergenerational Discounting."

59. A closely related argument points to the problem of offsetting effects: a regulation that imposes costs on certain individuals may induce them to reduce their savings. Discounting, here, serves not to indicate some additional option open to the government, but rather to indicate that the status quo involves private investment at some positive interest rate that will be reduced by the project.

60. For a discussion of the puzzles raised by policies that change the population, see, e.g., Parfit, *Reasons and Persons*, 351–441; John Broome, "Cost-Benefit Analysis and Population," in Adler and Posner, *Cost-Benefit Analysis*, 117.

61. Farber, "From Here to Eternity," 303 (internal quotation omitted).

62. Sunstein and Rowell, "On Discounting Regulatory Benefits," 13.

63. For general discussion of the VSL method that CBA employs to value lives saved or lost, see Freeman, *The Measurement of Environmental and Resource Values*, 298–321; W. Kip Viscusi, *Fatal Tradeoffs: Public and Private Responsibilities for Risk* (New York: Oxford University Press, 1992), 34–74; W. Kip Viscusi, *Rational Risk Policy* (Oxford: Oxford University Press, 1998), 45–68; M. W. Jones-Lee, "Safety and the Saving of Life: The Economics of Safety and Physical Risk," in Richard Layard and Stephen Glaister, eds., *Cost-Benefit Analysis*, 2nd ed. (Cambridge: Cambridge University Press, 1994), 290; David Pearce, "Valuing Risks," in Peter Calow, ed., *Handbook of Environmental Risk Assessment and Management* (Oxford: Blackwell Science, 1998), 345. Governmental use of VSL valuations is surveyed in Don Kenkel, "Using Estimates of the Value of a Statistical Life in Evaluating Consumer Policy Regulations," *Journal of Consumer Policy* 26 (2003): 1, 4–7; and W. Kip Viscusi and Joseph Aldy, "The Value of Statistical Life: A Critical Review of Market Estimates throughout the World," *Journal of Risk and Uncertainty* 27 (2003): 5, 53–56.

64. Ackerman and Heinzerling, *Priceless*, 62.

65. See, e.g., Ackerman and Heinzerling, *Priceless*, 61–90; Anderson, *Value in Ethics and Economics*, 195–203; Driesen, "The Societal Cost of Environmental Regulation," 587–589; Shapiro and Glicksman, *Risk Regulation at Risk*, 92–105; Sunstein, "Incommensurability and Valuation in Law," 837–839.

66. See Gary T. Schwartz, "The Myth of the Ford Pinto Case," *Rutgers Law Review* 43 (1991): 1013, 1020.

67. John Broome, "Trying to Value a Life," *Journal of Public Economics* 9 (1978): 91, 95.

68. On bequest functions, which allow for utility to be sensitive to postmortem wealth, see, e.g., James K. Hammitt, "QALYs Versus WTP," *Risk Analysis* 22 (2002): 985, 992–994.

69. For an analysis of VSL along these lines, see Matthew D. Adler, "Risk, Death, and Time: A Comment on Judge Williams' Defense of Cost-Benefit Analysis," *Administrative Law Review* 53 (2001): 271, 285–286.

70. Sugden, "Alternatives to the Neo-Classical Theory of Choice," 171. See Jack L. Knetsch, "Valuing Statistical Lives: The Choice of Measure Also Matters," *Journal of Consumer Policy* 27 (2004): 99.

71. See Matthew D. Adler, "QALYs and Policy Evaluation: A New Perspective," *Yale Journal of Health Policy, Law, and Ethics* 6 (2006): 1, 35–39.

72. See Cass R. Sunstein, "Valuing Life: A Plea for Disaggregation," *Duke Law Journal* 54 (2004): 385; Kenkel, "Using Estimates of the Value of a Statistical Life."

73. See Adler, "QALYs and Policy Evaluation," 30–35.

Index